BLACK FREEDOM AND EDUCATION IN NINETEENTH-CENTURY CUBA

*Caribbean Crossroads:
Race, Identity, and Freedom Struggles*

Black Freedom and Education in Nineteenth-Century Cuba

Raquel Alicia Otheguy

Lillian Guerra, Devyn Spence Benson, April Mayes, and Solsiree del Moral, Series Editors

UNIVERSITY OF FLORIDA PRESS

Gainesville

Cover: "Some Typical Cuban Faces—Santiago Cuba," by R. Y. Young, 1899. Library of Congress Prints and Photographs Division.

Publication of this work made possible by a Sustaining the Humanities through the American Rescue Plan grant from the National Endowment for the Humanities.

Copyright 2025 by Raquel Alicia Otheguy
All rights reserved
Published in the United States of America

30 29 28 27 26 25   6 5 4 3 2 1

Library of Congress Cataloging-in-Publication Data
Names: Otheguy, Raquel Alicia, author.
Title: Black freedom and education in nineteenth-century Cuba / Raquel Alicia Otheguy.
Description: Gainesville : University of Florida Press, 2025. | Series: Caribbean crossroads: race, identity, and freedom struggles | Includes bibliographical references and index. | Summary: "In this book, Raquel Otheguy argues that Afro-descended teachers and activists were central to the development of a national education system in Cuba and influenced the trajectory of public school systems in the broader Americas"— Provided by publisher.
Identifiers: LCCN 2024020851 (print) | LCCN 2024020852 (ebook) | ISBN 9781683404767 (hardback) | ISBN 9781683404934 (paperback) | ISBN 9781683404897 (pdf) | ISBN 9781683405061 (ebook)
Subjects: LCSH: Slavery—Cuba—History. | Black people—Education—Cuba—History—19th century. | Black people—Cuba—History—19th century. | Enslaved persons—Emancipation—Cuba. | Cuba—History—19th century. | BISAC: HISTORY / Caribbean & West Indies / Cuba | EDUCATION / History
Classification: LCC HT1076 .O84 2025 (print) | LCC HT1076 (ebook) | DDC 370.89/9607291—dc23/eng/20240820
LC record available at https://lccn.loc.gov/2024020851
LC ebook record available at https://lccn.loc.gov/2024020852

References to internet websites (URLs) were accurate at the time of writing. Neither the author nor University of Florida Press is responsible for URLs that may have expired or changed since the manuscript was prepared.

University of Florida Press
2046 NE Waldo Road
Suite 2100
Gainesville, FL 32609
http://upress.ufl.edu

Para Gabriel Andrés, Isabel Alicia, y Teresa Clementina

CONTENTS

List of Figures ix

Acknowledgments xi

Introduction: The Black Cuban Educational Tradition 1

1. Maestras Amigas and the Shaping of a Black Cuban Educational Ideology in Early Nineteenth-Century Cuba 25
2. Rebellious Teachers, 1812–1844 51
3. Racial Segregation in Cuba's First Law for Public Education 71
4. The 1878 Order to Build Schools for Children of Color, White Backlash, and the Effect on Black Teachers 88
5. Black Teachers, Sociedades de Color, and Separate Schools 110
6. The Directorio Central de las Sociedades de la Raza de Color and the 1890s Campaign for Equal School Rights 127
7. "No Division by Color": US School Inspectors and the Aftermath of the War of Independence 150

Epilogue: Race in Cuba's Schools, 1910 and Beyond 168

Notes 171

Bibliography 203

Index 227

FIGURES

1. Signatures of Juan José Benites and José Policeto Gómez   62
2. Teacher Eloisa Piñeiro, 1899   113
3. Eulogia Pérez article, 1903   115
4. Cuban municipal school building, 1899   155
5. Students and teachers of a public school for girls, 1899   160
6. Inspection report for School 4 in Recreo, 1899   161
7. Inspection report for School 1 in San Luis, 1900   162
8. Inspection report for School 2 in San Luis, 1900   163

ACKNOWLEDGMENTS

I am grateful to the many people and institutions that made the research and writing of this book possible. The Tinker Foundation field research grant funded my first research trip to Cuba as a graduate student, and the Turner Fellowship funded my doctoral studies. More recently, this book would not have been written without the National Academy of Education/Spencer Post-Doctoral Fellowship, which gave me a year without teaching and connected me to brilliant education studies scholars. Funding from the City University of New York including the Professional Staff Congress-CUNY awards, a Mellon-CUNY Black, Race, and Ethnic Studies Institute award, and the CUNY Faculty Fellowship Publication Program (FFPP) also provided crucial time and funding to work on this book. In Cuba, the Instituto Cubano de Investigación Cultural Juan Marinello sponsored my research and facilitated my academic visas; special thanks go to then-international relations liaison Henry Heredia for all his help.

Librarians in so many places have my unending gratitude for all their work in making our research possible. Thanks to the librarians at Bronx Community College, especially Tokunbo Adeshina, for their patience and dedication in chasing down books for me. Thanks also to the archivists and librarians at Stony Brook University, Columbia University, Yale University, New York Public Library, the Schomburg Center for Research in Black Culture, the Tuskegee University Archives, the New-York Historical Society, the National Archives and Records Administration, the Library of Congress, the Archivo Nacional de Cuba, the Archivo Histórico Provincial de Cienfuegos, the Archivo Histórico Provincial de Santiago de Cuba, the Biblioteca Nacional José Martí, and the provincial libraries in Cuba.

At Stony Brook, my adviser Brooke Larson led me to themes of race, nation, and education, which she beautifully examines in her own scholarship. I'm thankful to her and the rest of my dissertation committee, Jennifer Anderson and Paul Gootenberg at Stony Brook and Ada Ferrer at NYU. Stony Brook's amazing faculty and fellow graduate students all taught me so much about doing history. Thanks also to the college professors who taught me about race, empire, and history, especially Frances Negrón-Muntaner, Samuel Moyn, and Rashid Khalidi, and to my high school history teachers Maria Thompson (née Caragine) and James Caposella for providing those early sparks.

My thanks to editor-in-chief Stephanye Hunter and the entire editorial and production team at University of Florida Press for skillfully shepherding a first-time author and to the anonymous reviewers and series editor who engaged with my book so thoughtfully.

At Bronx Community College, the History Department faculty have created a warm home for me. I'm especially thankful to our former chair Tamar Rothenberg for her unflagging leadership, to Elizabeth Hardman, Prithi Kanakamedala, and Seth Offenbach for their mentorship, and for all the folks at BCC who build beautiful things in difficult circumstances. BCC students inspire me with their insight, curiosity, and commitment; I'm so lucky to be able to learn from them!

Many scholars have helped shape my thinking about this book over the years. I thank the folks in the NYU History of Education working group and the Yale Race and Slavery working group, the Cuba writing group with Angela Crumdy and Natalie Catasús, and Moustafa Bayoumi and the rest of the FFPP cohort for reading chapters of this book. Gracias to historian Félix Matos Rodríguez for his mentorship over many years. Katerina Gonzalez Seligmann has been teaching me about the Caribbean since we met in Gustavo Pérez Firmat's seminar twenty years ago. Gracias also to colleagues Takkara Brunson, Michael Bustamante, Adriana Chira, Aris Clemons, Anne Eller, Anasa Hicks, Jesse Horst, William Kelly, Ariel Lambe, Jennifer Lambe, Bonnie Lucero, Laura Muñoz, Melina Pappademos, Ethan Ris, Alexa Rodríguez, Daniel Rodríguez, Romy Sanchez, David Sartorius, Rainer Schultz, and Elizabeth Schwall for time spent in archives or at conferences together and for all your insight.

I am indescribably lucky to have dear friends from all walks of life who enrich my life in many ways and keep me whole. My thanks to the friends from Pelham for sticking with me through all the phases of our lives. Larissa Acocella left us too soon. Brittany Brandwein keeps my heart dancing. My comadre Lauren Mancia has been an essential interlocutor on much more than academics. Thanks to the New Haven moms for raising your children with mine.

This book comes from my heart, so it comes from my family. The late Dolores Corona started a conversation with me twenty-five years ago that continues with me to this day. Gracias a Katia Garay por ser mi familia habanera y a Martha Jiménez por cuidar a mis hijos. Muchos besos siempre a los Otheguy, Schwiep, Dunbar, González, y Catasús, and lots of love to the Pierponts. My brother, Eric García, and my sister, Emma Otheguy, will always be home, and we are so lucky that our accordion casa now includes Monica, Gianna, Charli, Tim, Alaya, Félix, y Paloma. Mis padres, Ricardo Otheguy y Ofelia García, nos quieren y se ríen con nosotros, y se tiran al suelo para jugar con sus nietos. There is always space at their table for another mystery guest. They have spent a career giving selflessly to their students and thinking deeply about language, su pueblo, and more. Los adoro, Mami y Papi.

Writing this book has overlapped with a decade of becoming a mami to Gabriel Andrés, Isabel Alicia, y Teresa Clementina. This book has shared headspace with baby wipes, bomberos, ballet, béisbol, and bedtime; sight words, sirenitas, step dance, and cenas; y las caritas luminosas de mis hijitos preciosos. I'm thankful to them every day, and to John, whose love makes everything possible and good.

Introduction

The Black Cuban Educational Tradition

In 1894 a group of Afro-descended Cuban activists accomplished something remarkable: the legal desegregation of public schools on the island of Cuba. This astonishing feat took place a full sixty years before *Brown v. Board of Education* would rule racial segregation in US public schools unconstitutional. Cuba lagged only a few decades behind some of the most progressive polities when it came to the timing of equal school rights; Massachusetts had desegregated public schools in 1855, for example. That Cuba would desegregate its public schools less than a decade after it fully abolished slavery in 1886 comes, at first blush, as somewhat a surprise. Beginning in the late eighteenth century and throughout the nineteenth, Cuba had experienced an expansion of the slavery-based sugar economy. It had become what scholars call a slave society, in which race-based slavery permeated the entire social order, as in the southern United States. Its desegregation of schools following more closely the northern states' timing than its fellow slave-society states in the US South is thus unexpected. But as this book will demonstrate, the success of the equal school rights campaign on the island was the culmination of persistent efforts across the nineteenth century by Afro-descended Cuban educators and educational activists to extend primary education to all Cuban children. The Black Cuban educational tradition was capacious in how it conceived of and pursued education as a tool of freedom and liberation for all. The 1894 desegregation victory was only one part of a long-standing and wide-ranging effort on the part of Black educators, intellectuals, parents, and activists to provide a sound and dignified education to all their children.[1]

In celebrating the 1894 desegregation order in colonial Cuba, the Black newspaper *La Igualdad* gestured to the history of Black educational endeavors that had led to it. The paper claimed that "the first thing it [la raza de color] did when its chains were broken was to create schools in which good-willed men taught children from each locality."[2] Similarly, the equal school rights campaign was a continuation of the campaign for the abolition of slavery, and like abolition, the struggle for education was an important part of the struggle for liberty. Indeed, the Black educational tradition was an essential element in the broader political movements for Black liberation in Cuba. But in dating the start of their account at the point of the abolition of slavery, when its chains were broken, *La Igualdad* was actually abbreviating the long history of the Black educational tradition. It is a history that should be traced back to the beginning of the nineteenth century and could likely be traced further back still. The article in *La Igualdad* also highlighted the role of male teachers and of schools outside of the home, suggesting that these educational efforts were only by and for Afro-descended men and boys in established institutions. But the newspaper's story left out other important aspects of the Black Cuban educational tradition: women teachers, racially integrated classrooms, Black-run separate schools, schools for girls, domestic spaces, free tuition, and even armed rebellion. These were some of the defining characteristics of the Black Cuban educational tradition. It is this longer, more participatory and complete story of Black Cuban education that I tell here.

Afro-Cuban educators—first the *maestras amigas* who taught young children in *escuelitas de casa* (informal schools in their homes), and later licensed teachers, militiamen-turned-teachers, teachers in the separate schools of the *sociedades de color* (mutual aid societies for people of color) and others—were the essential contributors to what I have identified as the Black Cuban educational tradition. In turn, the Black Cuban educational tradition and its practitioners shaped the emerging official Cuban public education system from its earliest moments. At a time when primary schools were not widespread, Black Cuban teachers taught children beginning with the lower levels that Cubans called *primeras letras*, the equivalent to the American reading, writing, 'rithmetic, and religion. At a time when Cuban schools charged tuition for all education, even at the primary level, many Afro-descended educators accepted children who could not pay. White Cuban Creoles (that is, born in Cuba) insisted that White girls should be educated at home or in schools that focused only on subjects deemed appropriate for their gender; Afro-descended Cubans created schools for girls as well as co-educational schools. An expanding race-based sugar economy intensified racial oppression throughout society, prompting White Cuban Creoles to use the developing school system to further firm up and institutionalize racial segregation, while Afro-descended Cuban teachers used their own schools to seat Black, *mulato* (mixed-race), and White children next to each other. As well, the sociedades de color created separate schools in order to give Black children access to the education that White Creoles and Spanish colonial authorities increasingly sought to deny them. Afro-descended Cubans also applied for teaching licenses, pushed for the expansion of access to municipal schools for all children, and lobbied for the desegregation of municipal schools. In some cases, Black and mulato teachers joined armed rebellions, linking education to these more radical strategies for liberation. In all of these educational activities, Afro-descended Cubans were using schooling to voice their oppositional politics to the racial discrimination of nineteenth-century Cuba and to advance a vision of racial equity and liberation for all Cubans.

Afro-Descendants in Nineteenth-Century Cuba

Most of the Black and mulato teachers and educational activists of the nineteenth century belonged to the island's *clase de color*, free people of color. Enslaved Africans arrived in Cuba starting with the sixteenth-century founding of the Spanish colony, and slavery persisted on the island until its final abolition in 1886. But due to the well-established practices of manumission and self-purchase (*coartación*), Cuba also had a substantial free Black and mulato population since the early colonial period. Afro-descended Cubans continued to pursue their own individual freedom and the freedom of their loved ones in the nineteenth century, in addition to working toward the general abolition of slavery. By the early part of the century, Cuba's free population of color, largely concentrated in urban areas, constituted 15–20 percent of the total population; in 1804, there were 90,000 free people of color on the island, out of a total population of 504,000.[3] In 1565, free Blacks made up 10–15 percent of Havana's free population.[4] Cuban-born Blacks and mulatos, especially women, were disproportionately represented among the free population, in contrast to the African-born, especially males, who were overrepresented among the enslaved.[5]

This free class included the recently manumitted as well as people who were separated from enslavement by several generations. Still, the ties between the enslaved and free communities were deep. Families and kinship networks often included both free and enslaved Afro-descendants, and free and enslaved people interacted in the island's cities as well as in the countryside. Moreover, and significantly, these groups were united as participants in many armed rebellions in the early part of the century.[6] The distinction between slavery and freedom by manumission or self-purchase was not always clear-cut; at times, some people could be only partially legally free, as recent scholarship by Adriana Chira and by Claudia Varela and Manuel Barcia demonstrates.[7] At the same time, some free people of color experienced significant socioeconomic mobility, becoming owners of property, including slaves.[8]

The Afro-descended Cuban teachers and students described in these pages were mostly legally free, but with close ties to slavery. Some of the island's Afro-descended teachers had been born free, but others had been enslaved and then manumitted, such as was the case of many of the maestras amigas, while others were freed with the abolition of slavery on the island in 1886. Legal freedom made a big difference when it came to access to formal education. Both slave codes and school laws suggested that enslaved people should be taught at least some religious content. But in fact enslaved people had limited or no access to the nascent system of public schools that would develop over the course of the nineteenth century, especially those in the expanding sugar plantation zones.[9] There are a few examples of free teachers of color attempting to provide schooling to enslaved people, but more research is needed to determine whether this was a widespread practice.[10] It was thus not until the abolition of slavery that the majority of Afro-descended children in Cuba—those who were enslaved—would have had access to formal schooling.

The *magisterio*, the teaching profession, sometimes functioned to provide free people of color with legal rights, social recognition, and economic mobility, the constellation of factors, along with adherence to Catholic and patriarchal mores, that endowed them with what Danielle Terrazas Williams calls "social legitimacy."[11] For many free people of color, formal schooling also held the promise of improving the lives of their children and uplifting their entire race. Yet the social legitimacy benefits of the magisterio and the promise of racial uplift through education were mostly available to men, and then only through formal channels such as receiving a teaching license from the Spanish colonial government and setting up a school. In the present work I bring to the fore other Afro-descended educators and educational activists who labored to provide schooling for their children while facing scorn or disdain, many doing so away from the official national school system. This was especially the case with the female teachers known as *maestras amigas*, unlicensed women teachers who taught children in their homes.

Free and enslaved Afro-descendants on the island were undoubtedly educating their children outside of the formal school setting long before the nineteenth-century movement for educational reform. Enslaved Africans brought with them the formal and informal education practices of West Africa.[12] Parents, grandparents, and other elders would pass on values and knowledge to their children at home, on the plantation, or in the street, in their associational life, and beyond. Afro-descended women almost certainly taught White children in these informal ways, too. Enslaved and free Black women worked as midwives to bring White children into the world, nourished them as *nodrizas* (wet nurses), and cared for young White children as nannies.[13]

Exploring those kinds of informal schooling provided by Afro-descendants is largely beyond the scope of this book, but echoes of these endeavors inform the debates about Black educators that I trace here. One of them had to do with doubts from Whites about the kind of knowledge that the maestras amigas passed on to children. As White elites, particularly the liberal Creoles, attempted to expand and formalize primary education on the island, they sought to distance it and differentiate from the multifaceted child care and educational efforts that women of color had long expended on the island, and to squeeze those women out of the educational labor pool. In doing so, Creole men in Cuba were drawing sharp distinctions between the kind of care work (often involving tending to young or female bodies) that they devalued and therefore found it acceptable for Black women to do, and the kind of formal education that they proposed to provide in the schools they aspired to create. Nonetheless, the maestras amigas persisted in teaching young children well into the twentieth century. And as the nineteenth century wore on, many women of color besides the maestras amigas joined the effort, becoming licensed teachers.

Regardless of their social status, all Afro-descended Cubans experienced intensifying racial discrimination during the nineteenth-century expansion of the slave-based sugar economy. In the last decade of the eighteenth century, enslaved people in the French colony of Saint Domingue, then the world's largest sugar producer, overthrew the system of slavery and then colonial rule, declaring the birth of the Haitian republic and ending the island's large-scale sugar export industry. Cuban planters eagerly took up the resulting slack in sugar production, importing more than a half-million enslaved Africans in the nineteenth century and ballooning sugar production sixfold between 1800 and 1840, when Cuba produced 160,000 metric tons of sugar. Upholding this expanded slave-based sugar economy required a hardening racial hierarchy throughout Cuban society. It became an important concern of White Creoles and Spanish colonial officials alike throughout the nineteenth century to control the newly enlarged slave population and to limit the rights and mobility of the free people of color.[14] At the same time, Creole elites were starting to focus on the problem of forging a modern nation out of a multiracial population containing increasing numbers of enslaved people. It was in large part this concern that gave rise to the attempt to set up a national public education system. The developing public school system thus became a crucial arena for the debate over the place of Afro-descendants in Cuban society and the emerging Cuban nation.

Education, Cubanidad, and Race

Before the nineteenth century, Cuba, like many other societies around the world, mostly educated only the rich. Wealthy children were taught at home or sent abroad. Monasteries throughout Latin America were tasked with maintaining primary schools, and Cuba's convents and monasteries were no exception.[15] The convents of San Francisco de Sales and the Ursulines had educated girls since the mid-seventeenth century, and the Belén school run by Jesuit priests and the school run by Bethlemite priests educated hundreds of children by the end of the eighteenth century. Aside from these schools run by religious orders, the data for Cuban schools at the turn of the nineteenth century is fragmentary. A 1790 educational census of Havana showed that only a small fraction, somewhere between 700 and 1,200, of Havana's 8,000 school-age children were being educated in about forty schools. Most of those schools (thirty-two) were schools for girls, run largely by freed Black and *mulata* women.[16] This staggering statistic and other examples like it support this book's central premise that the history of education in Cuba must begin with and center the role of Afro-descended Cuban educators.

But when the Creole elite landowning men of the Sociedad Económica of Havana received sanction from the Spanish crown to take charge of education in the early nineteenth century, they ignored their own evidence regarding how central Afro-descended Cuban women were in disseminating primary education on the island. Instead, these elites would spend the nineteenth century crafting a school system and a narrative about the school system that displaced Black educational activism, disparaged Spanish colonial educational policies, and centered themselves as the liberal creators of a modern school system and Cuban nation.

The nineteenth century was a period of deepening conflict between White Creole elites and Spanish colonial officials in Cuba. As White Creole opposition to Spanish colonial rule sharpened, movements developed for annexation to the United States, for autonomy, for self-rule, and finally for independence. In the thinking of White Creoles, political autonomy or independence required a modern nation with an enlightened populace. Entry into modernity and capacity for self-government, in their view, therefore required the development of a national education system. They bitterly accused the Spanish colonial government of underfunding education on the island and censoring the press and other publications to keep the island from rebelling, as Spain's mainland American colonies had done.[17] They portrayed themselves, by contrast, as liberal reformers who would shape the modern Cuban nation by implementing a national school system. This, in varying forms, is the narrative repeated in most nationalist histories of education of the island.[18]

But there is far more to tell than these conventional narratives would have us believe. By expanding historical inquiry to account for the educational experiences of Afro-descended Cubans, the present work brings a different story into view. Importantly, both Creole and peninsular educational policies articulated White-supremacist visions of the future. Whites across the political spectrum in nineteenth-century Cuba were united in their commitment to using the school system to cement an oppressive racial hierarchy, despite their growing rifts in other areas. In fact, as the following pages will demonstrate, at times the Spanish colonial government was more willing to concede educational access to Afro-descendants in Cuba than were White Creoles. The Spanish colonial government in nineteenth-century Cuba occasionally implemented liberal reforms as part of the repeated clashes between liberals and conservatives in the metropolitan government and in an effort to court loyalty in one of their only remaining colonies.[19] For Black Cubans, this meant that support for the Spanish empire was, at times, an effective method of making claims on the government, as David Sartorius has shown.[20] Still, as its school laws demonstrate, the Spanish colonial government, too, was largely committed to racial segregation in the developing educational system.

White Cuban Creole assertions about the slowness of the development of public education in Cuba were not entirely accurate. Throughout the

Americas and Europe in the nineteenth century, governments began to organize national systems of public education, some at faster clips than others.[21] Although Latin American republics had thrown off Spanish colonial rule by the 1820s, their pace in developing public school systems approximated that of colonial Cuba, with national laws providing for publicly funded schools that at first relied heavily on the municipalities, mandating compulsory primary education, and requiring towns to build schools.[22] The centralization of administration and finance occurred gradually. It was not until the rise of the *estado docente*, the teaching state funded by the export boom at the end of the nineteenth century, that Latin American nations saw the advent of a centralized public school system.[23]

Literacy in Cuba kept pace more or less with the rest of Latin America; on average, about 15 percent of the population in Latin America was literate in 1850, compared to 19 percent literacy in Cuba in the 1861 census.[24] There were also ideological convergences in the thinking about education between the elites of Cuba and those of the new Latin American republics. They all focused heavily on education serving to form republican governments, independent and coherent polities, and nations out of a heterogeneous population.[25] Educational thinkers such as Andrés Bello and Domingo Faustino Sarmiento disseminated educational philosophies, particularly the idea that common school systems were needed to create new citizens for the emerging republics of Latin America.[26] The role of educational policies, systems, and ideologies in the development of nations has been a major theme in the historiography of Latin American education, and this book offers the Cuban contribution to that literature.[27]

As conflict broke out in Cuba in 1868 and later in 1895, White Creoles had to formulate a national political vision that would compel Afro-descendants on the islands to support the bid for Cuban nationhood to replace the Spanish colonial apparatus. During the first war of independence (1868–1878), the Republic in Arms articulated an antislavery ideology and freed many slaves. The antiracist rhetoric of the *independentistas*, independence fighters, would become much more pronounced by the 1880s, leading up to the final war for independence in 1895. This rhetoric was powerful and achieved real results, contributing to the major presence of Afro-descendants in the war efforts and their inclusion in all ranks of the insurgent armies.

Ada Ferrer points out, however, that the White Creole independence activists' commitment to racial equality was deeply qualified and ambivalent. The discourse of raceless Cuban nationalism, what scholars have called the myth of racial equality, emerged out of the independence movements. While it may have allowed Afro-descendants some space to claim political rights, it also frequently had the effect of silencing race-based claims and decisively limiting the options for Black political and social organizing in the early twentieth century.

Building on extensive literature regarding racism in Cuban society, I show that a profound anti-Black conviction drove the White Creoles' efforts to push Afro-descended teachers out of the magisterio, to limit Black and mulato children's access to municipal schools, to resist integrating the growing public school system, and more generally to use educational policy to harden developing racial hierarchies. Despite the efforts of Cuban nationalists in the late nineteenth century to unite Black and White islanders against Spanish colonial rule, the history of Creole educational policies recounted here paved the way for continued anti-Black racism in the twentieth century that lingers still today.[28]

My research thus challenges more than the nationalist narrative of Cuban education that positioned White Creoles as liberal, modern reformers struggling against a backward, repressive Spanish empire. It throws into question too the nationalist mythology that linked liberal Creoles with a more progressive racial politics that would make possible political unity and legitimate Cuban sovereignty. Instead, I show that the liberal political ideology that motivated White Cuban Creoles to create a public education system was also profoundly anti-Black. They, no less than the Spanish colonial government, based their vision of Cuban society on White-supremacist ideology. In making this claim, I build on the labors of various scholars of Cuban history who have examined the nineteenth-century creation of a sense of *cubanidad,* Cuban national identity. The nineteenth century saw distinct, conflicting views of the Cuban nation emerge. One of the key axes of conflict was the issue of race and how race affected the possibilities of Cuban sovereignty. Modernity, in the view of White Cuban Creoles, was predicated on Whiteness and European cultural norms.

It cannot be lost sight of, however, that elites were not by any means the only players involved in the unfolding drama of the creation of a Cuban nation. Other groups such as workers, women, and Afro-descendants all contributed their visions of a national project throughout the nineteenth and twentieth centuries, as Lillian Guerra reminds us.[29] My work expands an extensive literature by scholars of Cuba that has traced the range of ways Afro-descendants in the nineteenth century resisted slavery, pursued equal rights, and shaped Cuban society. I do so by demonstrating that a key piece of Black political activism in Cuba was their commitment to education. Cuban historian Alicia Conde Rodríguez writes, "Education in Cuba has been a transcendental issue in the formation of the cultural values of the nation, even since [the nation] was still a project."[30] This was as true of Afro-descended Cubans as it was of White Creole elites. By bringing attention to the ways Afro-descended Cubans interacted with the educational field—in creating their own schools, in pressing for the desegregation of the public schools, and more—the present study shows that they were in fact creating alternative visions of Cuban nationhood. Through their teaching, writing, and advocacy, Afro-descended Cuban teachers and educational activists offered divergent views about what a modern Cuban nation and the public sphere could be. Through their educational activism, Afro-descended Cubans countered race science that suggested they were less intellectually capable than Whites; they acquired the literacy that allowed them to participate in and manipulate political systems, created community with other Afro-descendants, and joined in the most important intellectual debates of the day.

More than that, Black Cubans were at the forefront of the region's most progressive innovations in education, such as widely disseminating primary instruction, providing tuition-free schooling, educating girls, developing Black-led schools, and teaching Black and White children together. Black Cuban educators are shown here to not only have engaged in but more interestingly, often anticipated the transatlantic liberal currents of thought regarding education, race, and modernity. In this way, the pages that follow place the Black Cuban educational tradition at the center of the story of the development of national education systems in Cuba and in the Americas more generally. And they show too that Black Cuban educators were major contributors to shaping how all Cubans thought about and experienced the role of schooling in society and politics.

The Cuban Black Educational Tradition as Political and Intellectual History

This book presents the Black Cuban educational tradition as both a form of political activism and as revealing important currents of Black thought. In doing so, I draw on a deep well of Black studies scholarship throughout the Americas. Early work by nineteenth- and twentieth-century writers, intellectuals, and scholars from Rafael Serra to W. E. B. DuBois led to the 1960s establishment of Africana studies and Puerto Rican studies departments in the United States and the flourishing of Afro–Latin American studies in Latin America. Two strands of this scholarship are particularly relevant for the present study: the political activism of Afro-descendants and the history of Black thought in the Americas.

The historical scholarship on the political activity of Afro-descended people in the Americas has concentrated attention on the broad spectrum of political strategies they used. For example, resistance to slavery ranged from work slowdowns to *petit-* and *grand-marronage* to outright armed revolt. In the extensive body of work on Afro-descendants in the Cuban context, scholars have examined how the repression accompanying racial slavery, anticolonial struggles, and the post-independence myth of racial equality drew the contours of the political organizing options of Afro-descendants. Black Cubans nonetheless mobilized a wide range of political strategies. Some of the major strands of resistance to slavery and racial oppression emerged from African and African-derived religions and religious and ethnic groups, such as the Abakuá, the *cabildos de nación* (African ethnic organizations), the *cofradías* (Catholic lay confraternities), and free people of color involved in the militias.[31]

In the early twentieth century, Afro-descended Cuban men overcame the raceless national discourse that muffled complaints of racism by people of color enough to secure the right to vote. Black men voted, held office, used patronage networks to distribute resources, and often embraced patriarchal and bourgeois norms in order to prove their civilized status and uplift their race. These approaches have sometimes been characterized as overly accommodationist.[32] Such approaches have stood in contrast to the more radical approach of the race-based political claims of the hemisphere's first Black political party, the Partido Independiente de Color (PIC), which was met with a popularly backed state massacre of some thousands of Blacks in the eastern provinces in 1912.[33]

Black Cuban organizing around education in the nineteenth century involved a similarly wide variety of political and social approaches. Unlike what was to come in the post-independence period, in the developing public education system of the nineteenth century—one of the largest public institutions in Cuba—a series of school laws promulgated over the course of the 1800s established legal, de jure, segregation in educational institutions. These de jure segregation policies significantly affected the organizing options of Afro-descendants interested in education.

In the chapters that follow I present a sweeping range of responses by Afro-descended educational activists to these policies. Black teachers and families responded to the increasing formal racial segregation of the schools with approaches that encompassed two somewhat contradictory trends: an interest in Blacks' integration into the wider society as well as a concern with racially separatist organizing. Black and mulato Cubans in the nineteenth century created racially separate schools in black *sociedades*. But they also ran schools that accepted White children and those that sought to become publicly funded institutions. Black teachers sought to become licensed by the state and formed the Directorio Central de las Sociedades de la Raza de Color to lobby the colonial government to integrate the public schools. But they also rebelled against colonial rule and slavery. In the first half of the century, before the colonial school laws were enacted, some militiamen participated both in the magisterio and in armed rebellion, suggesting that for some free people of color in Cuba, involvement in education as political activism did not preclude pursuing more radical political options.

In addition to emphasizing the wide range of political strategies employed by Afro-descendants, historians have demonstrated that throughout the Americas, Afro-descendants were not simply reacting to conditions of oppression but were rather demonstrating agency and acting as central forces in the development of societies. Caribbean scholars of the early to mid-twentieth century such as C. L. R. James and Eric Williams (both Trinidadian) insisted that enslaved Africans and their descendants were the historical protagonists of world-shifting events such as the Haitian revolution and the industrial revolution.[34] In that same spirit, this work presents Afro-descendants' educational activism as decisively shaping the political and social landscape of Cuba.

Afro-descended Cubans interested in education were not only responding to or resisting segregation. They were also creating ideas and developing systems of education that preceded the de jure segregation policies that began to be implemented, piecemeal, in the early nineteenth century by Cuban Creole elite men and that were then further formalized when the Spanish crown started establishing the national school system. Thus, this is not only a story of Black resistance; it is a story of Black initiative and agency. Afro-descended Cubans' ideas and actions shaped the emerging school system and Cuban society itself, from the earliest moment of the history of education in Cuba and from the earliest moments of national formation.[35]

This book also contributes to the study of Black intellectual history, which has been reinvigorated in recent years.[36] Recent work on Afro-descendants' political activities in the Americas, particularly in the Caribbean, has sought to excavate their political consciousness, to open "windows into the cognitive world of the enslaved."[37] Building on a longer lineage of scholars of gender, slavery, and resistance in the Caribbean and the United States as well as on Cedric Robinson's foundational work, *Black Marxism*, scholars have in recent years looked in particular for the ideas and consciousness undergirding the actions of Afro-descended women in the Americas.[38] Jennifer Morgan has asserted that enslaved Africans and their descendants, and especially Black women, were theorists of power. Black women saw and understood the radically changing racial landscape before them (in Morgan's article, seventeenth-century Virginia; here, nineteenth-century Cuba), and as they tried to navigate it, they generated knowledge about it.[39] Aisha Finch, too, has centered enslaved Black women's roles in the "repeating rebellions" of early nineteenth-century Cuba in order to conceptualize their "anti-slavery epistemologies and ingrained structures of opposition" and their political consciousness.[40]

There were many pathways through which Afro-descended people acquired knowledge of the increasingly racialized world of nineteenth-century Cuba, not least of which was their lived experience of racial slavery and violence. Schools are also a way of disseminating knowledge and developing consciousness in young people and in adults. It is my contention that carefully examining the Black educational tradition in Cuba gives new insights into Afro-descendants' thoughts and theories of power regarding the world they lived in and how to survive it.

The conceptions of freedom revealed by the study of Black and mulato Cuban educators are also heterogeneous, from ideas of freedom that placed Black people in positions of authority and created separate institutions from Whites, to ideas of freedom as a revolutionary ethos emanating from the Black experience of slavery and racism, to freedom organized around ideas of citizenship and equality.

The history of Black education is Black intellectual history, as I first heard Vanessa Siddle Walker and Russell Rickford discuss.[41] Though Cuba has well-developed scholarly literatures on educational history and on Black history, these two fields have not significantly intersected yet. Then too, though the study of women's history has recently flourished in the field of Black Cuban history, it also needs to be brought to bear on the history of education.[42] The present study gathers together the insights of these various literatures to identify and trace what I call the Black Cuban educational tradition as it developed in the nineteenth century. My approach centers

Afro-descendants in the history of Cuban schooling, coupling the history of education—a history of ideas—with Black Cuban history, thus expanding the field of Black Cuban intellectual history.

In the United States, Black intellectual history has focused on Black educators and their schooling projects from the start.[43] If, as Earl E. Thorpe asserted long ago, "the central theme of Negro thought has been the quest for freedom and equality," then historians of Black education have shown that schooling was a central component of that quest.[44] It is from this historiography that my work has drawn much of its inspiration.[45]

The history of Black education in Cuba has remarkable overlaps with the history of Black education in the United States and throughout the Americas. The history of education in other Latin American countries has until recently not focused on Afro-descendants, but new work on Black education in Latin America, particularly in Argentina, provides useful points of reference.[46] Throughout the Americas, White officials and elites used the nascent public school system to implement structures of racial segregation in an effort to enshrine White supremacy. In other words, the desire for White supremacy was inherent in the liberal project of public-school building in the nineteenth-century nations and became more vehement, not less so, as the century wore on. In the United States and Cuba and to some extent in the rest of Latin America, inserting Afro-descendants into the history of education changes the story. It "shatters any pretensions we might have about the democratic and progressive origins of public education," Hilary Moss points out.[47]

Looking at the history of Black education in Cuba and the United States together as well as in other parts of Latin America also begins to present a picture of Black diasporic thought regarding the uses of schooling on the personal, community, and national levels.[48] In all of these national contexts, education played a central role in the struggle for emancipation from slavery and incorporation of former slaves into the polity. A diasporic view also reveals more nuanced aspects to the story of Black education, such as the sometimes painful but politically sophisticated ways that Afro-descendants pivoted between and balanced efforts at achieving public school integration versus creating Black-controlled schools.

In order to tell a Black Cuban intellectual history, it is necessary to look for "the people who do unexpected things in unexpected places."[49] Schools are perhaps not the most unexpected places to find ideas, given what students are sent there to do. But in the Americas in the nineteenth century, at exactly the same moment as public school systems were developing, slaveholding elites and their allies feared giving Afro-descendants access to education precisely because it might give them ideas. Ideas of rebellion. Ideas of ending slavery. Ideas of other possible worlds. Ideas of liberty. And so Black and mulato children were barred from the schools created by municipalities from Regla to Rochester. When Afro-descendants created their own schools, White elites in Cuba hardly considered that what was happening in those schools was intellectual labor that might one day be worthy of study. But Black and mulato Cubans continued with their education projects regardless, following their own ideas and creating the Black Cuban educational tradition that is recounted in this book.

Methodology

The archive has shaped the ways I look for intellectual history in unexpected places. Historians of education often study curricular content, textbooks, school calendars, students' accounts, and teachers' records to tell stories of specific pedagogical approaches, what students spent their days doing, and so forth. But for the study of the Black history of education in colonial Cuba, very little of that kind of material is available. The exodus of the Spanish government from Cuba in 1898 was chaotic, including the movement of documents. As Ada Ferrer tells it, records were tossed out the windows to be loaded onto carts and put on ships. Bundles of documents would fall off, be left where they lay, and eventually collected, haphazardly, into Cuba's first national archive.[50] The Cuban National Archive's card catalogues are not digitized, and the main collection for public education in the colonial period has a dearth of the kinds of materials often used in the history of education, such as curricular documents, textbooks, and student rosters.

There is even less material for the informal schools set up by unlicensed Afro-descended teachers or even for municipal and private schools in which licensed Afro-descended teachers sometimes taught. It is possible that this material is buried in the archive and that another researcher will find it. It is also possible that some Afro-descended Cuban families may have some materials related to schooling that have remained in family archives and may one day make them public when people feel that the state archives or private ones can be trusted to preserve their heritage. To date, however, there is little archival material directly addressing the experiences and perspectives of Black Cuban children, enslaved or free, in the official and unofficial schools of colonial Cuba.[51]

Nor did many Black and mulato Cuban teachers leave much in the way of published documentation about how they thought about the intricacies of teaching; no pedagogical tomes were authored by Black Cuban teachers in the nineteenth century. Publishing in Cuba was severely limited in the early to mid-nineteenth century; it was not until after the 1878 peace treaty ending Cuba's first and unsuccessful bid for independence from Spain that freedom of expression was extended to the island. Thus, even elite White Cubans found publishing on the island difficult; many of them were exiled for their writing and published books in New York instead of Havana.[52] In such a context, all teachers would have found it hard to write about teaching; Black teachers would have found it even more difficult. Furthermore, in the first half of the nineteenth century, many Afro-descended teachers were women with relatively low levels of formal schooling who might not have been inclined to publish theoretical texts. But that does not mean that they did not have ideas about how and why to teach.

Their ideas can be accessed by reading the extant archival materials against the grain, such as the racist diatribes leveled at them by White Creole education reformers. The fates of Afro-descended teachers, the willingness of Afro-descended parents to send their children to segregated municipal schools, the visions of a new world desired by rebelling teachers—all of these appear in the official archive obliquely, but no less convincingly. In many ways, then, this history of Black Cuban education finds ideas in unexpected places.

Those ideas become easier to excavate in the second half of the nineteenth century, when increased freedom of press led to a proliferation of Black newspapers, in which Afro-descended Cuban intellectuals frequently wrote about education.[53] The problem of recovering the history of Afro-descendants in the Americas is not always one of a scarcity of sources.[54] Nonetheless, even rich archival collections contain silences, violences, and power imbalances, as Michel-Rolph Trouillot and other scholars have pointed out.[55] To limit the story to one that can be told by the colonial archive of a slave state alone would be to reproduce the silencing and violence inherent in that archive. Scholars have thus persisted in telling the history of Black people in slave societies through innovative methodological approaches, such as paying close attention to the logic of the archive, listening for silences and noting absences, reading against the grain or with the violence grain, and even employing critical fabulation.[56]

In order to study the intellectual history of Black Cubans, we have to take into account how the practices of Afro-descended teachers—largely sketched out only in broad strokes in the official records by authorities who disdained their work—reveal their educational ideology. In the absence of a certain kind of archive so often used in the history of education and in a context of extreme racial oppression in a slave society, the relationship between praxis and ideology becomes an important methodological approach. "Practices and activities matter, too. . . . The distinctions between 'activist' and 'intellectual' or 'thinker' and 'doer' were often blurred by Black people who necessarily occupied both roles," write Brandon R. Byrd, Leslie M. Alexander, and Russell Rickford.[57] In this book I examine the broad outlines of the work of Black Cuban educators as it is recoverable in the official archive—who these teachers were, who they educated, in which spaces, for how much money, the censure or support they received from educational authorities—and from there, I make arguments about the ideas revealed by those actions.

It is my contention that a cohesive though changing educational ideology is discernible in the work of several groups of Afro-descended Cuban teachers in the nineteenth century, an ideology whose characteristics included a commitment to the widespread dissemination of primary education, the value of widespread primary education for the liberation of the Afro-descended and for all Cubans, tuition-free schooling, Black-run schools, racially integrated classrooms, education of girls, equal school rights, and more. These themes emerge repeatedly in this study of Afro-descended teachers, students, and schools over the course of the nineteenth century. They persist in the face of official censure of separate Black schools in the form of escuelitas; they persist as Black and mulato parents send their children to segregated municipal schools; they persist in the schools created by the sociedades de color; they persist as Black activists turn their attention to the battle for equal school rights; and they persist even in the face of war and US imperial occupation.

That is not to say that there weren't changes in the Black Cuban educational tradition over the course of the more than one hundred years chronicled in these pages. The cast of historical characters here varies. In the early nineteenth century, as White Creoles began their efforts to consolidate their control over primary education and disseminate it more widely, the mostly Black and mulato maestras amigas show up frequently in their records. Once the Spanish colonial government passed an educational law in 1844 and centralized administration of primary and secondary education, the maestras amigas become less visible in the archive, though they continued to teach well into the twentieth century and beyond. In the mid-nineteenth century, the record reveals teachers of color who received teaching licenses, especially the many militiamen of color who, accustomed to the official recognition and social mobility afforded them by one colonial institution, turned to another and sought work as teachers. Despite this group's commitment to the structures of the colonial state, some of them rebelled. In the late nineteenth century, the Black activists associated with the umbrella organization of the sociedades de color emerge as the main protagonists of a concerted civil rights movement that had the desegregation of public schools as its main priority.

All of these groups of Black educators were striving for Black freedom, but they came from different social classes and contexts, had different gendered experiences, and used different strategies. Some of them had racially separate schools; others participated in and demanded access to the developing public school system. The maestras amigas were from a lower social class than the militiamen or the middle-class members of the sociedades de color. They were disdained by White Creoles, and teaching does not appear to have been a route to significant social mobility for them, although it likely brought in some income. Unlike the maestras amigas, the militiamen garnered some respect from some White Cubans. They received official recognition from the colonial state and were usually from a higher social class, having amassed both financial and social capital through their militia service and the prominent place it afforded them among other Afro-descendants. But in the early nineteenth century, as slave rebellions rocked Cuba and the rest of the Americas, some militiamen-teachers rebelled. The militiamen-teachers who took up arms desired a more fundamental and rapid change in their society, and yet they sometimes returned to teaching after rebelling. This suggests that their view of education, too, may have been more radical than that of other Black and mulato educators who may nonetheless have shared their hopes for a Cuba without slavery, colonialism, and racial oppression.

By the end of the nineteenth century, the middle-class Afro-descended Cubans of the sociedades de color were pursuing a two-pronged approach to freedom and education. Slavery had ended but colonialism remained, along with the racial hierarchies these had created. Black educators in this period both created separate schools and lobbied to desegregate the official school system. Their views of education often hewed more to a racial uplift approach, like many other Afro-descendants in the late nineteenth century. They were confronted with a recently freed majority of Afro-descendants with no formal education, and they were convinced that education could help many of the social ills they faced. They also criticized the White supremacy in the colonial institutions, such as education, that they worked within, but these Black educators were significantly less radical in their critiques than the earlier militiamen who rebelled and also less radical than the maestras amigas who figuratively thumbed their noses at the educational authorities. Thus, it is important to reach to the early nineteenth-century origins of the history of the Black Cuban educational tradition to recover more female, lower-class, and radical elements of an educational tradition that would, toward the end of the century, achieve some impressive goals by working within as well as outside of the official educational system.

In all of these cases, education was central to how Afro-descended Cubans thought about their future, their children, and the possibilities of freedom in Cuba. The Black Cuban educational tradition was, from the beginning and across the nineteenth century, liberatory. Its proponents insisted that Afro-descended children and adults were capable and worthy of reading, writing, and learning. In doing so, they contradicted the ideological underpinnings of nineteenth-century White supremacy, and they insisted on a place for themselves in one of the most important developing public institutions in Cuba.

Chapter Outline

In chapter 1, I examine the work of the maestras amigas, mostly Black and mulata women without teaching licenses who provided early education to neighborhood children in what were called *escuelitas de amigas* or *escuelitas de casa*, informal schools in their own homes. It is in the escuelitas de amigas where the earliest antecedents of a national public education system are seen. Specifically, it is in the classrooms of the maestras amigas that some of the earliest roots appear of the idea that Cuban national schools should be racially integrated, co-ed, and tuition-free. The maestras amigas educated girls and boys, White children and Afro-descended children, regardless of whether students could pay a modest fee. Though there is almost nothing in the way of archival records left by these women or their schools, I read against the grain of the copious criticism leveled at them by White reformers of the Sociedad Económica in order to uncover their educational ideology and center their contributions to Cuban educational thought.

Similarly, in chapter 2, I contend that the actions of some Afro-descended male teachers who participated in armed rebellions against slavery and the colonial state reveal something about these teachers' ideas regarding the connections between education and the struggle for liberation. In the first half of the nineteenth century, Cuba experienced many rebellions by enslaved and free Afro-descendants. These "repeating rebellions," posits Finch, reflected and fueled the development of a Black political consciousness. Among the thousands of Black and mulato men who were arrested for rebellion were men who had previously worked as teachers or who would open schools after they served sentences of imprisonment or exile. In some cases, these Afro-descended teachers participated in multiple rebellions. I trace the stories of these rebellious teachers to explore the role that education played in Afro-Cubans' politics of opposition. Like armed insurrection, schooling allowed Black Cubans to envision a new world order for the future and a path toward personal and collective liberation.

As the public school system in Cuba developed over the course of the nineteenth century, Afro-descended Cuban teachers had to deal with racial segregation enshrined in educational law. As in the United States, authorities meant for school segregation to be a tool of racial oppression.[58] The first decree of the colonial government in Cuba regarding education (1842–1844) allowed children of color access to education but required separate schools to be built for them where necessary. In chapter 3 I follow the debates about race and schooling that played out in this and subsequent laws, rulings, and decrees. In addition to exploring how the requirement for racial segregation affected students of color, I look at its effects on teachers of color. Though reformers throughout the first part of the century sought to push these teachers, such as the maestras amigas, out of their jobs, the creation of a segregated public school system also created an opportunity for other Afro-descended teachers. Examples were men involved in the militias obtaining teaching licenses from the Spanish colonial state. I use the application of a Black former militiaman to examine how Cuban authorities weighed the imperatives of racial segregation embodied in the law against the dangers and necessities of courting Black loyalty.

In 1878, the same year that Cuba's first anticolonial revolution ended in failure, the Spanish colonial government issued a decree requiring each town in Cuba to build a separate school for children of color. Although this decree continued in the racial segregationist vein of the 1842 law, it also represented a push to substantially expand access to public education for children of color, even if in a segregated setting. Furthermore, in a demonstration of how much the colonial authorities were willing to confront White Creoles, the central government decreed that if a municipality didn't build a separate school, it would be forced to admit children into the existing ones. Chapter 4 centers on how Afro-descended Cubans seized on that order, petitioning the central and provincial governments to force municipalities to comply. Although the order was widely ignored, it had a considerable on-the-ground impact, as many towns created either new segregated schools or mixed-race schools by allowing children of color to enter schools previously reserved for White children. This expansion of access to the municipal schools did not benefit teachers of color, however, as most of the teachers in these new schools appear to have been White.

In chapter 5, I turn back to the separate schools created by people of color outside of the official school system. In the aftermath of the peace treaty ending the failed war for independence (1868–1878), sociedades de color proliferated, and many of them focused on education. The separate schools of the sociedades de color gave employment to Black teachers and allowed Afro-descended children to be taught in spaces free of the White supremacy that was coming to characterize the developing public school system. But many of the sociedades de color also admitted White children and provided free tuition, in a continuation of earlier trends in the Black Cuban educational tradition. The repeated characteristics of Black separate schools suggests that the Black Cuban educational tradition represented a cohesive set of ideas regarding the purpose of schooling and its relationship to society and to the liberation of both Black and White Cubans.

But even as they created separate schools within their sociedades de color, Black Cubans continued to insist on a desegregated public school system. In chapter 6, I tell the story of the Directorio Central de las Sociedades de la Raza de Color, an umbrella organization of Black mutual aid societies that sued the Spanish colonial government for failing to comply with the 1878 decree requiring them to build separate schools for children of color. The Directorio asked the Spanish authorities to desegregate all public schools. In 1894, after a concerted legal and public campaign, they won their suit. The Spanish colonial government ruled that all municipal schools should be open to children of color, and Black newspapers urged their readers to send their children to school while documenting instances of discrimination and White resistance. The simultaneous efforts of Afro-descended Cubans to create their own schools to fill the gaps left by the public school system and to valorize Black teachers and students while at the same time insisting on admission into the municipal schools has parallels to the work of African Americans in the US North who similarly pushed for both separate schools and equal school rights. "Both forms of activism transformed educational history for the better by rejecting White supremacy and insisting on the inherent dignity and worth of Black children and the central role of public education in the Black freedom struggle," Zoë Burkholder writes about the United States. In the US and Cuban contexts, Afro-descendants took their ideas about what liberation looked like, how their societies should be structured, what the relationship was between the people and the state, and what the relations were between different groups of people with significant power differentials. They put these ideas into practice in the institutions they themselves created while also insisting on shaping the institutions White Creoles were attempting to use to oppress them.

The educational efforts of Black Cubans were interrupted by the last Cuban war of independence, which began in 1895, only one year after the desegregation ruling. Following three years of warfare, Cuba was occupied by the United States for four years (1898–1902), during which the occupying government sought to rebuild the public education system. In chapter 7 I describe the clash of racial strictures that resulted when US school inspectors, expecting to find segregated public schools, were baffled to find schools that were racially integrated. Though US colonial officials attempted to create a new public school system from scratch, the history of public education on the island meant that Cubans had their own ideas about what public education should be and acted accordingly, even under the noses of the US authorities. In the efforts of Afro-descended Cubans to shape a Cuban national education system that was free, widespread, and racially integrated, the legacy continues of the early nineteenth-century maestras amigas' educational ideologies and the influence of the Black Cuban educational tradition.

The epilogue briefly presents the subsequent failure of desegregation of the schools in the early twentieth century, as middle- and upper-class Whites fled public schools for private ones. It was this situation that Fidel Castro's revolutionary government sought to remedy when it nationalized the school systems in 1961, outlawing private schools and successfully integrating the public school system. The Revolution's integration campaign, however, came at the expense of shutting down many separate Black schools and organizations, thus destroying the educational opportunities that Black Cubans had built for themselves over decades in the face of great racial oppression. Today, racial disparities in the public school system are on the rise again in Cuba, as in the United States, showing how much the story told in this book needs telling, in hopes that we can learn from the efforts of those who came before us.

In the nineteenth century, Afro-descendants throughout the Americas, including in Cuba, used education as a vital tool in the pursuit of freedom and equality. The education of Black children and adults constituted a serious blow to the heart of the White-supremacist logic that shaped the Americas in the nineteenth century. In daring to imagine that the edifice of nineteenth-century colonial Cuba, built on slavery and sugar, could be remade differently, that modernity could be traveling on a different road, Afro-descended Cuban educators were producing ideas and knowledge about their contemporary world and imagining the next possible one to come.

A Note on Terms

There are many terms in this book that have been kept in the original Spanish, such as *maestras amigas*, *escuelitas de casa*, *sociedades de color*, and *magisterio*. They are evocative in the original, and I don't want to lose that in translation or to subvert my own translanguaging practices.[59] I italicize and define each Spanish (and French and Latin) term the first time it appears to signal to the reader that it may be unfamiliar, but subsequent mentions are not italicized.

Although the book is primarily about free Afro-descended Cubans, I use "Afro-descendants," "Afro-descended Cubans," and "people of color" to denote all Cubans of African ancestry, whether free or enslaved. In the nineteenth century, free Afro-descended Cubans were usually referred to in Spanish as *la clase de color*, *gente de color*, or *la raza de color*. These labels encompassed two related racialized groups: *morenos*, also referred to as *negros*, and *pardos*, also referred to as *mulatos*. I have chosen to use the terms *mulato* and *mulata* without translating them because the English term would be offensive to many, whereas the terms in Spanish are still in use by Cubans today. As scholars of race have always insisted, racialization is a historical process, and any label will denote a location-specific historical moment. As the nineteenth century wore on, the pressures of White supremacy holding up the slavery-based sugar system meant that the people called *negros*, *morenos*, *pardos*, and *mulatos* were more often racialized as a single non-White group. They faced similar constraints and increasingly acknowledged their shared African ancestry and contemporary social position in opposition to White supremacy. Consequently, as the timeline of the book advances, I more frequently refer to all Afro-descendants as Black. I call it a Black Cuban educational tradition in part as a nod to this process of racialization and to tie this freedom struggle to the educational freedom struggles of other Black people in the Americas.

1

Maestras Amigas and the Shaping of a Black Cuban Educational Ideology in Early Nineteenth-Century Cuba

In her testimonial *Reyita: The Life of a Black Cuban Woman in the Twentieth Century*, María de los Reyes Castillo Bueno describes two years of her life in the late 1910s or early 1920s during which she taught in a "little school in a private house" in the eastern part of Cuba. Though she was only fifteen years old, had little formal education, and was not a licensed teacher, she bought primers to study at night and taught what she had learned to the sixty-two students who enrolled in her school. "They called it 'La Escuelita,'" she recalls. Although Castillo Bueno was able to charge some students tuition and thus earn a little money, she noted that "the families of the few Black pupils in my little school couldn't afford the monthly fee, and I didn't charge them when I saw their eagerness to learn."[1]

Castillo Bueno's school was one example of a centuries-long Cuban tradition of escuelitas de amigas, small in-home schools for very young children that existed outside of the official education system. The women who taught in them were known as maestras amigas, many if not most of whom were, like Castillo Bueno, Afro-descended. Maestras amigas often charged a fee to the families that could afford it but usually educated the students of families that couldn't afford tuition as well. And like Castillo Bueno's school, these schools' students often included both Black and White children.[2] Indeed, in the first half of the nineteenth century, Afro-descended women were pioneers in establishing racially integrated, tuition-free schools, creating the kind of equitable access to schooling that eludes the Americas today.

In the nineteenth century, the national public education systems that were being developed throughout the world were characterized by tuition-free primary schools, usually financed by governments, and available to growing numbers of children, whose presence was in turn required by compulsory attendance laws.³ Equal access to those schools remained a hotly debated and unresolved issue well into the twentieth century and beyond, especially for Afro-descended children after de jure segregation policies replaced slavery regimes in many parts of the Western Hemisphere and in cases where children had to work for much of the day and year.⁴

In Cuba, the story of the rise of the national education system usually begins in the late eighteenth and early nineteenth centuries with the Real Sociedad Económica de la Habana (also called the Real Sociedad Patrótica de la Habana and later the Sociedad Económica de Amigos del País). The Sociedad Económica was a group of White Creole men who saw themselves as liberal reformers intent on bringing modernity to Cuba. After its founding in 1793, the group was granted a royal charter to take charge of education on the island; in 1816 it formed an education section. The members sought to establish more primary schools that could educate more lower-class children, operating on the idea that a modern country needed an enlightened populace, and that could only be achieved through the formal education of the masses. Besides more primary schools, they sought to offer more schools free of tuition to maximize access to all classes of Cuban society. But crucially, the Sociedad Económica sought to deny schooling to Cuba's large Afro-descended population. For its members, a modern society was a White one. Thus, the modest expansion in free primary schooling achieved by the Sociedad Económica in the first half of the nineteenth century only benefited White children.

Despite the prominence of these White liberal educational reformers in the nationalist historiography and existing literature on the history of education in Cuba, the Sociedad Económica's own records point to a very different beginning to the story of national education systems and educational ideologies that would develop on the island: the escuelitas de amigas run by maestras amigas like María de los Reyes Castillo Bueno and her predecessors. In Cuba at the turn of the nineteenth century, before the existence of national public education laws or a comprehensive system of schools on the island, it was the maestras amigas who provided much of the kind of education usually attributed to the influence of liberal transatlantic currents of thought about schooling and their White proponents in Cuba. Escuelitas de amigas were often racially integrated, and many of them were either co-educational or only for girls. They often provided an education with no tuition cost to children's families. In other words, Black and mulata women were at the forefront of the free education movement that would come to dominate the Cuban educational landscape in the nineteenth century, a push that was the defining issue for implementing national public education in Cuba and part of a wider Atlantic circulation of liberal ideas about mass education. They were also pioneers in educating girls and providing a racially integrated education. Thus, Black women educators' work and ideas are central to the history of education in nineteenth-century Cuba.

Afro-descended Cuban teachers faced significant challenges. The push for mass education in Cuba in the 1800s took place within a sociopolitical context that included a growing sugar economy, an expanding slave system, an increase in the number of Africans and Afro-descendants on the island, and an effort to shore up Spanish rule as colonial officials faced challenges from local Creole Whites and rebellions by enslaved and free people of color. As official schooling options for children expanded, first under the control of prominent Creoles associated with the Sociedad Económica and then, after 1844, under the control of the colonial authorities, education became an ideological battleground for Creoles and Spanish government officials to express their differing ideas about Cuba's future. These groups engaged in a protracted struggle over educational policies, even as both at times advocated for ostensibly liberal measures such as the implementation of a free educational system that would help to modernize Cuban society. These educational debates contributed to the rise of national consciousness while revealing that the groups were using the educational arena to manage their anxieties about the growing Afro-descended population in Cuba, time and again enacting segregation policies that would allow them to exert control over people of color. Despite the palpable tension and open contest for power between Creoles and colonials, in the educational arena they demonstrated shared commitment to Whiteness at the expense of students and teachers of color.[5]

Afro-descended teachers, however, were not silent observers of the contest for power in the educational arena between liberal Creole Whites and colonial officials. Instead, Afro-descended teachers actively shaped the ideologies about education and Cuban identity that circulated in the early nineteenth century. Two groups of teachers of color are of special interest here: the maestras amigas, mostly Afro-descended women who taught little children informally and without a license in their homes, and the former militiamen of color who became teachers.[6] Afro-Cuban teachers established schools that were significantly more equitable than those the Creole educational reformers implemented. Examining these teachers reveals much about how Afro-descended Cubans used the educational system to articulate their own visions of freedom in nineteenth-century Cuba and how they contributed to the emerging Cuban national ideology that would come to the fore in the 1868 war of independence.

Free people of color in mid-nineteenth-century Cuba used education to respond to the growing racial discrimination of the period. The rebellion by enslaved Africans in Saint Domingue (1791–1804) decimated the French colony's sugar industry, which had until then been the largest producer in the world. Cuban sugar planters saw this as an opportunity to expand their own sugar production and imported hundreds of thousands of enslaved Africans to labor on Cuban sugar plantations during the nineteenth century.

As the rise of the slave-based sugar plantation led to a shoring up of racial hierarchies throughout Cuban society, Afro-descended teachers endeavored to foster a sense of identity and community with other people of color by disseminating literacy that they had painstakingly acquired to other people of color, children and adults. These Afro-descended women teachers also taught White children in their schools, resisting the official trend toward segregation by sitting White and Black children next to each other, suggesting that they were interested in developing a racially integrated Cuban society. Lastly, the maestras amigas of color were also particularly committed to extending education to every child regardless of income. In fact, it was maestras amigas who were at the forefront of disseminating free primary education on the island in accepting students for no fee long before Creole educational reformers seized on the same idea. In the actions of free teachers of color in the nineteenth century, they demonstrated with clarity a pattern of resistance to official efforts to degrade and oppress them but also a distinct Afro-Cuban contribution to the contours of an emerging Cuban educational and therefore national ideology.

The maestras amigas faced particular animosity from the White Creoles involved in the education section of the Sociedad Económica. The organization's records do not ignore the role of women of color in early childhood education but rather mention them frequently, always disparagingly. In the disdain for the maestras amigas expressed by members of the Sociedad Económica, it is possible to discern a fear of the type of knowledge the women passed on to little children. The curricular content of the maestras amigas of the turn of the nineteenth century is not available in the archive, but the clash between elite White Creole men and lower-class, sometimes previously enslaved, free Afro-descended women raises intriguing questions about what these women were teaching the children and why White men were so opposed to it. Was Black literacy understood to be a threat to White power? Were women-of-color teachers a threat to White male teachers' job prospects? Were maestras amigas teaching West African religious maxims instead of Christian ones? These questions are impossible to answer with the extant archive, but the vitriol contained in the records of the Sociedad Económica suggests that the very fact of women of color teaching in the primary education space, along with the content of their teaching, might have had the power to destabilize the systems of oppression being painstakingly constructed by White Cuban men. In this way, then, the maestras amigas were challenging White supremacy and advancing visions of a more liberatory Cuban future.

The Sociedad Económica, the Spanish Colonial Government, and the Struggle for Control over Cuban Education

It was in what they considered to be a particularly bleak educational landscape that the White Cuban Creoles associated with the Sociedad Económica began to work. Many of its members were proponents of the constitutional rule that existed intermittently in Spain, and they advocated for economic liberalism and political autonomy for the colony.[7] The Sociedad Económica's royal charter to take charge of education on the island meant that education became one of the few institutional spaces in Cuba controlled by White Creoles rather than Spanish colonial officials. Subsequently, Sociedad Económica members would clash repeatedly with Spanish authorities over the issue of education, claiming that Spain used schooling to control the island's people and underfunded education generally.

From the early to mid-nineteenth century, the Creoles involved in the Sociedad Económica grew in their conviction that the expansion of education and in particular of primary education was necessary to allow Cuba to develop into a modern society that could lay claim to political autonomy from the Spanish empire. "Here we know that primary and secondary education is as necessary as food . . . and that a society that doesn't provide a general education to its individuals . . . does not deserve to be called civilized," proclaimed Domingo del Monte, the secretary of the sociedad's education section.[8] These men wanted to construct a particular kind of education system, one in which children went to schools instead of being educated at home and poor children could go to school for free so as to widely disseminate learning at the primary level.[9]

In the calculation regarding education, modernity, and political autonomy, race played a major role. Many White Creole elites, especially the planter class, supported the Spanish colonial government as a defense against the abolitionist zeal of the British empire and against the threat of insurrection from their rapidly expanding enslaved population, while some White Cuban intellectuals by the early nineteenth century had begun to articulate an ideology in favor of a separate Cuban national identity and varying degrees of political autonomy. These White intellectuals understood that slavery and colonialism were intertwined phenomena, and they came to oppose the continuation of the slave trade as well as, in some cases, even of slavery. These men did not envision a racial democracy, however; at best, they envisioned a racial mixture that would lead to a Whitened population on the island since only Whiteness, in their view, could foster a modern, independent polity. Thus, though some White Cuban intellectuals, many of them associated with the Sociedad Económica, sought political autonomy and modernization, they envisioned that imaginary modern Cuban nation as White. When they worked on issues of education, their preoccupation with the issue of race was evident, as was their quarrel with Spanish colonial officials.

Free Education as the Vanguard of Educational Reform

In the early nineteenth century, neither the Spanish colonial government nor the White Creole men of the Sociedad Económica had much in the way of educational advancements to lay claim to. In 1837, the Sociedad Económica took an educational census of the island that showed there were 210 schools on the island for White children, meaning only 5 percent of all school-age children in Cuba were attending schools.[10] Most African and Afro-descended children were enslaved in the 1830s and did not receive any schooling at all. And there was little in the way of official educational options for free children of color by the 1830s, in part due to the Sociedad Económica's priorities.

One of the Sociedad Económica's major initiatives for the development of primary education was to provide free education to children who could not afford it. "Primary education should be universal and therefore should be free for those who cannot pay," declared Sociedad Económica member Juan Justo Reyes.[11] Indeed, the idea of free primary education was central to expanding liberal notions of education in the nineteenth century, and Cuba was no exception. In the earliest years of its work, the education section solicited donations from wealthy White Creoles to fund the tuition of children in extant schools; one such was an 1818 donation by Desiderio Herrera that covered tuition, paper, and other supplies. Sometimes, influential White Creoles were able to convince local municipalities to take over the funding of free schools; in Santiago de Cuba a school that had been created in 1798 by Juan Manuel Carvajal was funded by the *ayuntamiento*, the town council, by 1806.[12] The education section itself also funded tuition for at least twenty students in the neighborhood of Jesús María in Havana. A branch of the Sociedad Económica in Puerto Principe supported six schools with 330 boys and five schools with 164 girls.[13]

In the 1820s there were 140 schools on the island, but only 16 of them were free, a situation that Sociedad Económica members noted and strove to rectify.[14] In an 1830 report, Reyes noted that "the Education Section, struck by the importance of its mission and by the eminent service needed by the homeland, dedicated itself to promote, by all means possible, the creation of free primary schools, which would serve to diffuse the immeasurable benefit of a Christian and literary education to every last class of society."[15]

Later, another Sociedad Económica member, Antonio Bachiller y Morales, would label the period 1833–1846 as one of "expansion and improvements" in the field of education because of an increase in the number of schools and credited the expansion of tuition-free education. Bachiller positioned these tuition-free schools as the necessary precursor to a plan for public schools in every town that would be the "realization of the longed-for project of the Sociedad: to generalize free education to all corners of the island, having demonstrated that vice is always the companion of ignorance."[16] Thus, for the Sociedad Económica, expanding education on the island was necessary for an enlightened, virtuous people to develop into a modern society, and the first step in doing so was to provide free education where possible.

Free education required funding, and this issue became a major flashpoint in the disputes between the Spanish colonial government and the White Creoles of the Sociedad Económica. In the first three decades of the nineteenth century, the Sociedad Económica struggled to get the government to provide funds for free primary education to children. In the 1820s, the Havana city council withdrew the Sociedad Económica's funding for schools, opining that poor children were served by the free school available in each monastery. In response, Francisco Filomeno "had to make [the mayor] understand the necessity of attending to education." Finally, repeated demands by the Sociedad Económica were met by the government, allotting the organization 8,000 pesos, only half of which could be used for schools.[17]

These clashes over funding continued apace, and the members of the Sociedad Económica continually interpreted them as evidence that the Spanish colonial government was not enlightened enough to understand the importance of education. In another episode in the 1830s, the Spanish colonial official Vicente Vázquez Queipo claimed that what free primary education was available in Cuba was due to the generosity of the Spanish colonial government. This prompted José Antonio Saco, a Cuban intellectual and the head of the Sociedad Económica's education section, to respond furiously. Saco pointed out that although some small amount of funding came from the Spanish colonial government, the Sociedad Económica mostly received funding from dues paid by the members and income from the *Diario de la Habana* newspaper, which it owned. "Since the funds of the Sociedad do not come solely from the colonial government, it is clear that the free primary education granted by the Sociedad is also not exclusively paid for by the government," Saco pointed out. He went on to argue that the Spanish colonial government's claims of generosity and benevolence fell short: "the government receives enormous contributions from the Cuban people, and in allocating a minimal and insignificant part of those contributions to the education of a few poor children, the government is not conducting an act of generosity, but rather fulfilling a sacred obligation imposed by religion and society." Without adequate Spanish colonial spending, White Creoles in Cuba struggled to raise funds and consolidate control over the education system, hindering the school system's ability to advance a national project.[18]

The Sociedad Económica, Gender, and Racial Segregation in Educational Policy

The Sociedad Económica's activities in support of an educational enterprise that would bring Cuba's educational system in line with wider transatlantic developments in education coincided with the rise of the slave-based sugar system. White Creoles involved in education, wary of the growing Black population in the early nineteenth century, used the educational system they were taking such pains to expand for the purpose of marginalizing free people of color. Education became a marker of civilization that for White Cuban Creoles was marked by European or White customs and was used to further distance White Creoles from the increasing numbers of Black Cuban Creoles.[19]

The Sociedad Económica's push for expanded and free primary education in the early nineteenth century purposefully left out people of color, a goal made explicit by its members who desired to "prohibit the learning of letters and its teaching to people of color."[20] The expansion of education in Cuba mostly benefited White children as the Sociedad Económica established more schools that charged tuition and a few tuition-free schools for poor children. In a country with limited educational options, children of color found it even more difficult to access schooling.

In the late eighteenth century, some free Afro-descendants had been able to access schooling. A 1792 survey found that the best seven schools in the capital city of Havana educated 552 students, 408 of them White and 144 of them pardos and morenos.[21] Some free children of color had been able to access an education before the early nineteenth century, but by the 1830s, schooling options were being steadily foreclosed to more of them. This was because de jure racial segregation became a desired educational policy for White Cuban Creoles who were interested in disseminating free primary education in Cuba. Despite expressing an interest in making primary education available to all classes of Cuban society and providing tuition-free schools, the members of the Sociedad Económica elevated their commitment to White supremacy over those goals. In fact, their conviction that racial segregation should be enacted in education grew apace with their interest in spreading education generally.

An 1804 rule book for teachers published by the Sociedad Económica education section allowed each teacher to decide whether to admit Black children, and many Creole teachers decided not to. In 1809 the group went further, urging that Black children not be educated and encouraging their expulsion from schools. Racially integrated schooling would only be tolerated in the escuelitas de amigas, which fell outside of the purview of the official school system being developed by the Sociedad Económica.[22]

In 1816, the year the Sociedad Económica formed its education section, there were 49 schools within the Havana city walls attended by 883 White boys, 164 mulato boys, and 248 Black boys, 183 White girls, 67 mulata girls, and 72 Black girls. There were 19 schools in the neighborhoods outside of Havana's city walls attended by 464 White boys and 33 students of color.[23] Evidently, White boys had the lion's share of access to the limited education system that existed, although children of color made up about 30 percent of the students inside the city walls. Sociedad Económica records do not specify whether the children of different races went to school together within city walls except in Belén, with 1,225 White students and 69 students of color. This accounting likely included every kind of school, since the Sociedad Económica had not created any oversight or licensing system yet.

Its members' interest in expanding primary education through tuition-free schools conflicted with their interest in enshrining White supremacy in Cuban society. In an 1830 report, Sociedad Económica member Reyes explored the question "Can people of color attend White schools?" His answer was a resounding no; he acknowledged that the "resolution [to this question] departs from the general rule established [in the section on who should attend free schools]; but this exception, if it is one, is not dictated by the Sociedad, but rather by nature."[24] Reyes not only departed from the goal of disseminating primary schooling as widely as possible but also ascribed a cause to this prioritization, blaming nature and not the group of White Creoles in charge of education during this period, for the efforts at implementing racial segregation in Cuba's schools. Nature was thus used to explain away the tension inherent in the Sociedad Económica's educational reforms.

White supremacy, in the view of Reyes, required racially segregated schools. Reyes went on to explain that schools for children of color should be directed by people of color themselves, although these should be licensed by the government and ecclesiastical authorities and overseen and inspected by the Sociedad Económica.[25] In the 1820s, the Sociedad Económica attempted to establish a dedicated private school for children of color that would have provided access to education to some children, but members again revealed their interest in racially segregating the educational sphere.[26]

Thus, the expansion of free schooling effected by the Sociedad Económica largely excluded children of color. In 1802 a Havana school for boys had thirty White and eight Afro-descended students, among whom only fourteen White children received free education.[27] In 1835 the Sociedad Económica established free schools in Matanzas and in two neighboring towns, but this expansion of free public schooling was only for Whites; the group's regulations for the schools in Matanzas province stipulated that only children from White families would be admitted to the schools.[28] In the same year, the Sociedad Económica paid for the education of 540 White children in Havana and did not pay for the schooling of any children of color at all.[29] In 1837 the Sociedad Económica paid the tuition fees of 535 of the 3,093 White children in Havana schools but did not fund any of the 234 students of color.[30] For the White Creoles associated with the Sociedad Económica, the notion of fostering a civilized, enlightened populace through schooling only extended to the White population and purposely left out the enslaved and free population of color.

An 1837 report by the Sociedad Económica shows a decline in the number of children of color attending schools, although it is possible that this report excluded informal or unlicensed schools from its census. Of the approximately 9,000 students attending the island's schools, only about 500, less than 6 percent, were children of color. At a time when enslaved and free Afro-descendants may have outnumbered Whites on the island, there were only about a dozen schools for children of color and 210 for White children.[31] In Havana province there were 123 schools for 3,093 White students and 7 schools for 340 students of color.[32] In the same year in Santiago de Cuba and the rest of the eastern province, there were 45 schools for White children, and 7 schools for children of color.[33] In the fifteen years between 1836 and 1851, Cubans added 150 new schools for Whites, for a total of 366 licensed schools, but the number of schools for Blacks remained the same, namely 12.

The Sociedad Económica's efforts took their toll; in the fifty or so years between the end of the eighteenth century and the middle of the nineteenth, the proportion of free colored elementary school students dropped from 25 percent to less than 5 percent.[34] White Creole educational reformers' desire to limit the expansion of primary education to Whites and to implement racial segregation in Cuba's educational system adversely affected children of color's ability to acquire schooling.

Gender also played a role in the Sociedad Económica's educational policy. It established schools primarily for White boys but also pursued education for White girls as a part of its civilizing project. Historian Matt Childs demonstrates that the education it offered to girls would be provided in separate schools and focus on domestic skills such as sewing rather than academic subjects. The gendered focus of the curriculum would mitigate the risk that schooling might prompt White Cuban women to abandon their roles as wives and mothers; instead, educating women in domestic tasks would help further the Sociedad Económica's project of civilizing Cuba through education, since mothers were the first teachers of their children.[35] The ideal of White female education also served its White-supremacist project by widening the educational gulf between White and Afro-descended girls in Cuba.

Free People of Color and Teaching in Early Nineteenth-Century Cuba

Black children were not the only ones affected by the Sociedad Económica's interests in using education to uphold a racial hierarchy, and the White Creole men of the Sociedad Económica were not the only Cubans interested in education in this period. In the early nineteenth century, free adults of color in Cuba were deeply involved in the teaching profession, the magisterio. Indeed, free people of color were at the forefront of disseminating the tuition-free primary education that elite White men identified as being sorely needed even as they ignored Afro-descendants' contributions. Ironically, Sociedad Económica members themselves inadvertently revealed that the increase in free education in this period was due not only to their organization's own new free schools but also to the maestras amigas, most of them Afro-descendants, teaching in escuelitas de casa.

The Sociedad Económica's activities were carefully and self-consciously recorded in its various publications and those of its literary-minded members. These materials crafted a self-congratulatory narrative centering their efforts at expanding free primary education in Cuba. But there were other actors on the educational stage of early nineteenth-century Cuba, and the Sociedad Económica's own records often unwittingly highlight the contributions of Afro-descended teachers.

For free people of color in Cuba, the teaching profession was an important arena of work. And it was these Afro-descended teachers, reviled and sidelined (but never ignored) by Sociedad Económica members, who did the most to advance the liberal cause of tuition-free primary education in nineteenth-century Cuba. They were also at the forefront of creating a racially integrated society by teaching children of color and White children in the same classrooms. Some of their escuelitas were co-ed, too, challenging the Sociedad Económica's notion of what an education system should look like. In all of these ways, the maestras amigas were creating a Black Cuban educational tradition that anticipated the most progressive aspects of transatlantic liberal educational thought and stood in opposition to the patriarchal and racist educational project that the Sociedad Económica was advancing.

Despite the consolidating racial categories and hardening racial hierarchies caused by the early nineteenth-century sugar boom in Cuba, racial categories were still fluid enough then to allow free Afro-descendants to develop livelihoods, wealth, and important social networks. Free people of color worked as artisans and traders; they were dockworkers, domestic laborers, tailors, dentists, militiamen, and teachers. In some cases they held apprenticeships.[36] Some free people of color, including formerly enslaved men and women, became slaveholders themselves.[37] Unlike elite White women, free women of color worked inside and outside of the home, as wet nurses, domestic servants, midwives, laundresses, and teachers.

Even though Spaniards and White Creoles considered these jobs to be devoid of honor, free people of color engaged in them and derived from them considerable meaning and, in some cases, considerable sums of money. The work thus allowed them to create their own sense of honor and to resist the degraded place that society had designated for them. Free people of color who participated in the economy did so in order "to dispute [their] place in the world of free men."[38]

The magisterio was a particularly important area of work for free people of color. Like the arts and trades, teaching primary school was disdained by White people who had therefore left the field of early or primary education, like the arts and trades, to la clase de color at the turn of the nineteenth century, much to the chagrin of the White Creole educational reformers. It was this trend that the Sociedad Económica members were trying to change by pushing Afro-descended women out of Cuban education. But as their records showed, the maestras amigas were already widely disseminating primary education at little to no cost and developing the Black educational tradition that is recounted in this book.

Afro-Descended Maestras Amigas

Some women of color managed to become licensed teachers in the early nineteenth century. The poet Juana Pastor received a license in 1835 to open a primary school for female children of color. Ana del Toro and María Faustina Peñalver were also licensed teachers in Havana in this same period.[39] Still, it was difficult for people of color to become licensed teachers during this time. Between 1830 and 1844, while the Sociedad Económica was still in charge of education on the island, there were only eight mulata women and six Black women who were licensed on the island of Cuba, for a total of fourteen.[40] Six men of color also received titles in those years, during which time there were 178 White teachers (60 women and 118 men).[41] Notably, there were more women teachers than men teachers among the Afro-descended group, as compared to the White teachers, where men outnumbered the women significantly. This may suggest that women of color, in addition to presenting path-breaking educational ideologies and practices, may also have been the vanguard of feminizing the profession.

Despite the presence of a few licensed Afro-descended teachers in the first half of the nineteenth century, many more women of color became informal and unlicensed teachers, opening small schools within their homes. These escuelitas de amigas and escuelitas de casa were something like modern-day kindergartens, teaching basic reading and writing skills, as well as catechism to small children. Maestras amigas had practiced in Spain since the seventeenth century, and escuelitas were found in the nineteenth and twentieth centuries in various parts of the Americas. Like the ones in Cuba, they were usually informal community schools run by women in their own homes.[42]

Most teachers of the escuelitas de amigas in nineteenth-century Cuba were Afro-descended women. Afro-descended women provided a lot of the care for wealthy children in colonial Cuba, and the escuelitas de amigas may be another instance of this trend. Oftentimes Afro-descended women, many of them enslaved, nourished and cared for White children as wet nurses and nannies. This practice led some White Creole men to despair that White women were surrendering their moral and religious influence over their children to women of color.[43] "If a mother finds it necessary to give her child a wet nurse, her vigilance should be doubled, regardless of how much affection the wet nurse demonstrates, since no one—no one—can adequately replace the lively interest of a good mother, and the smallest neglect by a wet nurse can cause unpleasant consequences," wrote the doctor Ramón Zambrana Valdes in the *Revista de la Habana* in the 1850s, encouraging White Cuban women to breastfeed their own children.[44] The role of Afro-descended women in young children's lives continued from early physical nourishment into the sphere of early education. In 1793, the majority of existing escuelas de amigas in Havana (twenty-three of thirty-nine) were run by women of color.[45] In 1814, there were fifty escuelitas de amigas in Havana.[46]

The escuelitas de amigas were run by and attended by lower-class Cubans, and the teachers and the students were Afro-descended, although the students also included White children. The teachers and students of these escuelitas were usually described as being poor. The 1817 educational survey conducted by Sociedad Económica member and friar Félix González noted that the escuelitas de amigas were "humble classrooms where poor girls and boys and of both races learned to read and write."[47]

For the maestras amigas, teaching was not a particularly lucrative position. They did not make enough money to pay overhead costs for a separate building. Their lack of teaching licenses from the authorities also suggests that they did not have the social status or the funds to apply for and receive them. Most amigas who taught in their homes charged a small fee to the few students who could afford it, but more commonly they educated students for free.[48] Still, the reference to "decency" suggests that it was a job that granted them a position of dignity among other Afro-descendants and their White neighbors who sent their children to the maestras amigas' schools. In her 1841 teaching license application, María Faustina Peñalver, a free Black woman, stated that she wanted to support herself and her family "through such honorable means, with the decency and composure that is so advisable in society."[49]

Despite the Afro-descended maestras amigas' attempts at securing a line of work that would provide some security and social legitimacy, they faced significant opposition and malicious derision from the White Creole men of the Sociedad Económica. In records from the 1820s, they complained that because "teaching was seen [by White men] if not with disdain, at least with significant abandon, teaching the young becomes the recourse of destitute who barely know the alphabet, and women of color and some wretched widows are called to be the minervas of the fair sex."[50]

Inadvertently, the records of the Sociedad Económica show that the primary education field in the early nineteenth century was dominated by women of color who filled the teacher shortage left by white men's disdain of the magisterio. Rather than acknowledge the important role women of color played in the history of Cuban education, the White Creole men of the Sociedad Económica lamented the women's presence in the magisterio and derided their capacity to teach, describing maestras amigas as barely literate, as well as the content of their teaching. In his 1817 report, González claimed that children only attended the maestras amigas' schools "to entertain themselves making kites."[51] Such condescending dismissals often came on the heels of descriptions of how much these students were actually learning and the significantly large proportion of Cuban students who were only able to attend primary schools thanks to the maestras amigas.

Sociedad Económica records not only threw the content of the maestras amigas' teaching into doubt; they also cast aspersions on their motivations for teaching. One member described the maestras amigas by asserting that "in general some poor Black women have set themselves up as Amigas who have no other way of sustaining themselves with decency."[52] In suggesting that the women were only teaching because they had no other way of sustaining themselves with decency, the report suggested that the mostly Afro-descended maestras amigas were not motivated by the same lofty political and pedagogical concerns that animated the White Creole men of the Sociedad Económica.

Though free men of color, particularly those serving in the militia, garnered some respect and social status from White Cuban society, women of color who became teachers patently faced more animosity. Bachiller conceded grudging respect to male teachers who were also militia members, whose schools, he wrote, "taught first letters with the consent and applause of the corporations of the country." He presented female teachers of color much differently, assigning them considerably more racial difference than he attributed to male militia teachers. Bachiller complained about the escuelitas de amigas that were mostly staffed by women of color as "the most debased and ignorant race, teaching the Caucasian one." He went on to lament that because the teaching profession in the early nineteenth century required no license and no prerequisite, the teachers were "people who were not only ignorant to the point of stupidity but also people of unclean habits and ambiguous race."[53] He protested that people previously employed as cigar rollers or midwives deigned to open "a so-called establishment" without any prior requirement or vocation besides hunger.

For Bachiller, the lack of professional standards for the magisterio de primeras letras, or early education, allowed free people of color to become teachers despite being motivated only by what he considered to be selfish material or social concerns. Besides professional standards, racial hierarchies also were violated by having female teachers of color. Bachiller's presentation of female teachers of color makes clear the disdain with which the women were treated by Creole White Cubans associated with the Sociedad Económica who tolerated them at best and more often attempted to push them out of the teaching force as part of their reform of education.

Maestras Amigas at the Forefront of the Tuition-Free Education Movement

Beyond creating roles for themselves separate from racial slavery, Afro-descended maestras amigas were advancing an important public service, namely educating and caring for many Cuban children, both Black and White. Maestras were also advancing the agenda of providing tuition-free primary education that the men of the Sociedad Económica articulated as being crucial to modernizing Cuban society and underpinned the nineteenth-century efforts to expand educational access and develop national school systems in the Americas.

The escuelitas of the maestras amigas played a crucial role in making early education accessible free of cost in the years before national public education was established on the island. Indeed, Black and mulata women were at the forefront of the free education movement that would come to dominate the Cuban educational landscape in the nineteenth century, a push that was part of the implementation of national public education and of a wider Atlantic circulation of liberal ideas.

That escuelitas de amigas played an important role in propagating tuition-free primary schooling is clear from records of the Sociedad Económica even as its members denigrated the mostly female teachers of color and the schools' curricular content. In 1790, most of the primary schools in Havana other than convents were escuelitas primarily for girls, and most of the schools were directed by free Black and mulata women, according to Bachiller.[54] By 1830, after the Sociedad Económica took charge of education on the island and began to advance its mission of tuition-free primary education, it counted a total of 12 tuition-free schools in the city of Havana, both inside and outside the city walls, 5 schools serving 664 boys and 7 schools for 547 girls. At the end of this educational census, the report noted, "There are, in addition to these, ten escuelas de amigas for both sexes inside the city walls, and seven in the exterior neighborhoods, in which they only teach work and Christian doctrine, with other very light principles of education to children of a very young age. The number of those who attend these rudimentary schools is more than 120 in the interior, and 129 in the exterior ones."[55] Though the report relegated these escuelas de amigas to a side note, in Havana there were considerably more escuelitas de amigas than there were tuition-free schools sanctioned by the Sociedad Económica. Most escuelitas de amigas accepted children who could not pay tuition fees. Thus, it is clear that free women of color's schools presented a considerable and important part of Cuba's tuition-free education landscape in the early nineteenth century.

There were likely many more escuelitas de amigas taught by maestras amigas than official records reflect, as Reyes himself mentioned in his report: "I think the number of [escuelas de amigas] is at least double what appears in the census, but I have not been able to acquire sufficient data on the matter."[56] Other Cuban intellectuals also referenced the ubiquity of escuelitas de amigas providing tuition-free education. José Antonio Saco obliquely referred to them when he mentioned free schools "not paid for by the Government or by the Sociedad [which] educated for free a considerable number of poor children."[57]

White Creoles were sometimes forced to tolerate the escuelitas de amigas despite their disdain for Afro-descended maestras amigas, precisely because the escuelitas were providing tuition-free primary education. This reluctant tolerance highlights how even its members understood that their most important priority was being significantly advanced by women of color. In the 1830s, after an overly zealous inspector shut down several unlicensed schools in a poor neighborhood outside of Havana's city walls, Bachiller told Sociedad Económica members that they could not create obstacles to tuition-free education and thus had to tolerate and learn more about the maestras amigas. "We should not place obstacles to the creation of large numbers of schools. And without funds to support them, we cannot require the guarantees that you demand," he advised. A subsequent commission found that the maestras amigas had wide-ranging qualifications and responsibilities.[58] Bachiller's book *Apuntes para la historia de las letras y de la instrucción pública de la isla de Cuba* makes frequent mention of the escuelitas de amigas generally and of the Afro-descended maestras amigas in particular, underscoring their importance to the history of education on the island of Cuba.

That women of color were at the vanguard of nineteenth-century modern educational ideas is plainly evident in the writings of White Cuban educational reformers who nonetheless described these teachers' actions in very different terms informed by racial and gender animus. Reyes found that the teaching in schools before the Sociedad Económica took charge of education was "defective and reduced, being commonly limited to reading, writing, arithmetic, and catechism." He saved his harshest criticism for the teaching in the schools "for girls, which was, if possible, more imperfect. Many of these schools were directed by pardas and morenas," he explained, "and in most of them they only learn how to pray and sew, in some of them to read and catechism, in few of them to read, and only here and there math and grammar. In almost all of these schools was a mix of classes and conditions, in many, also the sexes."[59] In Reyes's telling, the sex and race of the teachers (Afro-descended women) and the mixed-race composition of their student body has explanatory power for why these schools taught fewer subjects than he found desirable. Decades later, Bachiller echoed Reyes in lamenting that "in the most advantaged schools for boys, they don't get past integers in mathematics, and in the many schools for girls, directed by free Black and mulata women, they only learn to read."[60] Again, the curriculum of the maestras amigas' schools was denigrated for being under the direction of Afro-descended women.

Maestras Amigas and Lessons in Race and Gender

Afro-descended maestras amigas drew the ire of the men of the Sociedad Económica because of the latter's outright racism but also because the teachers' educational project challenged the liberal Creole model for a national education system in various ways. And yet it is in these violently racist and sexist lamentations that the full scope emerges of the ambitious educational project advanced by the Black and mulata maestras amigas.

The men of the Sociedad Económica envisioned schools that would be the predecessors to public schools, that is, schools in the public sphere, as well as funded by the government. The private-public divide in Cuba, as in many other places in the Americas in the early nineteenth century, was a deeply gendered divide. Men operated in the public sphere and women in private ones. Women of color and working-class women constantly confounded this dichotomy by working in the domestic sphere or by traversing the streets for their work while White upper-class Creole women stayed indoors, leaving their homes only with proper chaperones and at appointed times and places.[61]

The maestras amigas' schools likewise violated this gendered divide between private and public. These women were doing work that affected a broader Cuban public, but their schools were literally in their homes. In fact, even many official schools in Cuba were located in the homes of teachers. In 1831, Del Monte, the education section secretary, praised the teachers who allowed poor children into their homes and even to their tables, suggesting that the schools were located inside the teachers' houses.[62] But only the escuelitas de amigas were considered escuelitas de casa, while men's schools were not similarly labeled even if they were actually located in the men's dwellings, suggesting that women teachers doing public work in their homes rendered the entire enterprise uncomfortably domestic, gendered feminine, and in violation of the public-male, private-female divide in Cuban society. Thus, the Afro-descended maestras amigas, by virtue of their racialized and gendered status and the work they undertook, doubly challenged the dominant society's norms. In their personhood and in their work, they were forging a different Cuban public sphere.

Liberal Creole reformers were interested in education primarily because it was a way to shape a specific kind of Cuban public; it was a way to mold society into what these men envisioned as modern—a White, male-led, enlightened public that would be deserving and capable of political sovereignty. But as the men of this class expanded sugar production on the island, Cuba's population became Blacker. White Creoles attempted to solve this problem using racial segregation measures, including in the educational sphere. The schools the Sociedad Económica established were mostly for White boys and strictly segregated by race and by sex.

Having Afro-descended women teachers teach White children as well as Black children violated the efforts at racial segregation that the Sociedad Económica was advancing. Indeed, it was precisely the racially integrated nature of the student body at the escuelitas with teachers who were women of color that drew the ire of Creole educational reformers. The integrated schools of the maestras amigas ran contrary to the general push toward segregation in Cuban educational policy that began with the sociedad in the early nineteenth century and would continue in the public education laws of the mid-nineteenth century.

The escuelitas de amigas, unlike the Sociedad Económica's official schools, sat boys and girls and children of all races right next to each other. These co-educational, integrated classrooms therefore disseminated the benefits of formal education more broadly across sectors of the Cuban population, decidedly fostering a different kind of Cuban public and a different vision of a possible Cuban modernity.

For White Creoles, the first problem posed by the maestras amigas was that Black women were teaching at all, whereas White men were ignoring the field of primary education. The second problem was that Black women were teaching White children. Bachiller complained that people of an inferior race were teaching Caucasians. The problem there was in part one of perceived inability, as in documents describing maestras amigas as barely literate. But Sociedad Económica members also were concerned about teachers of color being in a position of authority over White students, thus violating the racial hierarchy the men were pursuing. In 1827, the chair of the education section of the Sociedad Económica insisted, "We should under no circumstances allow a person of color the right of ordering about a White person by virtue of being their teacher; on the contrary, we should take away the illusion that they could in any way be in charge, nor White people obey them."[63] The men feared that Afro-descended women teachers would destabilize the White-supremacist social order the White Creoles were working so hard to impose. Put another way, the very fact of Afro-descended women teachers teaching White children challenged White supremacy in Cuba.

Besides having teachers who were of a different race, the students of the escuelitas were also usually racially diverse. The escuelitas de amigas usually included White, Black, and mulato students. Ana del Toro, described as a morena, a Black woman, taught Black, mulato, and White children of both sexes, as did the parda (mulata) teacher Victoria Nazaria. A mulato male teacher, Martín Lujarzo, taught sixty-four students, a mix of Whites, Blacks, and mulatos.[64] All three of their schools served both boys and girls. Bachiller y Morales described the escuelitas de amigas run by Black women for children of different races this way: "This peculiarity produced another one, which then the Sociedad set out to destroy: the confusion, in one setting, of all colors and castes, promoting in this way from infancy that element of moral corruption that is wrought from the inevitable familiarity of young people from diverse conditions in countries of slavery."[65] Reyes likewise noted of the escuelitas de amigas that students "in almost all of them were a mix of classes and conditions, in many, also the sexes."[66]

For Bachiller and other members of the Sociedad Económica, the early nineteenth-century increase in African and Afro-descended people on the island was a dangerous consequence of the expansion of the sugar production industry, which enriched the Creole White planter class, many of them members of the sociedad. These men were full of fear and paradoxical desires. They wanted to expand primary education on the island to prove Cuba to be a civilized society capable of autonomy or self-rule, but they were fearful that expanding education to women and people of color could overturn the social order from which their own class benefited. Racial segregation in education was therefore essential to mitigating the dangers of the liberal spread of schooling. Maestras amigas challenged that goal, filling their classrooms with White and Black children.

In addition to being racially integrated, the escuelitas de amigas educated girls, and these schools were often co-educational. They also seem to have dominated the educational landscape for lower-class girls and girls of color. The men of the Sociedad Económica, on the other hand, either focused strictly on male education or, if they provided girls an education, did so in separate schools where they could focus the curriculum on domestic training instead of the education boys were receiving. The escuelitas de amigas do not appear to have altered the curriculum for the boys and girls who were in their schools together. It's possible that the escuelitas de amigas were particularly responsible for educating the girls of the lower classes, to whom sociedad members were not interested in spreading primary education. Bachiller noted with dismay that the escuelitas de amigas appeared to primarily serve girls: "there were many schools, mostly for girls, directed by people of color."[67]

Childs has shown that to the extent White Creoles were interested in girls' primary education, it was to demonstrate to the world that Cuba was a civilized country. White girls would be educated in the domestic tasks deemed appropriate to their gender and race, and the White Creole men of the Sociedad Económica would try to prevent Black girls from receiving an education. The escuelitas de amigas challenged this arrangement by particularly focusing on girls' education, including educating Black and mulata girls. For Afro-descended women and girls, learning to read and write might allow them to challenge systems of social control and oppression. For the maestras amigas, consolidating positions of dignity in Cuban society became more difficult as the White Creole men of the Sociedad Económica sought to control the primary education arena.

Conclusion

For maestras amigas, running escuelitas de casa put them on a collision path with Spanish Creole and colonial authorities rather than allowing them to gain benefits through the state, as militiamen-turned-teachers did. Escuelas de amigas were unofficial and therefore did not engage directly with or gain recognition from the colonial bureaucratic state. They do not appear to have been able to consolidate much personal wealth from their teaching endeavors because they often educated children without charging tuition. And they encountered scorn and disdain from White Creole educational reformers who resented them and tried to push them out of the teaching profession.

And yet, even the Sociedad Económica acknowledged the important role of free women of color as teachers in the early nineteenth-century educational landscape. Maestras amigas were at the forefront of providing free education, a deeply held desire of White Creole men involved in education as well. The women provided a racially integrated education to boys and girls, often in co-ed settings. Doing so ran counter to the official segregation trends in educational policy in nineteenth-century Cuba. The maestras amigas were enacting their own vision of a Cuban society and future in which primary education was widely available and free of cost, women could do work beyond domestic tasks, and boys and girls of all races could learn to read and write together. This was a revolutionary educational agenda that went far beyond the liberal goals of White reformers at the time.

Maestras amigas faced the hardening of a racial hierarchy throughout society, rising discrimination, and the implementation of racial segregation policies in the service of nominally modern and liberal educational agendas. The Sociedad Económica's push for racial segregation in schools evidences this trend to construct White supremacy through education. Enslaved and free Afro-descendants banded together to resist their oppression, sometimes through armed insurrection but other times, as the experience of teachers of color shows, through education.

Beyond resisting oppression, Afro-descended teachers' experiences also reveal much about why free people of color pursued the teaching profession, what they valued in the educational system, how they were able to use education for themselves as individuals as well as for their communities, and how they saw the place of free people of color in the wider Cuban society. The maestras amigas were creating a vision of what Cuban society should be, despite their very marginalized place within it, by providing free education to children at a time when free education was increasingly seen as essential to creating a modern society but was not provided by the official educational system. Afro-descended Cubans used the educational system to help children of color as well as to sit those children next to White children in the classroom and extend education to as many Cubans of all races as possible. This educational project, one in which race-based solidarity could coexist with a racially integrated Cuban society, should be understood as an important Black freedom project, led by working class Afro-descended women.[68]

The Sociedad Económica's efforts to segregate schools and professionalize the teaching force targeted the maestras amigas who taught in the escuelitas de casa. It began to purposefully push the amigas de color out of the teaching profession in the early nineteenth century and sought to replace them with White male instructors in a larger shift to license and professionalize the teaching force.[69] As part of its regulation of public education, the Sociedad Económica required that public schools should teach religion, reading, writing, grammar, and arithmetic as a way to automatically disqualify the escuelitas de amigas, which apparently did not include all these subjects.[70] Women of color who desired to teach with official sanction were also rejected; in 1827 the city council of Havana denied the free Black woman Ana del Toro a teaching license (though she appears to have run her own escuelita without a license).[71]

In the 1840s the Spanish colonial government passed its first law for public education on the island and removed education from the purview of the Sociedad Económica. Spanish colonial authorities, however, shared the White Creole members' commitment to constructing White supremacy in nineteenth-century Cuba, and Afro-descended teachers faced continued challenges under the new educational plan.

The maestras amigas come in and out of the official sources after the Sociedad Económica was removed from its role in the Cuban education system, but the women continued to teach well into the twentieth century and likely beyond. Even in the 1840s, as the new education system was being implemented, the maestras amigas continued their work. In December 1844, Santiago de Cuba had twenty-one schools in addition to the Colegio de Santiago, with a total of more than 2,000 students. There also were thirty-nine escuelitas de casa in Santiago de Cuba, although they taught fewer students each, mostly girls of color, who learned how to read, count, pray, and sew.[72] Five years later, in 1847, a report suggested that there were 342 primary students in two public schools paid for by the town council and one paid for by the Sociedad Económica, in addition to 257 students in "escuelitas amigos de niñas y niños."[73]

Despite the 1844 law's purpose to systemize primary education and centralize control in the hands of the Spanish colonial authorities, the reach of the public school system was still limited enough that the White Creole men of the Sociedad Económica continued their work in the education sphere, and the escuelitas de amigas continued to operate with Afro-descended teachers and students.

The 1844 education law coincided with the Escalera rebellion of 1843–1844, the latest in a long string of resistance actions mounted by enslaved and free Afro-descendants in the first half of the nineteenth century. Finch has argued that these repeating rebellions are indicative of a development of Black consciousness in Cuba. Maestras amigas might well have been a crucial part of this process of *concientización*, consciousness-raising. Racialized people and women did not, and do not, need to read to understand their own oppression. But reading and writing, the primeras letras education that the maestras amigas were reviled for, can certainly help people make sense of their world and work with bureaucratic states. And the act of learning to read and write together, in classrooms that were integrated in race and sex, can also be revolutionary and emancipatory. In the Americas, enslaved people did not need literacy to rebel. But some insurrections were led by literate people such as the carpenter José Aponte, who in 1812 led the rebellion commonly known by his name. As maestras amigas continued to disseminate primary education across more sectors of the population than the Creole men, their work may have contributed to a Black consciousness or even to the rebellions.

As the Spanish colonial government began to centralize and develop a national school system, maestras amigas become hard to trace in the historical record. White Creoles in the Sociedad Económica in the early nineteenth century were particularly opposed to these teachers because they lacked preparation or licenses, because they were Black and mulato, and because they taught White children as well as Black children. Presumably, the public education system that began in the 1840s, which relied on professionalization and bureaucratization, continued the push against the amigas who taught at home. In this, the women's experience was likely similar to that of midwives whom colonial officials tried to force out of the field of midwifery in the era of the Escalera rebellion by requiring further education and licensure, as historian Michele Reid-Vazquez has described.[74]

But maestras amigas did not disappear. The development of the public education system was slow to expand and provide sufficient schools for all the children on the island. Penetration of public education was particularly slow in the countryside until more than a century later, when the 1960s literacy campaign made rural teaching a priority.[75] Thus, female teachers of color continued teaching small children in their home, filling the gaps that the public education system was not able to reach for more than a century. Escuelitas de amigas, many taught by Afro-descended women, continued well into the twentieth century, as the example of Reyita demonstrates. Reyita recounted that she taught small children in her home on multiple occasions in the early to mid-twentieth century. She also sent her own children to escuelitas de casa in the absence of other educational opportunities.[76]

There are other traces of maestras amigas in the twentieth century. Scholar Denise Blum recounts an interview with a Cuban woman named Caridad, whom she describes as "a petite mulatta," who opened an escuelita in her living room in 1942.[77] Caridad's school was shut down by revolutionary authorities in 1968, but she estimates that over the years she taught about eighty-five students. Government officials wanted her to teach in the public schools instead, but Caridad refused, suggesting that for women of color, teaching in their homes gave them an independence that could not be found in the official school system. Caridad explains, "I never have liked being told what to do, and I was working for a man, and I did not like my work conditions, so I quit my job and said, 'I am going to start a school.'"[78] That independence is reflected in her school's curriculum as well. Caridad taught arithmetic, reading, writing, geography, spelling, and history, and her school also functioned to diffuse Afro-Cuban cultural and religious norms that were frowned upon by the Revolution.[79]

In Caridad's story are echoes of the 1830s clash between Black women teachers and official school authorities. Like Reyita and Caridad, other female teachers of color likely continued operating schools at home well into the twentieth century, but under the radar of educational officials. The continuity of the teaching work by maestras amigas, many of them women of color, suggests that they successfully resisted the top-down imposition of educational reforms such as segregation measures by creating Black-run schools separate from the official public school system.

2

Rebellious Teachers, 1812–1844

In the first half of the nineteenth century, many militiamen of color in Cuba also became teachers. For male teachers who were able to obtain teaching licenses, the school system, like the militia, offered formal recognition from the Spanish colonial authorities and acknowledgment of their work from White Cuban society. Thus, these free people of color were able to articulate for themselves and for society at large a social status distinct from the one generalized by racial slavery. For Afro-descended teachers, the magisterio, the teaching profession, offered a way to cultivate common cause and community with other Afro-descended people, especially in the face of intensifying racial animus in an expanding sugar-based economy. The Black educational tradition being forged by the militiamen-teachers, therefore, combined separate race-based schools with strategies for racial integration into the wider Cuban society.

But these two colonial institutions, the militia and the magisterio, were not enough to contain the political aspirations of some Afro-descended men. Rebellions against slavery and Spanish colonialism in which both enslaved and free Africans and Afro-descendants participated rocked Cuba in the first half of the nineteenth century. Among the rebels were several men who participated in several rebellions and who, in between armed conflict and periods in jail, also taught school. Armed rebellions were political acts in which the participants envisioned a different political and social future for themselves and other inhabitants of the island. The converging of rebellion and teaching in the stories of these men suggests that we should understand the educational activities of Afro-descendants in Cuba as political acts, and radical ones at that. Furthermore, the extent to which the Black Cuban educational tradition might have informed the political consciousness of Afro-Cubans bears consideration, especially among those who chose to rebel against the slave-based colonial order.

Afro-descendants in nineteenth-century Cuba were articulating educational ideologies and offering educational opportunities that eschewed the narrow parameters and expectations for education set by White Creole and peninsular authorities. This emerging Black Cuban educational tradition challenged, sometimes head on, the steady hardening of racial strictures in Cuban society in the first half of the nineteenth century. In the case of militiamen-teachers who also participated in conspiracies against the government, the pairing of education and armed conflict suggests that for Afro-descendants in Cuba, schooling was a mode of developing a politics of opposition, of expressing political protest, and of constructing an alternative political and social world.

The documentary record for the schools of Black and mulato Cubans in the early to mid-nineteenth century is scarce, and the curricular content of their schools is particularly difficult to recover. Many Afro-descended teachers such as the maestras amigas did not have licenses to teach school. Cuba's press and civic society was constrained by Spanish colonial laws until the first war of independence ended in 1878. In the absence of newspaper editorials, curricular content, memoirs of teachers, and similar material, the early educational history of Afro-descended Cubans must be excavated in different ways. The pairing of two activities—teaching and rebellion—in the lives of several militiamen of color can provide insights into the ideologies being developed by some Afro-descended teachers in early nineteenth-century Cuba and how teaching school fit into their views of Cuban society and politics.

Military Service, Gender, and People of Color

The militias in Cuba, organized into White, Black, and mulato corps, were a particularly important institution for free people of color in the colonial period. Militias in colonial Cuba were organized in the sixteenth century, and by the late eighteenth century the battalions of pardos (free mulatos) and morenos (free Blacks) made up more than 30 percent of colonial militias. Most free men of color in Cuban cities were either members of militias or were indirectly connected to them in some way. By 1770, one out of every five adult males in the free population of color was a member of the militia. Two-thirds of all free men of color between the ages of fifteen and fifty belonged to them.[1]

For free men of color, the militia offered a chance at social mobility, specific rights, and a broader place in Cuban society. Men in the militias were covered by the *fuero militar*, the military code that guaranteed them the right to bear arms and gave them access to military courts. They received pensions after they retired and had access to loans as well as medical and burial benefits. Moreover, fuero rights extended to the families of militiamen. Often, these Black and mulato battalions would bring together most of the men in a particular neighborhood, so that neighbors lived and served together, underscoring the centrality of militia service to Black community life in Cuba. Militiamen of color were also sometimes able to accumulate wealth; some were slaveholders and property owners.[2] Many militiamen of color became leaders within their communities by taking advantage of the rights and opportunities available to them through their military service and extending those rights to their families and neighbors.

Militiamen of color were often also members of religious societies called cabildos de nación that were organized around African ethnic origins. Militia service was one way to distinguish oneself within the cabildo, thus gaining leadership rights in that organization as well as through the militia. Although only free men of color could belong to the militias, enslaved and free women and men could belong to cabildos. Afro-descended women numerically dominated the cabildos, were able to vote for leaders of their cabildos, and likely influenced which men ascended to leadership positions within them. Like the militias, cabildos may have been a route to literacy, since cabildos sometimes had schools, and some left records written by their literate members.[3]

Perhaps most importantly, militia service offered an experience of legal equality before the Spanish state; by the late eighteenth century, the legal rights and privileges of militiamen of color were, at least according to the letter of the law, the same as those of White militiamen.[4] Spanish colonial society in Cuba was a hierarchal one, but expressing loyalty to the Spanish crown allowed colonial subjects to assert themselves as political subjects and enter the public sphere. Militias were a key site for the expression of what Sartorius has called "loyal subjectivity" for free people of color.

Loyal subjectivity was a gendered mode of political inclusion, Sartorius has noted. What the Spanish colonial government prized in free people of color was "military valor, skilled occupational status, and social relationships that included, among other things, 'authority over subordinates,'" the kinds of behavior and relational status more readily available to men.[5] The militias of color figured prominently in the military defense of Cuba during the British occupation and in other moments. By virtue of their gender, some free men of color like those in the militias could claim political subjecthood in the Spanish colonial state. Loyal subjectivity was not as available to free women of color such as maestras amigas. However, the faithfulness of free men of color was increasingly called into question over the course of the nineteenth century, and these loyal subjects sometimes found that the state did not reciprocate their expressions of fealty.

"Milicianos y Maestros"

Importantly, participation in the militias may have served as one of the earliest forms of Afro-Cuban access to literacy and instruction, aside from the escuelitas de amigas. Militia service broadened the geographic horizons of participants, since it sometimes required travel, thus allowing militiamen of color to become acquainted with the workings of the Spanish empire and other political systems. Furthermore, militiamen read royal decrees and wrote petitions directed to Spanish officials asserting their rights. Suspected rebels in the 1812 Aponte Rebellion in Cuba, many of whom were members of the Black and mulato militias, were found to have copied and circulated royal decrees.[6] The connections between military service and literacy may account for the number of militiamen who became licensed teachers in the nineteenth century.

Teaching offered strong parallels to the way militiamen were accustomed to constructing their lives; it provided another highly effective path to personal social status in relation to the Spanish colonial government and the wider Cuban society. For some, teaching provided an additional source of income. Free men of color who taught school, therefore, assumed a very different social position than that available to the female Afro-descended maestras amigas. The magisterio, no less than the militias, afforded the men recognition from Cuban authorities. Many of them, unlike maestras amigas, were granted licenses to teach school. This official sanction was a far cry from the treatment of maestras amigas whose escuelitas existed outside of the developing official school system. The difference between the treatment of Afro-descended maestras amigas and militiamen-teachers was highly gendered.

But both men and women Afro-descended teachers used teaching to extend the benefits such as literacy they accrued to the Black community. Militiamen-teachers identified with and expressed their loyalty to the Spanish colonial state but also to other people of color. Black-run escuelitas de amigas that admitted both White and Black students evinced an interest in racially separate organizing on the one hand and racially integrated policies on the other; likewise, militiamen of color who became teachers could work toward positions of dignity for themselves in Cuban society while simultaneously accruing those benefits for other free people of color and in doing so, forging racial solidarity. Through their teaching, Black educators demonstrated a concern for the well-being of other people of color, especially children, and an interest in serving as community leaders. This was a social practice to which members of the Black and mulato militias were well accustomed.[7]

Militiamen-teachers' educational endeavors exhibit a confluence of race-based solidarity and organizing combined with a focus on a place for Afro-descended Cubans within the structures of the colonial state and White Cuban society. As militiamen, they were granted recognition, status, and rights by the Spanish authorities. When they became teachers, they received licenses to teach. Some of them participated in the exams by White Creole educational authorities. Like the maestras amigas, militiamen of color teachers often educated both White and Black students.

And yet, their schools were usually primarily for children of color. When the militiamen-teachers rebelled, they did so with other Afro-descendants, including people who were enslaved, people with different levels of education, and people who were born in Africa. The militiamen-teachers in these ways held a common identity with other Afro-descendants while at the same time thinking about how Cuba could be a place for both Afro-descendants and Whites. This dual approach, with all its inherent tensions, was one of the hallmarks of the Black Cuban educational tradition throughout the nineteenth century.

The Black Educational Tradition of the Militiamen-Teachers

By the early nineteenth century, men of color who had participated in militias were particularly well represented among schoolteachers. Historian Pedro Deschamps Chapeaux lists León Monzón, Lorenzo Meléndez, Pilar Borrego, Matías Velazco, Mariano Moya, Doroteo Barba, José Calzada, and Roberto Florencia as members of battalions of pardos and morenos who became teachers from 1820 to 1845. Some of these men, though probably not all, received licenses to teach from the educational authorities of the Sociedad Económica.[8]

Gabriel Doroteo Barba was one of the most celebrated Black teachers of the early nineteenth century, and his biography well illustrates the social and financial ties of the overlapping membership of the militia, the cabildos, the trades, and the magisterio. Barba was a captain of the *batallón de morenos* (Black battalion) and had served in a military campaign in Florida. Like many military men, he had married into a wealthy family of color, and his wife had brought a substantial dowry, including an enslaved woman, to the union. Barba began teaching in 1803, and by 1833 he boasted of two separate schools, both for children of color, one for each sex. His success suggests that for Barba and perhaps other militiamen of color, teaching could be a lucrative profession. The accumulation of wealth suggests that he was perhaps not educating as many students free of charge as the maestras amigas had. His son would become a militia member as well as a skilled artisan, and his daughter would marry a man who was a Black militia captain, demonstrating how free people of color in Cuba developed strong social networks among Black and mulato artisans, tradesmen, cabildo members, and militiamen.[9] Barba's consolidation of personal wealth and status was significant. But by teaching, he was also extending to the community's children some of the benefits he had accrued.

The militiamen-teachers' work suggests what education might have meant to them. For the militiamen, the magisterio became a way to achieve or extend personal status and wealth. For example, Gabriel Doroteo Barba made enough money from his first school to enable him to open a second one, keeping his educational institutions going for thirty years. By the same token, the militiamen appear to have charged students tuition to attend their schools. Many of them likely catered to a Black and mulato urban middle class of tradesmen and people associated with the militias who could afford to pay tuition for schooling.

Although the militiamen worked in racially segregated military corps and many of their schools were just for children of color, they had some interest in racial integration. Several of them had racially integrated schools; that is, they taught both White and Afro-descended children. There are several prominent examples. Lorenzo Meléndez's school on Corrales Street in Havana boasted 120 students, and forty of them were White. Roberto Florencia, who had been a captain of the moreno battalion, had forty students of color as well as some White students.[10] These examples suggest that militiamen-teachers resisted the trend of hardening racial categories and subsequent segregation in the nineteenth century, creating solidarity with White Cubans as well as Afro-descended Cubans. In addition to providing schools for children of their own class, la clase de color, Afro-descended teachers often educated White children who apparently were not being served by the various schools created by religious organizations or by the White Creole teachers often associated with the Sociedad Económica.

Other kinds of mixing occurred in the militiamen's schools. Gabriel Doroteo Barba appears to only have taught free children of color. But in 1828 he had advertisements for his school in the *Diario de la Habana*, offering after-hours (from prayers at five in the evening to eight at night) catechism classes for enslaved Africans and Creoles whose masters didn't have the time to teach them as they were required to do.[11] Though it is unclear whether any enslaved students ever attended, his audacious advertisement—as well as other historical data such as the participation of free people of color in slave uprisings—demonstrate that the free community of color in Cuba kept close ties to the enslaved community. Barba's class privilege as a man who had been able to accumulate wealth and his social status as a militiaman clearly put distance between him and the growing enslaved population of Cuba. And yet here he was offering enslaved students the rudimentary education that slaveholders were supposed to provide but usually did not.

Still, in other ways, some militiamen appear to have been more conservative than the female maestras amigas in their educational projects. They do not appear to have provided much tuition-free education, the way the maestras amigas were noted to have done. The militiamen-teachers' schools were more likely to serve only boys or at least not be co-educational schools, and they also seem to have adhered to the kind of education that was considered appropriate to whatever group they were working with. Lorenzo Meléndez's and Roberto Florencia's respective schools were only for boys, and both of them taught some White boys along with boys of color. Gabriel Doroteo Barba had a school for girls and a school for boys, only for children of color and not co-educational. In them, the children received "an education corresponding to" their gender. The enslaved people he taught would learn only "Christian doctrine."[12] Adhering to the social norms of White Cuban society appears to have allowed the Afro-descended militiamen-teachers to escape the scrutiny and scorn that White Creole educational reformers leveled at maestras amigas, who were more transgressive in providing the same primary education to children of both sexes and races in the same classroom, often without charging tuition.

Black militiamen-turned-teachers, who often built up wealth through their trades and teaching, were able to access corporate rights from the Spanish colonial government. They experienced gender and class privilege that allowed them to maintain some social distance from racial slavery and to imagine a future in which their lives would not be ruled by racial hierarchies. But the pedagogical work of these teachers also shows them sharing common identity with and drawing closer to other people of color, particularly children but also sometimes adults of color and even enslaved people. The early nineteenth century saw a spate of slave rebellions in which free people of color assisted; among them were men who also taught primary school.

Militiamen and the Connection between Rebellion and Teaching

The intensification of Cuba's race-based social hierarchy in the nineteenth century following the expansion of the slavery-based sugar plantation system in the wake of the Haitian revolution affected not only Cuba's expanding enslaved population but also the free people of color. This intensifying racial oppression was met by significant resistance from enslaved and free Afro-descendants. Slave rebellions, some in which free people of color also participated, occurred annually in 1795–1799, then in 1812, 1823, 1824, 1825, 1827, 1832, 1833, 1834, 1835, and again annually between 1837 and 1844. The 1843–1844 rebellions were met with even more repression than usual, since authorities suspected British abolitionists, free people of color, and enslaved people to be working in concert.[13]

Spain increasingly doubted the loyalty of all the inhabitants of its "ever-faithful isle" in the nineteenth century, but forms of loyal subjectivity still held some currency in this period.[14] Some free people of color continued to use loyalty to colonial institutions such as the militias and the magisterio to pursue rights, recognition, and social mobility. Others chose to rebel. And some may have done both over the course of one lifetime, suggesting that Afro-Cubans' search for liberation was multifaceted and flexible. Most armed rebellions in this period were led by enslaved people, and most of the leaders and participants in slave rebellions were West Africans, as historian Manuel Barcia has shown. However, Cuban-born free people of color also rose up and were particularly well known for their leading roles in the rebellions of 1812 and 1843–1844.

The political goals, ideologies, and motivations of the rebellions of enslaved Africans and their descendants in the Americas have garnered considerable scholarly attention despite the challenges of employing archival methodology in the reconstruction of that history. Cedric Robinson, searching for the "ideological source of their revolts," has proposed that the

"Black radical tradition was an accretion, over generations, of collective intelligence gathered from struggle."[15] Cuban scholar Gloria García, looking for that to which the specific forms of marronage and rebellion could be attributed, begins her book countering planters' explanation of enslaved people's ingrained barbarity by casting a wide net: "Había algo más," she evocatively states.[16] Finch finds that the rebelliousness of this period that she calls "the repeating rebellions" was something that enslaved people were aware of and carried memories of, thereby fueling the development of a Black political consciousness. The rebellions were not exactly the same, nor were the participants always the same, but the patterns and repetitions are evidence of "the antislavery epistemologies and ingrained structures of opposition" developed by Afro-descendants in Cuba. Finch calls her work "an attempt to identify the political and epistemological structures that linked together disparate events of Black protest which together undergirded the question of the recurrent."[17] The repeating rebellions could link entirely different participants and movements, but occasionally, as Finch and others have pointed out, the same people rebelled on the same plantations or appeared to be involved in protest actions on different plantations. There are also examples of free people of color being indicted in several different rebellions.

Interestingly, several of the people who were accused by Spanish authorities of rebelling multiple times were, in addition to being members of militias, also known to be licensed teachers. Here, then, is a wrinkle in the fabric of the repeating rebellions: Afro-descended people who dipped in and out of armed opposition also had a foothold in the world of Black Cuban education. If there is a pattern to be discerned in the repeating rebellions, it must account for these Afro-descended men's forays into teaching as well as into armed conflict. For these militiamen-teacher-rebels, education and rebellion were both strategies of liberation and a kind of political action. Like rebellion, education formed an important strand of the politics of opposition and likely informed the structures of knowledge and understandings that fueled such protest. In this story, therefore, education appears as a tool of liberation with radical possibilities.

Schooling among Afro-descendants itself may have played a central role in the evolution of a shared Black consciousness in nineteenth-century Cuba. No formal learning has been necessary for oppressed people to be aware of their own oppression, and many if not most of the enslaved people who rebelled in nineteenth-century Cuba were likely illiterate. But the maestras amigas and militiamen-turned-teachers had been particularly active since the late eighteenth century; it is possible that their dissemination of literacy could have helped with the basic reading and writing skills that enabled some Afro-descended people in Cuba to encounter texts that could inform them about antislavery movements, allow them to reflect on the power structures they lived under, and communicate with others. In addition, teaching, like participation in the cabildos and militias, gave people leadership experiences that may have emboldened them to seek power and leadership in other spheres. It was precisely the effects of Afro-descended teachers' positions of authority over White children that Sociedad Económica members expressed fear about in the early nineteenth century.[18]

Slaveholders and colonial authorities throughout the Americas articulated a link between literacy and rebellion. South Carolina passed the 1740 Negro Act forbidding people from teaching slaves to read or write and from employing them as scribes. The law was passed in response to the 1739 Stono Rebellion, which was understood to have been motivated by an edict passed by Spanish colonial authorities in Florida offering shelter for maroons. This suggests that there was an understood link between literacy and rebellion and specifically that literacy allowed for an understanding of geopolitics and an awareness of broader antislavery movements and potential allies in the fight against slavery. Literacy was a way for those in the African diaspora to connect to broader antislavery networks. In the United States, public opinion in the nineteenth century continued to link literacy with rebellion. After the 1831 Nat Turner rebellion in the United States, almost every state passed a law prohibiting enslaved people from learning to read and write.[19] The converse was also widely understood to be true, that emancipation needed literacy to be completed. "The alphabet is an abolitionist. If you would keep a people enslaved refuse to teach them to read," stated an 1867 *Harper's Weekly* article.[20]

Unlike laws in the United States, there were no specific laws against slave literacy in colonial Cuba. But the well-documented evidence of Black people's pursuit of literacy and schooling during and after slavery throughout the Americas demonstrates that education and armed rebellion must be understood as liberation strategies that were pursued by Afro-descendants throughout the Atlantic world. They need to be parsed in order to understand the specific nature of freedom that Black Cubans were pursuing, especially by those Black Cuban teachers who participated in both liberation strategies in one lifetime.

Freedom Teachers

In 1828, two captains of the militia for pardos and morenos in Matanzas, Captains Juan José Benites and José Policeto Gómez, wrote to the captain general (sometimes also called governor general) of Cuba directly, asking for permission to open a private school for la clase de color. The purpose of such a school would be to teach Christian religious maxims and primeras letras, basic reading and writing skills. They wrote, "Not being able to look upon with indifference the lack of a school where this class of individuals may be inspired by the maxims of our sacred religion and the teaching of the basics of reading and writing that are so necessary in the arts and trades, we ask your excellency to . . . concede [to us] the right to establish a school in this city."[21]

In this letter the militiamen of color were relying on their experience of loyal subjectivity to claim rights for themselves and for their communities. They wrote directly to the highest-ranking Spanish colonial official in Cuba, the captain general, and not to the governor of Matanzas province or to any other provincial or local authority including the education section of the Sociedad Económica, which was in charge of education on the island in the 1820s. The two men identified themselves as officers in the militia with certain corporate rights to whom the Spanish colonial officials had a responsibility. They noted that the purpose of the school would be to teach Christian religion and reading and writing because those were important for the trade jobs so often done by free people of color. In other words, these two captains were drawing directly from the tradition of loyal subjectivity, as free men of color appealing in ornate language to the highest colonial authority, drawing on their experience as militiamen in the service of the colonial government, and noting the benefits the colonial government would derive from free children of color learning to read and write so they could work in trades.[22]

The florid language of the document suggests that these militiamen were familiar with the rhetoric of loyal subjectivity, even if their shaky script, especially that of José Policeto Gómez, speaks to the limited access to formal education they may have previously received (figure 1).

The letter suggests that the militiamen had further expectations of the Spanish government in Cuba, too. Not only did they write directly to ask the captain general to open a school, but they further asked "his excellency also to assign the corresponding rights to these teachers [presumably a teaching license], since it is not just that they remain inactive as they have

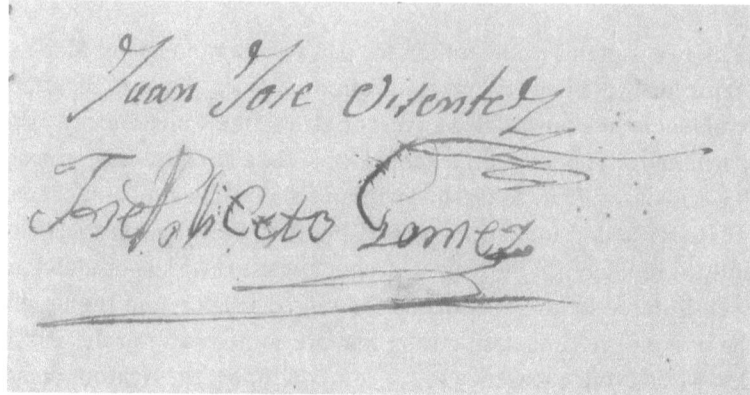

Figure 1. Signatures of Juan José Benites and José Policeto Gómez on their request to open a school, 1828. Benites and Policeto Gómez to Francisco Dionisio Vives, captain general of Cuba, documents, 1828, MS span 52, folder 921, José Augusto Escoto Cuban History and Literature Collection, circa 1574–1922, Houghton Library, Harvard University. https://nrs.lib.harvard.edu/urn-3:fhcl.hough:100006568.

for years, without taking into account that your excellency would generously agree to this just and proper request."[23] It is apparent that these free men of color expected that the Spanish colonial state might acquiesce to justice and rights and that the teaching profession and educational sphere was a vehicle for rights and recognition. Obtaining a teaching license was understood as a right or franchise granted by the government. In doing so, they may have been attempting to transfer the experience of social mobility and rights from one colonial institution (the militias) to another (the magisterio).

Neither their embellished rhetoric nor their appeals to justice nor their practice of appealing directly to the captain general guaranteed the success of their request, however. This is because the captain general forwarded their letter to none other than the education section of the Sociedad Económica "with the purpose that the Section should make the corresponding arrangements," presumably to bestow a teaching license on the militiamen and allow them to open the school. The Sociedad Económica objected, however. The education section "lacked all notice regarding the aptitude, conduct, and morality of the applicants" and recommended that the application "be returned to the interested parties," who should gather "reports from the diputación patriótica [the local chapter of the Sociedad Económica] of that city."[24] For the Sociedad Económica, the direct connection between the militiamen of color and the highest colonial authority in Cuba appeared to be a dangerous one since it was not mediated by local hierarchies that kept free people of color oppressed through standards of reputation and certain kinds of conduct. For the organization's members, loyal subjectivity was not enough to grant the rights of the magisterio to these free men of color.

With his concern about the "aptitude, conduct, and morality" of the militiamen, the vice president of the education section was appealing to only thinly veiled notions of White supremacy rather than to the loyalty that might have concerned the captain general. But in the early nineteenth century, the Spanish colonial authorities in Cuba were more and more suspicious of the loyalty of all Cubans, White and Black. The 1820s, 1830s, and 1840s saw a spate of rebellions by White and Black Cubans. In June 1824, Spanish authorities foiled an attempted rebellion in Matanzas for which they arrested, along with two White people, Black militia captain José Policeto Gómez, the very same man who four years later requested permission to open a school. No enslaved people appear to be involved, and Cuban historian Carlos Trelles refers to it as a rebellion in favor of Cuban independence, though French historian Alain Yacou calls it an antislavery rebellion. One of the participants, a Spaniard, was deported, but Gómez somehow managed to escape punishment and four years later was still in his position in the militia and asking for permission to open a school.[25] Fifteen years after this petition to be granted a teaching license, in 1844 he was arrested for participating in what became known as the Escalera rebellion of 1843–1844, tried, and once again exonerated.[26]

Gómez seems to have had a penchant for escaping punishment for rebellion. Or perhaps he had roused unfair suspicion by the colonial authorities who arrested him, only to exonerate him twice. But if colonial authorities were correct about his participation in conspiracies against slavery and colonialism, it is interesting to note that he attempted to turn to teaching in between these two rebellions. José Policeto Gómez shows up in the archive as a suspected rebel against the Spanish colonial government and as a loyal subject asking for teaching rights from the Spanish colonial government. He appears to have had an interest in reading and in rifles, in racial uplift through education and in rebellion, in loyal subjectivity through the militias and the magisterio, and in liberation through literacy and armed revolt.

Deschamps Chapeaux briefly gestures to the connection between the militias, magisterio, and rebellion. In his 1971 *El negro en la economía habanera del siglo XIX*, a section titled "Magisterio y conspiración" chronicles the experiences of León Monzón and Pilar Borrego. Both were "militares y maestros," militiamen and teachers. They were members of the batallón de morenos, the battalion for free Blacks. And they were cabildo members, likely in the cabildo San Benito de Palermo, although Borrego may have also been a member of Nuestra Señora de Belén. Monzón and Borrego rebelled with Aponte in 1812 and then again 1839.[27]

Pilar Borrego (sometimes written as Borrero) was a second lieutenant in the firefighting corps of the free Black militia and a teacher. León Monzón was also a teacher and a captain in the same militia. Monzón had been a member of the militias of color since 1800. Both men were indicted in the 1812 Aponte Rebellion and sentenced to four years of prison in Puerto Rico. The 1812 Aponte Rebellion has received much attention specifically for the use of texts and illustrations among the rebels, some of whom were literate, including the rebel leader José Aponte himself.[28]

Militiamen who were implicated in the 1812 rebellion were granted amnesty by the king only two years later, in 1814, and allowed to return to their battalions, an occurrence that might have cut Monzón's and Borrego's prison terms short. They returned to Cuba, and Monzón, at least, returned to his militia and was made a captain in 1829. Borrego may also have done so. Both returned to teaching. It is unclear whether Monzón taught school in the years between 1814 and the late 1820s. But in 1832, with notions of expanding primary education circulating throughout the Atlantic world, and within the Cuban context of the educational work of Afro-descended maestras amigas and the White Creole men of the Sociedad Económica, Monzón applied for and was granted permission to open a school.

And yet in 1839, only seven years later but more than a quarter century after the 1812 rebellion, the two men were arrested again. They were accused of conspiring to overthrow slavery and Spanish colonial rule in a scheme led by Monzón himself, assisted by Borrego and others, that extended into the eastern region of Guantánamo. Other rebel leaders were enslaved people, members of the Abakuá religious society, and members of cabildos.[29] Authorities found documents, booklets, books, and pictographs in Monzón's house, demonstrating the importance of texts and literacy to this rebellion just as they had been during the 1812 rebellion. These included proclamations by the militias of color supporting Spanish constitutional rule and books about republicanism and constitutional rule, suggesting that Borrego, Monzón, and their supporters were familiar with and hoping for a future of specific ideas of political liberty and that such an ideological circulation was made possible in part by their literacy.[30]

Judicial authorities expressed their shock and dismay at the collaboration between Monzón, "a man who, due to his rank and circumstance, we would not assume would enter into these meetings without a marked and momentous goal," along with dockworkers, domestic laborers, artisans, enslaved people, and Abakuá practitioners. The collaboration between free people of certain elevated status and enslaved people, between Blacks and mulatos, was unimaginable to Spanish colonial authorities. The attorney defending Monzón used this understanding of the class divisions between free people of color and enslaved people in his defense: "It is well known to all, that the same dividing line that exists between white and black . . . you can be sure exists between the naïve free man [of color] and the African slave. Nothing in the record suggests a link or correlation between my defendants and the seven blacks in question."[31]

For authorities in Cuba, clear demarcations between enslaved and free people of color and between Blacks and mulatos were necessary to keep Afro-descendants from banding together against slavery and the colonial system. Spanish authorities also understood there to be important class and cultural differences among Cuban Afro-descendants, including along lines of place of birth, religion, and language. Creole Afro-descendants who spoke Spanish and practiced Christianity may have been more likely to develop political relations of loyal subjectivity with the Spanish colonial state. This latter group of loyalists was sometimes also in possession of wealth and able to read and write; it was these men and women who received licenses to teach school from the Cuban educational authorities.

In the 1839 rebellion and others, authorities were horrified to find African-born and Creole (Cuban-born) Blacks and mulatos working together. Authorities may have assumed that literacy, education, and status might work to fragment Afro-descendants along class lines and maintain the loyalty of the higher classes.[32] But in the case of Monzón, literacy and education appear to have been working precisely in the opposite way. Monzón and Borrego participated in important Spanish colonial institutions such as the cabildos, the militias, and the magisterio. They were literate men with significant social standing within their communities and the colonial institutions they participated in. And yet, instead of literacy and standing distinguishing them from other Afro-descendants, Monzón and Borrego were also committed teachers, disseminating their hard-earned literacy to children of color. And in their armed resistance activities, they made common cause with Afro-descendants who were understood by the Spanish colonial authorities to be very different from these men.

Thus, the educational efforts of Afro-descended Cubans may have been crucial to the development of a shared consciousness that bridged the divide between Black and mulato and between enslaved and free and propelled an increasingly unified group to imagine different political and social futures in Cuba. In this, Monzón's experience echoes that of Gabriel Doroteo Barba, who taught enslaved and free Afro-descendants, blurring the line between them by extending schooling to what were assumed to be different groups and bolstering racial solidarity. The mixing that occurred in Afro-descendant classrooms served to destabilize the racialized categories that Spanish authorities and White Creole Cubans were working so hard to define and uphold.

The defense attorney's effort to draw this distinction for Monzón did not exonerate him. Monzón and Borrego, along with other collaborators, were sentenced to prison and then to permanent exile. Cuban historian Juan Risquet wrote that they were exiled to La Coruña in Spain, where they continued to dedicate themselves to the magisterio, and they opened schools "in which more than a few of those who may deny the virtues and talents of la clase de color received an education from these sons of Cuban slavery."[33]

Borrego and Monzón were firmly rooted in all of the most important institutions for free people of color in nineteenth-century Cuba: the militias, a colonial institution that allowed them a place of dignity, mobility, consolidation of wealth, and the demonstration of loyal subjectivity; the cabildos, another colonial institution where free people of color could be in community, organize, celebrate, and worship; and the magisterio, yet another colonial institution that allowed them recognition from the Spanish colonial authorities, positions of respect, and opportunities to disseminate literacy to Black children and sometimes also White children.

None of these institutions were enough, however, to secure their loyalty to the Spanish colonial state and the system of racialized slavery that the state enabled. If Spanish colonial authorities were correct, then Borrego and Monzón rebelled not once but twice, once as young men and the second time as middle-age men. They endured prison and exile not once, but twice. And after each time, they turned back to the magisterio, to teaching. The persistence of education in these men's lives suggests a firm commitment to other Afro-descendants in Cuba, even ones whose status may have been very different than theirs, as in the collaboration with enslaved people and workers in the 1839 rebellion. It also suggests that formal education, in all its facets, played a crucial role in binding the Afro-descended community together and in developing a political consciousness that understood freedom in particular ways. The maestras amigas' and militiamen's curricula are largely unknowable to us, but we know they were teaching their students how to read. They may also have taught them about west African religious beliefs along with political organizing strategies and about the anti-Black racism that was cohering with renewed virulence in the nineteenth century.

Matías Velazco was another Havana militiaman of color who was also a teacher. He was a first sergeant of the batallón de pardos (free mulatos) and had been in the militia since the campaign on Florida. He had been born enslaved by his White father, a priest who educated him and his brother and later freed them. Velazco opened a school in 1823 in the Havana neighborhood Jesús María, where he taught White and Black students together. His brother, Eugenio Velazco, was also a teacher, in addition to being a poet, and had a school in the Los Sitios neighborhood of Havana. Matías was arrested during the Escalera repression of 1844 for conspiring with the rebels; by that point he had been teaching for twenty years. In 1856 he either reopened his school or was still teaching on Someruelos Street in the Jesús María neighborhood.[34]

Like Gómez, Velazco survived being accused of being a rebel. Like Monzón and Borrego, he seems to have had a serious commitment to teaching as well as to militia service and perhaps also to armed rebellion. Again, the close ties between the militia and the magisterio for these men suggests that they were experimenting with what colonial institutions could grant them in mobility and rights. But the added factor of rebellion suggests that education itself was understood to be a multivalent tool that could lead to liberation, much the same way that armed rebellion could. It also suggests that for these men, literacy and the experience of teaching school tied them closer to other Afro-descendants, leading to the development of a shared consciousness that rejected the social divisions encouraged by Spanish colonial authorities, and challenged both racial slavery and Spanish colonialism head on, at times through armed rebellion.

Conclusion

Militiamen who also taught school were building the Black educational tradition by demonstrating a commitment to extending the benefits of literacy and social standing that they acquired through participation in colonial institutions to Afro-descended children. For militiamen-teachers and maestras amigas alike, teaching was a way to build common cause and to identify with other Afro-descendants. Thus, education was an expression of their hopes for Black and mulato Cubans' future as well as a tool with which to bring that future into effect.

Teaching was a highly gendered experience for Afro-descendants in the early nineteenth century. The loyal subjectivity that allowed free men of color to receive benefits and recognition from the Spanish colonial authorities and White Cuban society was not available to the maestras amigas. Teaching provided militiamen of color a path to social mobility, prestige, and income. For maestras amigas, teaching was often uncompensated and earned them only the disdain and censure of White Creole educational reformers. For that reason, the maestras amigas' schools were set apart from the official system, allowing them often to push the boundaries of what was acceptable in Cuban society—educating girls, sometimes in co-ed settings; sometimes having racially integrated classrooms; providing schooling for free. Perhaps most importantly, it allowed them to run their schools away from the oversight of White Creoles who did not consider their schools to be part of the developing official school system. The militiamen, on the other hand, often received official sanction to teach and admiration for doing so from Cuban authorities. Perhaps for that reason they tended to hew more closely to the Cuban patriarchal norms that required boys and girls to be taught separately; they were less committed to providing a tuition-free education since they could experience social mobility from charging school fees, and they taught children and adults only those subjects that were deemed appropriate for their groups.

The limits of loyal subjectivity and its diminishing rewards, as seen in the militias of color and the magisterio, though, may have been part of what prompted Afro-descended militiamen-teachers to take up arms. Then too, literacy and the experience of participating in their educational projects may have provided the ideological basis and political consciousness that undergirded the activities of these rebellious teachers. The combined experiences of Gómez, Velazco, Monzón, and Borrego in rebellion and education are repeatedly woven together like strands on a braid, suggesting how militia service and the magisterio, how rebellion and education, might have been interconnected.

Teaching involves children who will grow up into what could be a different world. The literacy that is taught in primary schools provided a basis to begin to decipher state bureaucracies, transnational ideologies such as those of constitutionalism and republicanism, and information about circulating antislavery movements and networks. Armed rebellion, though, suggests a desire for a totally new order, one free of racial slavery and colonial rule. For the rebellious teachers, Cuba's future had the potential to be free of colonial rule and slavery, and people of color had the potential to acquire literacy and knowledge. These positions ran counter to the hardening racialized labor regimes and racial science of the early nineteenth century.

The Black Cuban educational tradition shaped Afro-descended children, likely transmitting not only literacy but a shared Black identity and political consciousness that may have contributed to the rebellions of the early nineteenth century. Though they did not have to contend with anti-literacy laws like Afro-descendants in the United States, Black and mulato Cubans did have to deal with a White-supremacist project shared by Creole and peninsular elites and made manifest in the developing national school system. The Black educational project was thus set against and sometimes apart from the racial oppression intended by White educational authorities in Cuba. Afro-descended teachers in Cuba, providing primary schooling to Afro-descended children, sometimes in racially separate or segregated schools, were developing a Black Cuban educational tradition that had specific contours and expressed hopes for the future of Cuba. It was a project "set against the entire order of things," as Jarvis Givens articulates for his concept of the "fugitive pedagogy" of African Americans in the United States.[35]

Like fugitivity, marronage, and rebellion throughout the Caribbean and the Americas, the teaching projects of Afro-descendants in Cuba must be seen as projects of political liberation. This is especially so when we consider the choice to become teachers alongside the rebellions of the militiamen. Not only could Afro-descendants in Cuba be freed of slavery, but they could be freed of the racist discourse already in full swing in the nineteenth century that suggested that Afro-descendants were intellectually inferior. Thus, the consciousness being developed by the repeating rebellion, and by the Afro-descended teachers in nineteenth-century Cuba, was capacious, wide-ranging, and capable of prompting profound and radical change. For the militiamen-rebel-teachers, the magisterio and schooling appear to have been avenues to radical social change, as full of potential as armed rebellion. The educational tradition being developed by Black and mulato teachers, therefore, was a liberatory one.

3

Racial Segregation in Cuba's First Law for Public Education

As the White Creole men of the Sociedad Económica in Cuba jockeyed for power with the Spanish colonial government and denigrated the important work of the mostly Afro-descended maestras amigas, they attempted to use liberal institutions and policies to foster a Cuban society that could take its place among what they considered to be the modern nations of the world. The education section of the Sociedad Económica desired to create a primary education system that could reach even poor people in Cuba, which meant that they would have to be educated for free. Only if they were able to reach the lower classes through education would they be able to bring about an enlightened, modern society, they contended.

However, the organization's members wanted to educate only a specific sector of the Cuban population: White and male. Insofar as they were interested in educating girls, it was for domestic skills only. And if they occasionally thought to educate free children of color, they too would be educated in separate schools and with a different, less ambitious curriculum. Enslaved children, they asserted, need only be taught Christian doctrine. But the White Creole men of the Sociedad Económica, tied as many of them were to the sugarocracy of the island, made no effort to penetrate the plantation world to educate enslaved children. In all, the school system that the men of the Sociedad Económica attempted to establish demonstrates their interest in having a patriarchal, White-supremacist Cuban society.

In this, they were challenged by the maestras amigas, who, falling outside the purview of the educational bureaucracy's licensing rules, continued teaching in their homes well into the twentieth century and likely into the twenty-first century. White Creole Cubans and Spanish colonial authorities also faced even more direct challenges to their authority from enslaved and free Afro-descended rebels who conspired to overthrow slavery or the colonial government or both. There were at least a handful of Black and mulato men who moved in and out of the militias, the magisterio, and the judicial system as they were prosecuted, jailed, and even executed for rebelling against the government. These Afro-descended militiamen-maestros' pairing of teaching with rebellion suggests a Black political consciousness of striving toward liberation through various means, and schooling was one of them.

Liberal reforms and the use of liberal institutions to establish White supremacy were the purview of more than the Creole men of the Sociedad Económica. In the nineteenth century, the colonial government in Cuba was at times inspired to implement liberal reforms as a result of the repeated clashes between liberals and conservatives in the Spanish metropolitan government; the reforms included allowing freer trade, more autonomy to local governing bodies, and extending individual rights to colonial subjects. Building a national education system was no exception. In 1844 the Spanish colonial government removed the Sociedad Económica from its position in charge of education and passed the first law for public education in Cuba, the Plan General de Instrucción Pública para las Islas de Cuba y Puerto-Rico (hereafter Plan de Instrucción Pública).

The maestras amigas existed outside of the licensing system, so this change in educational administration may not have affected them much. However, Afro-descended teachers who sought official licenses within the new educational administrative system of the Spanish colonial authorities faced new challenges as the onset of an ostensibly liberal educational system dovetailed with a hardening racial hierarchy.

The 1844 Plan de Instrucción Pública was the first law of a centralized national education system that would continue to develop through the nineteenth century. It came exactly at the same time as a wave of rebellions by enslaved and free Afro-descendants in Cuba culminated in unprecedented repression by colonial authorities against Black and mulato Cubans.[1] In line with this racial oppression, the public education plan enshrined de jure racial segregation in Cuba's public schools. Its emphasis on racial segregation and the Spanish colonial authorities' increased repression of free people of color in the aftermath of the Escalera rebellion of 1843–1844 meant that in the years that followed, Afro-descended teachers experienced foreclosed avenues for mobility and recognition through colonial institutions such as the militias and the magisterio. These colonial institutions, which had once served to bind Afro-descendant men to the colonial state, were now viewed with suspicion by Spanish authorities who worried that allowing free men of color access to arms and literacy might lead to rebellion. Instead of courting the loyalty of free people of color, the colonial government used the newly centralized education system after 1844 to construct a firmer basis for racial segregation in Cuban society.

However, the continued interest of free people of color in the magisterio suggests that for them, schooling still held liberatory potential, although the authorities wanted to use it for a different purpose. For free Black and mulato educators working in the mid-nineteenth century and following what was already becoming a Black Cuban educational tradition, schools provided the opportunity to disseminate literacy and build community with other Afro-descended Cubans as well as with White Cubans. The dissemination of literacy and the consolidation of community in the face of racial oppression would be important aspects of how Afro-Cubans pursued freedom within and outside of Cuba's political system.

In other words, teaching continued to be an exercise in lifting as they climbed.[2] Through their teaching, Black educators demonstrated a sense of identification with and concern for the well-being of other people of color, especially children. But the ability of teachers of color to leverage a social position in which the Spanish colonial state officially recognized them—such as being granted a license to teach—was compromised by the increasing racial disdain evident in the policies of racial segregation in the educational sphere of the 1840s and 1850s.

A New Law for Public Education in the Escalera Era

After the 1843–1844 rebellions and lasting through the 1860s, in a period that Reid-Vazquez has termed "the Escalera era,"[3] the Spanish colonial government tortured, executed, sentenced to hard labor, and deported suspected rebels, enslaved and free. It also enacted a new slave code and restrictions on the activities of free people of color in Cuba, thereby affecting all Afro-descendants on the island, not just those involved in the rebellion.[4] The Plan de Instrucción Pública of 1844 came at the same time as these developments.

In theory, the plan might have provided a new avenue of membership in colonial society that free people of color could participate in. But the Spanish colonial government displayed conflicting tendencies about how to govern Cuba and especially Cubans of African descent. New efforts to control free people of color such as the post-Escalera laws and racial segregation in the new education law overlapped with continued efforts to court Afro-descendants' loyalty. Colonial officials worried that the spread of liberal ideas to Afro-descendants on the island and in particular public education might undercut their loyalty. In an 1860s report to the metropolitan government, the outgoing Captain General Francisco Lersundi wrote that the spread of education was part of "the diabolical system" that would compromise two of the most robust pillars of Spanish power, namely free people of color and rural people.[5]

Despite these misgivings, in 1844 the Spanish colonial government enacted the first law for public education in Cuba and Puerto Rico. Finalized by royal order dated October 27, 1844, the Plan General de Instrucción Pública para las Islas de Cuba y Puerto-Rico set forth nominally progressive measures such as establishing at least one primary school in every town of a certain size and shifting the administration of education from private institutions to the central government and financing it through municipal budgets. The administration of the nascent education system was not centralized under the captain general's control but rather through local and provincial commissions whose members were appointed by the captain general.

The 1844 public education law brought to the fore the conflict between White Cuban Creoles increasingly interested in constitutional liberalism and some measure of self-rule and a modernizing Spanish empire desperate to hold onto its remaining few colonies. Throughout the early nineteenth century, the Spanish colonial government responded forcefully to White Cuban Creoles' interest in autonomy or annexation to the United States, giving extraordinary power to the captain general and exiling political Creole dissidents. But the nineteenth century was also punctuated by periods of constitutional rule in Spain that was sometimes extended to Cuba. Educational policy became an outlet for colonial authorities to exercise control over the island while also experimenting with liberal measures; Creoles, too, sought to implement educational policy as a way to shape Cuba's political and social future. In practice, though the central government changed the administration of education significantly with the 1844 law, it provided little funding and opened few new schools.[6] In the meantime, the Sociedad Económica continued to function in the educational space. In 1848 its Santiago branch established a free school for poor children.[7]

Despite their conflict, the colonial officials and White Creoles shared an interest in exercising power by developing a modern, liberal school system of the sort that was expanding throughout the Americas and Europe. They also shared a commitment to White supremacy. The Plan de Instrucción Pública therefore advanced measures of racial segregation in the educational sphere. The plan called for Afro-descended children to be educated in racially separate schools that would teach fewer subjects. Though the law was silent regarding the licensing of Black and mulato teachers, the professionalization measures in the law worked to preclude teachers of color from the expanding public education system. Licensing requirements were onerous or impossible for many people of color to meet. Women also faced special challenges becoming licensed teachers. The first Cuban educational law placed significant barriers to teaching and learning for free Afro-descendants on the island. Thus, the construction of a national school system in colonial Cuba went hand in hand with the de jure implementation of White supremacy.

Racial Segregation in the 1844 Plan General de Instrucción Pública para las Islas de Cuba y Puerto-Rico

The first public education law in Cuba covered both public and private education. Schools would be considered public if they were funded in full or in part by the towns or the central government. Even in public schools, children paid tuition unless they could prove to the city council that they were poor. The law required the establishment of an elementary school in every town with more than one hundred residents. Elementary primary education would include religious and moral principles, reading, writing, arithmetic, and Spanish grammar. Subsequent laws for public education in Cuba, in 1863 and 1880, added more progressive measures such as making education free to the students and requiring attendance for children ages six to ten. Separate schools would be created for girls "where resources permitted," and the subject matters would be the same as that for boys, "with the modifications demanded by their difference in sex."[8]

The 1844 Plan de Instrucción Pública nominally advanced a liberal agenda of national public education, but it was criticized by White Cuban Creoles for taking power out of their own organizations and centralizing it in the hands of the captain general. Previously, education had been one of the few areas in the hands of White Cuban Creoles, namely through the royal decree giving the Sociedad Económica control over the island's education. The new law removed the sociedad from its role as head of public education, creating instead an Inspección General de Estudios (later called the Junta Superior de Instrucción Pública) that was subsumed under the captain general's authority and populated by people who were proven to be pro-Spanish.⁹ Creoles accused the Spanish colonial government of using the public education system as a tool of repression and control rather than of liberation, and they bemoaned the backwardness of Cuba's educational systems.¹⁰ Though the plan for Cuba was based off of Spain's Plan de Instrucción Primaria of July 21, 1838, and in some cases copied verbatim, the colonial plan centralized control over education in the hands of the captain general of Cuba and required schools to use only those textbooks that had been approved by the government.¹¹

The Spanish colonial government's priority in the mid-nineteenth century was often to control its remaining but rebellious colonies. In the aftermath of Latin American independence movements culminating in the 1820s and in order to keep political control over the island, Spain governed Cuba under military rule punctuated by periods of constitutional rule. Information control was a crucial aspect of this effort at political control. At times, the press and education were tightly controlled by a government that feared that any reform, local autonomy, or individual rights for Creoles would mean that Cuba would follow in the wake of mainland Spanish America.¹² The Spanish colonial government betrayed a deep ambivalence about the liberal expansion of public education as enshrined in the 1844 law.

The dangers of allowing White Creoles to become educated became a concern for Spanish colonial officials, but the dangers of educating Blacks also was as much a concern for them as it had been for White Creoles. Despite the tensions between White Cubans and the Spanish colonial government, both groups feared the growing Black population of Cuba and used education as a forum to express their anxieties about the racial situation in Cuba, with segregation in educational policy as a tool to limit Afro-descendants' access to schooling and participation in Cuban society. Afro-descended teachers and children were impacted by the public education law, which called for the racial segregation of children in primary schools and placed onerous licensing burdens on teachers of color.¹³ Would free people of color be able to express loyal subjectivity through the educational bureaucracy now that it was more squarely controlled by the Spanish authorities?

The 1844 plan addressed schools for children of color in chapter 6 of the royal order. While the law specified that a primary school would be built in any town with more than one hundred residents, it said that *separate* schools for free children of color would be created in towns that needed them, in the judgment of the colonial head of the island. In other words, the law called for the creation of racially segregated schools and centralized the decision making about whether such racially segregated schools were even needed.[14] This measure at least provided for the possibility of educating free children of color, should communities be allowed to build a school for them, but it required separating children of color from Whites. Thus, the first law creating a national education system enshrined racial segregation, moving away from the model of education provided in the escuelitas de amigas. Some schools established by the Sociedad Económica also had been racially segregated, but the organization's measures and recommendations for its schools were piecemeal and ad hoc. The Spanish colonial government's Plan de Instrucción Pública hardened and nationalized the racial segregation efforts begun by the members of the sociedad's education section.

Under the law, segregated schooling led to discrepancies in educational content; it mandated that schools for children of color would teach fewer subjects (religion and morality, reading, writing, and arithmetic) than White schools. Elementary schools for White children, on the other hand, would also teach Spanish grammar, and the superior schools would add Christian doctrine, religious history, grammar and spelling, and principles of agriculture, industry, and commerce.[15] Tuition would be the same for children of color and White children, with the same exceptions for any children whose families could certify their poverty. Cuba's first law of public education thus enshrined de jure racial segregation in the school system as well as more limited education for free people of color.

The 1844 colonial education plan affected Black teachers as well as Black children. It removed teacher licensing and examining responsibilities from the control of the Sociedad Económica and made the requirements for teachers more stringent. Chapter 3, article 13, required that elementary schoolteachers be at least twenty years old, have obtained a license after being examined, and present evidence of their "buena conducta" (good conduct) and "limpieza de sangre" (blood purity). Teachers would be paid a salary according to the law, although in practice municipalities were frequently behind in paying teachers and could charge tuition to students.[16] Teachers had to be examined, but examining commissions would only be located in Havana, Santiago de Cuba, and Puerto Rico. Furthermore, the examination of teachers was shifted from the Sociedad Económica to provincial commissions that were located only in the provincial capitals. It was not until 1857 that local commissions for exams were created.[17] In addition, teachers had to pay twenty-five dollars to receive their teaching title or license, too much money even for many White applicants.[18] These requirements placed high barriers of entry into the magisterio for all teachers and particularly for teachers of color.

Black teachers' entry into the official teaching profession was also complicated by the plan's call for the creation of teacher-training schools just for men that in fact were not created until 1857, when the first such school for men opened in Guanabacoa.[19] It was not until 1890 that a school for women teachers would be established in Cuba.[20]

The requirement for "limpieza de sangre" was an odd inclusion. What had originally been a marker of religious orthodoxy distinguishing Christians from Jews in Spain had become, in Spanish America, a racial marker denoting African ancestry. Still, it is a term and concept that was shifting and declining in importance in Cuba by the 1840s, when the Plan de Instrucción Pública was created. Blood purity requirements began to disappear in Spain beginning in the 1830s, and from 1865 to 1870 purity ceased to be a requirement for most offices on the peninsula.[21] Proof of limpieza de sangre was required in the 1844 education law but was omitted from the 1863 law. Blood still mattered to Cubans, Sartorius argues, but its meaning shifted: "Blood's universality could foster political unity as much as blood difference could reinforce stratification."[22] African ancestry did not therefore always preclude free people of color in this period from becoming teachers. Still, the determination of limpieza de sangre was subject to oversight by White educational authorities who would look for evidence of conduct and status they considered appropriate; this element of personal discretion potentially allowed them to bar any Afro-descendants who did not adhere to Christian patriarchal norms.

Spanish colonial authorities did not know quite what to do with Black teachers in this period. The conflict between White Creoles and Spanish colonial officials and the need for Spanish officials to court the loyalty of Afro-descendants on the island would sometimes clash with the intensifying race-based social organization of the period. During an era in which the colonial state brutally repressed enslaved and free Afro-descendants alike, some teachers of color managed to acquire licenses to teach. Nonetheless, educational legislation in the second half of the nineteenth century used schooling to further impose racial segregation and consolidate a racial hierarchy on the island.

Licensing a Black Teacher: The Case Study of José Moreno

In 1856, just a dozen years after the passage of the 1844 education plan, José Moreno applied for a teaching license from the Spanish colonial government in Havana.[23] José Moreno was described as a moreno, that is, a free Black man. In nineteenth-century Cuba, this term was distinguishable from pardo, which meant mulato, a person of mixed African and European ancestry. Though the Plan de Instrucción Pública codified racial segregation for students in that it required them to be educated in separate schools, it did not specify who should teach in the segregated schools for children of color. Should they be White teachers or Afro-descended teachers? Thus, Moreno's application, a case of first impression, gave rise to a firestorm of debate within the colonial government in Cuba over the issue of racial segregation in education. In response to Moreno's application, authorities in Cuba attempted to use the 1844 plan as the basis for an expansion of racial segregation to include racial segregation in the teaching force.

In the correspondence and other paperwork related to the application, Spanish colonial officials expressed concerns about an expanding liberal ethos that included education and about the place of people of color in Cuban society. These documents reveal that in the mid-nineteenth century, White officials in Cuba were adopting a philosophy of de jure racial separation in public education and that they were using the schools to firm up national divisions along racial lines.

José Moreno was a fifty-two-year-old man from Havana who, like other male teachers of color in this period, had been a second sergeant in the now-defunct Black militia. Moreno's application lists his father as a militiaman who had reached the rank of commander, highlighting the generational importance of the militias for free people of color. The Black and mulato militias had been disbanded in 1844 during the Escalera repression. By 1856 the Spanish colonial government was attempting to reinstate the Black and mulato militias, though it had to resort to a draft after free people of color failed to flock back to the militias. Moreno's parents, both Moreno by surname, were legally married. Therefore, Moreno, as a legitimate son, had been baptized in the Catholic Church and registered in the baptismal book for pardos and morenos. He was a member in good standing of his local parish and produced various documents vouching for his good morality and conduct, including having limpieza de sangre.[24]

In his solicitation letter, Moreno wrote that he had been inspired to pursue his interest in teaching after hearing Captain General José Gutiérrez de la Concha speak a few months earlier at the Real Colegio de Belén, Havana's most important seminary and school, run by Jesuits. Moreno was inspired when the captain general spoke of the importance of "literacy and Christian education, which produced good morals, worthy heads of households, and loyal men to defend the Church and the homeland."[25] Using the captain general's logic, Moreno framed his arguments in his application for a teaching license in terms of the benefits to the Spanish colonial state. In this appeal to the highest Spanish authority on the island, Moreno was deploying the language of loyal subjectivity. Such a position was surely utilitarian for Moreno, a way to get authorities to concede what he wanted. However, it also suggests that the magisterio itself fit into the framework of loyal subjectivity, that in teaching, Afro-descended men could receive recognition from the colonial state and social prestige. If for some militiamen teaching was a way, along with armed rebellion, to challenge the Spanish colonial government, for other militiamen the magisterio provided a continuation of the practice of loyal subjectivity. Still, subjectivity was a difficult political relation to sustain in the Escalera era, as new laws, including the Plan de Instrucción Pública, intensified racial segregation and limited the mobility of people of color.

The Government Debate over Race and Segregation in Public Education

The correspondence generated by Moreno's application involved the Negociado de Instrucción, the new administrative body in charge of public education under the authority of the captain general, and its head, A. de Villanueva; the members of the Real Audiencia de La Habana, a consultative body; the Provincial Commission of Primary Education of Havana, which, like the Negociado de Instrucción, had been established by the 1844 education law; and several other parties. Their exchanges reveal how authorities thought about education as a tool for social control.

For those most closely involved in its evaluation, Moreno's application related directly to the requirement in the 1844 plan that separate schools be built for children of color. But the application was treated as a case of first impression by educational authorities because it posed a new question of what to do about Black people who wanted to be teachers instead of students. The law had not directly addressed the issue of who would teach in the racially segregated schools or whether people of color were allowed to become licensed teachers. Thus, the decision reached about Moreno's application had the potential to set precedent and shift the course of race relations in the public school system in Cuba.

Understanding the far-reaching implications of Moreno's teaching application, the officials involved in discussions of the application considered far more than the specific case of Moreno. They explored broad issues of education for people of color. They weighed the benefits and drawbacks of racial segregation in schools and in the teaching profession. The letters surrounding this one application give insight into how officials were thinking about race and education; they reveal not only the final decision but also the specific questions that were taken into consideration. The case of Moreno also demonstrates that racial categories, laws, and customs were fluid, changing, and overlapping in this period and that authorities were weighing multiple factors as they considered the extent to which racial segregation laws should be enacted in the Cuban education system.

Much of the paperwork produced by Moreno's application was only tangentially about Moreno himself. Villanueva, the head of the negociado de instrucción, acknowledged that Moreno's personal qualifications were all that they should be. Moreno had submitted his baptismal record, testimonies as to his being an active member of his local parish, and a person of buena conducta, including a letter from the bishop. Moreno was even understood to have limpieza de sangre, a condition required of licensed teachers.

Rather, Moreno's file reveals the other issues raised by his race. The 1844 law was clear on who would attend Black schools but left unstated who would teach in them, an ambiguity noted by the head of the Negociado de Instrucción: "The Plan establishes schools for people of color, but it does not prohibit or authorize, apparently, that Professors should be of the same quality."[26] If racial segregation was the main priority, could White teachers teach Black children? Could Black teachers teach White children? With this question in mind and acting as a representative of the governor of Cuba, Villanueva requested reports from the Provincial Commission of Primary Education in Havana and the Real Audiencia.

In addition to widening the scope of the inquiry beyond Moreno's individual application to the broader issue of race in the public school system, the letters show a concern for setting cohesive policy. This interest in establishing precedent further reveals a general anxiety about the future of the place of people of color in Cuban society and about colonial officials' ability to control them. In his letter to the Provincial Commission of Primary Education, Villanueva wrote about what race teachers of Black schools should be, "It is necessary to determine as much for this case as for the following cases that may occur." This problem had not occurred before because, according to Villanueva, "this is the first case, at least since the undersigned is in charge of the education section, in which a Black man applies for a teaching title."[27] Such a statement suggests that the Plan de Instrucción Pública, with its onerous licensing burdens, may have barred other teachers of color from applying for licenses. In the 1830s, in contrast, several teachers of color had received teaching licenses through the Sociedad Económica.

The Provincial Commission of Primary Education in Havana was the first to submit its report. It recommended that Moreno be given a teacher's license because it would allow for a Black teacher to teach Black students. The commission's foremost consideration, stated the report, was "the separation ... with which, according to the general Plan of Public Education, the schools for people of color must be established."[28] In other words, it reiterated the segregationist policy enshrined in the 1844 law.

The commission went on to say that there were "few people of color capable [of teaching], as is proven by there not having been more than one Black and two mulatos authorized with titles since the previous term." Here, the commission ignored the barriers to entry into the teaching force that White colonial authorities had erected, blaming the low number of Black and mulato licensed teachers on natural ability, that is, on their race. Focusing on licensed teachers also ignored the decades-long work of the maestras amigas. In this case, then, the educational policy served to naturalize racial categories of inferiority. The commission report went on to say that it would be unlikely that many other Black men would attempt to acquire teaching licenses. Given these considerations—the perceived lack of Cubans of colors' aptitude and interest in teaching and the need to maintain racial segregation in schools—the Provincial Commission of Primary Education recommended that Moreno be allowed to sit for his licensing exam.[29]

The commission's report reveals a deft crafting of educational policy in the service of White supremacy. The law nominally provided the possibility of schooling free children of color, but it prioritized racial segregation in the educational sphere. In prioritizing racial segregation and erecting barriers to Black teachers, the 1844 plan invoked notions of Blackness as an inherent category associated with a lack of ability, in this case, an inability to teach and learn. Allowing a Black man like Moreno to apply for a license was therefore not an act of racially equitable treatment before the law but a doubling down of the priority of racial segregation.

Having received the commission's report, Villanueva forwarded it to the governor captain general with his own comments. In his comments, the head of the Negociado de Instrucción echoed the commission in suggesting that very few Whites would be willing to teach in separate Black schools: "The plan allows schools for [children of color], it's true, and therefore it is necessary that their teachers be of the same race, given that traditions, instinctive repugnance, and perhaps the indispensable need of White dominance makes it impossible that [Whites] should teach them."[30] Given the constraints imposed by White supremacy, therefore, Villanueva thought Black teachers should be allowed to teach in Black schools.

By using the language and rationale that he did, Villanueva was also making discursive justifications for segregation in the schools, furthering racial divisions in rhetoric as well as in practice. He naturalized racial discrimination, mentioning White people's "instinctive repugnance" and the "indispensable necessity" of White supremacy. Notably, no specific instance of a White person refusing to teach Black children had actually given rise to the pronouncements in these documents. The Spanish colonial official was simply reaffirming his own ideas about the structures of racial segregation in schools and in Cuban society writ large.

Upholding segregation had been the focus of Villanueva's initial inquiry and of the commission's report. However, Villanueva also expanded on the issue of extending education to people of color generally. He wrote on behalf of the education section that "the difficulty for this bureau consisted less in Moreno's personal aptitude and more whether it is advisable or not to extend education to the class of color."[31] Villanueva was not just reviewing Moreno's application. His concern was not even limited to whether Black people could be teachers. Rather, for him, there was a broader problem with whether Black Cubans should be able to access education. In the end, Villanueva acknowledged "the danger of giving people of color the means to acquire the enlightened conscience of education" but considered "the greater danger to be the ignorance in which the population of color in Cuba was sunk."[32] Thus, though the expansion of education to include people of color, as the 1844 law had nominally done, was understood to be dangerous, Cuba needed more schooling so as to avoid the greater danger of ignorance.

Here we see how some White authorities considered education and especially public education to be a flexible strategy of governance and social control. This was especially useful given the Spanish colonial government's varying strategies on how to prevent people of color from rebelling, either through loyal subjectivity or through racial oppression. For the head of the Negociado de Instrucción, an "enlightened conscience" resulting from education was a danger, but so was denying people of color an education. Educational policy was therefore crafted to speak to the contradictions in the colonial government's stance toward free people of color in Cuba.

Villanueva, unlike the provincial commission, contended that there would be many more free people of color requesting teacher's licenses because of the larger social context of education in this period. "It is possible that the emigrations that many of them have passed through, their lives in a city like Havana, and more than anything, the irresistible spirit of the era, would awaken interests until then asleep," he wrote, suggesting that many free people of color were not native born and perhaps gesturing to the revolutionary ideas emanating from Haiti. His reference to the spirit of the era might also suggest that Villanueva was aware that the 1844 education plan had represented an important step in Cuba's educational history but that he was concerned that the spread of education was not something the authorities could control. Coinciding with a period of social unrest in Cuba, this phenomenon demanded a clear response from the government, whether to check it or encourage it.

The head of the negociado de instrucción, probably on behalf of the governor of Cuba, also requested a report from the Real Audiencia Pretorial on whether it was advisable to allow teachers' licenses to people of color, "or if these should instead be held only by White teachers."[33] Writing on behalf of the Real Audiencia Pretorial, the head of the treasury responded to the captain general's request for a consultative vote and to the commission's report. He wrote that "grave disadvantages could present themselves, particularly in the future . . . with the admission as teachers of primary education and of the primary education of people of color, since it could inculcate in their schools maxims that are not conducive to the social state of the island." The reference to "maxims" suggests that the treasury head understood Afro-descended Cubans to be culturally different others whose customs were not the same as those of the White society of the island. Furthermore, he understood schools to be places of exchanges of ideas and perhaps of potential contagion.

Still, the treasury head rejected the need to set a precedent. He suggested that "for the moment, it doesn't seem that we should deprive one man of color from teaching those of his class," given that the central government had the ability to take measures later if officials didn't find it suitable to have people of color as teachers. This suggests that teaching or getting an education was not understood to be a guaranteed right; rather, it was a privilege allowed by the government that could be easily rescinded. He further suggested that the colonial governor of Cuba could charge the Provincial Commission of Primary Education with keeping a close eye on the schools of people of color. Thus, the new administrative educational system could be used by the colonial authorities to surveil Black teachers and Black students.

The documents generated by José Moreno's teacher application reflect a society turning to liberal institutions such as national public education systems to construct racial hierarchies and racist notions in order to keep its free Afro-descended population under control. Formal segregation measures in the public education system allowed Spanish authorities to mitigate what they feared would be a liberatory effect of education on Blacks and to control the place of Blacks in a Cuban society that was understood as normatively White.

However, the example of José Moreno, like the history of the Afro-descended teachers who preceded him, also tells us about the strategies of adaptation and liberation pursued by free people of color in Cuba. Ultimately, José Moreno was allowed to sit for his exam. In August 1856 he passed, paid the fee for the license, and presumably was able to begin teaching children of color. In his application for a teaching license during the heart of the Escalera era, we see the resilience of Cuba's free Black population. For militiamen in particular, accustomed to prestigious social standing and to taking on positions of leadership within their Black communities, the nineteenth century brought challenges that they met head on, sometimes by rising up in armed rebellions, sometimes by attempting to enter the teaching force. For free people of color in Cuba in the early to mid-nineteenth century, education became a multi-use tool, one that allowed them to address the issue of their place within wider Cuban society as well as attending to their own communities. They seized on the nascent public education system to create alternative visions for Cuba's racial and national future, even while the Spanish colonial government used the same public education system to solidify racial segregation and limit Blacks' access to education.

Conclusion

During the Escalera era (1840s–1860s), teachers of color faced a new public education system and bureaucracy that further institutionalized racial segregation, an intensifying racial hierarchy, and an unprecedented wave of repression by the Spanish colonial government. The devastation and violence visited on free people of color required them to take stock of their options for political, social, and economic participation in society. For teachers, this reevaluation would happen at the same time as the newly created national public education system imposed new segregationist policies. In the 1862 census, there were only 11 male Black licensed teachers out of 484 total male teachers, and out of 53 total female teachers, only one mulata licensed teacher.[34] Teachers of color were thus left out of the formalization of the national school system following the 1844 law. The Spanish colonial government no longer rewarded loyalty and participation in colonial institution with rights, recognition, and social standing as it had previously done through the militias and the magisterio. Instead, it used the new school system during the Escalera era to harden racial categories and racial segregation, not loyalty, to ensure social control of free people of color on the island.

But as the maestras amigas showed, teachers of color did not need licenses to do their work, nor were rights and recognition the only rewards of teaching. Despite the brutal repression of the Escalera era, this period was also one in which enslaved and free people of color continued to act on alternative ideas of social order and visions of Black freedom. Free people of color in urban settings were increasingly radicalized and politicized by the curtailing of rights in the Escalera era, and they had a long history of education, training, and subjectivity to draw from.[35] By 1861 free people of color had again doubled their number and maintained a proportion of 15–20 percent of the total population. Despite being caught up in the brutal Escalera repression of 1844, they were able to rebuild their class economically in its aftermath.[36]

Teachers of color, too, continued to think of themselves as political subjects who could create their own freedom, not only for themselves but also for the students of color that they created common identity with.[37] One of the most famous Afro-descended Cuban teachers worked in this era. Antonio Medina was a poet, writer, and newspaperman who later became the famous and beloved teacher of Juan Gualberto Gómez, Miguel Gualba, and other Black intellectuals of the late nineteenth and early twentieth centuries. Medina applied for a teacher's license in 1862. Though he did not have the funds to pay for his application fees, which he requested be waived, he included the rest of the documentation, such as the letter from the bishop, parish priest, and chief of police vouching for his good manners and conduct. Medina was granted the license and went on to open a Catholic school for children of color called Nuestra Señora de los Desamaprados in which many important future intellectuals of color were educated.[38]

In the mid-nineteenth century, as Cubans were struggling to shape their society and develop the anticolonial and antislavery ideologies that would inform the 1868 war of independence, the contributions of Afro-descended schoolteachers were notably at work. Militiamen of color continually positioned themselves vis-à-vis the colonial authorities in a way that insisted that the Spanish colonial government owed them recognition as free subjects. Through the militia, they received rights and benefits. As teachers, they applied for licenses, a form of recognition from the official educational bureaucracy whether Creole or colonial. This recognition allowed them to gain social status and promoted an idea of a Cuba in which free people of color had equal access and rights and a social place well outside racial slavery. Teachers of color were also at the forefront of expanding nominally liberal and modern ideas such as free education for all children, even before this was a project undertaken by White Cuban Creoles and later Spanish colonial authorities. The maestras amigas were some of the earlier proponents of free schooling, educating children in their homes for no fee. Lastly, militiamen of color and maestras amigas sometimes demonstrated a commitment teaching all children, White and Black, together in their classrooms. Their openness demonstrated a vision of a racial confraternity in Cuban society well before the Cuban independentistas of the late-nineteenth-century wars of independence seized on the idea. Teachers of color in nineteenth-century Cuba advanced these visions of freedom in Cuba even while faced with growing racial discrimination and de jure racial segregation policies in the educational realm.

4

The 1878 Order to Build Schools for Children of Color, White Backlash, and the Effect on Black Teachers

In the second half of the nineteenth century, colonial educational policies in Cuba continued to expand the apparatus of what would gradually become a national school system. Racial segregation had been enshrined into school law in the 1844 Plan de Instrucción Pública. To what degree that racial segregation should be adhered to as an organizing principle became a point of contention among peninsular and Creole White Cubans, as did how much access free children of color should have to the developing public school system. Despite these efforts at racial segregation, however, free people of color broadened their participation in primary schooling in the second half of the nineteenth century by entering the public school system as students and teachers in greater numbers than ever before and by pursuing independent schooling, often within their mutual aid societies.

From 1868 to 1878, Cuban separatists fought against Spanish colonial rule in the Ten Years War of independence. Municipal schools were closed until 1871 by order of Cuba's captain general. As part of the peace settlement that ended the war, the Pact of Zanjón, several peninsular laws were applied to Cuba, among them an administrative reorganization of the island's provinces and towns, a law ensuring freedom of assembly, and the application of the 1876 Spanish constitution to the island.[1] The changes to the social and political context of the post-Zanjón years led to a flurry of activity in the educational realm, too. Crucially, the Spanish colonial authorities used the issue of race in the public school system to court Black Cubans' loyalty and to confront White Cubans in the city councils.

Beginning in 1878, the Spanish colonial government ordered ayuntamientos (city councils) across Cuba to establish more schools for children of color, under the penalty of desegregating the municipal schools if they failed to do so. Afro-descended Cubans seized on this order, petitioning authorities to comply and build schools for children of color. But many local city councils and school boards resisted the order, arguing that they did not have a need for or sufficient funds to build schools for children of color, while they simultaneously refused to desegregate the public schools. Ultimately, despite the colonial government's order, most municipalities did not provide schools for children of color, nor did they admit children of color into the schools designated for Whites.

The 1878 order had a significant effect nonetheless. In the years following the order, many towns did establish schools for children of color or allowed children of color to enter previously White schools as now mixed-race schools. These towns included Alfonso XII, Baracoa, Bejucal, Cabezas, Camajuani, Cardenas, Cimarrones, Esperanza, Guanajay, Guines, Havana, Macagua, (Corral Falso de) Macuriges, Matanzas, Marianao, Palmira, Perico, Ranchuelo, Sabanilla del Encomendador, San José de las Lajas, Sagua la Grande, Santa Ana, Santa Clara, and Santiago de Cuba.[2]

The establishment of new schools for children of color may have had paradoxically detrimental effects on the Afro-descended magisterio, the teaching force, since almost all of the licensed teachers nominated by the city councils and appointed by the central government for the new schools were White. Thus, the expansion of educational access for children of color did not correspond to more employment for Black teachers. This new arrangement represented a shift against the logic that had dominated José Moreno's licensing application, although there had been no consensus on the issue when Moreno applied for a teaching license in the 1850s. The segregated schools for children of color that some towns built had, for the most part, White teachers. This meant that racial segregation was not strictly adhered to. However, it also meant that Black and mulato teachers were not given employment in municipal schools. A very few municipal schools for children of color do appear to have had teachers of color. But for the most part, the magisterio de color seems to have found employment in the growing numbers of *escuelas particulares*, private schools that were being established by mutual aid societies of the 1870s and 1880s. Thus, even during this modest expansion in access to the public education system for children of color, teachers of color were being pushed out of the public system. In response, they organized their own schools.

The Ten Years War, the Pact of Zanjón, and the Abolition of Slavery in Cuba

By the 1870s, Creoles in Cuba across the political spectrum in Cuba advocated for some amount of reform of the political system. Creole separatists were fighting the first Cuban war for independence from Spain, and some were in exile planning to continue the insurrection against Spain. Their aims were a transformation of the political and social order in Cuba. Reformist Creoles involved in local government, on the other hand, were usually still somewhat committed to the social status quo, although they were often also interested in implementing the liberal reforms that swept through the Americas in this period.[3] The Spanish colonial government in Cuba itself was greatly affected by these shifting political loyalties and tried desperately to hold onto Cuba as its prized remaining colony along with Puerto Rico.

In this effort, the Spanish government's position toward its Afro-descended subjects fluctuated. Spanish authorities sought first to sow discord among Cubans by portraying the 1868 bid for independence as a race war and later sought to court Black Cuban loyalty by extending them some concessions and rights.[4] In addition, the colonial government in Cuba was at times inspired to implement liberal reforms as a result of the repeated clashes between liberals and conservatives in the metropolitan government; some of those reforms entailed allowing freer trade, giving more autonomy to local governing bodies, and extending individual rights to colonial subjects.

The issues of the abolition of slavery and the place of Black people in Cuban society also heated up in this period. During the Ten Years War, insurgents had been ambivalent on the abolition of slavery and eventually declared the enslaved to be freed but with severely curtailed movement and rights. Nonetheless, freed people of color in insurgent-controlled lands moved decisively to determine their own fates. In response to the tepid abolitionism of the Cuban insurgents and to the antislavery movement within Spain itself, in 1870 Spain passed the Moret Law, freeing all children born to enslaved people after 1868 and all enslaved people over the age of sixty. The Spanish crown also freed some 16,000 enslaved people who had fought for the Spanish military during the Ten Years War. Finally, in 1880, the Spanish government passed a law that established an eight-year period of gradual abolition under a system of *patronato*, an apprenticeship that allowed slaveholders to continue to extract labor from the formerly enslaved people on their plantations.⁵ These measures were forced by the actions of enslaved people themselves as well as by the social upheaval of the war that made it imperative for Spain to continue to court the loyalty of people of color on the island.

This political and social upheaval also prompted Creoles and Spanish alike turn to new forms of racial control; in this period, Whites in Cuba would turn the public education system into an arena of debate and conflict over the place of free Afro-descendants in the island's society. When the Spanish colonial government forced White Creoles to build schools for Afro-descended children, threatening them with desegregation of the existing municipal schools if they failed to comply, some White Creoles in the municipal governments responded accordingly, creating new racially segregated municipal schools, while many smaller towns with only one school simply desegregated their existing schools. The insistence on racially segregated public schools on the part of many White local governments and school boards demonstrates the difficulty that the Cuban separatist movement would have in gathering disparate elements of Cuban society around a notion of a raceless Cuban nation as it organized its next bid for independence. And the White-supremacist policies implemented in these formative years of the Cuban school system planted the seeds of racial segregation in schools and other public arenas that would plague the new Cuban nation well into the twentieth century and today.

The Spanish Colonial Government's 1878 Order on Schools for Children of Color

After the foundational 1844 law structuring public education, policies surrounding primary education continued to evolve, and racial considerations played an important part in how policies were developed. In 1857 Cuba's first teacher-training school for men opened in Guanabacoa. In 1863 a new school law was promulgated for Cuba under the direction of José Gutiérrez de la Concha, Cuba's former captain general and then head of Spanish overseas possessions. The law was intended to bring Cuba's and Puerto Rico's 1844 education plan in line with the 1857 education law for the peninsula. The 1863 law called for more nominally progressive measures such as making primary school obligatory for children six to nine years old, requiring municipal governments to provide school funding in their budgets, and fining parents for their children's truancy.⁶ Article 182 of the 1863 school law said that each town, according to its size, should build a school for children of color. The law specified that the primary elementary instruction for Afro-descended children would be free of charge and "directed essentially to the moral and religious aspects." This paralleled the law's section on enslaved Africans and their children whom the slave owners were encouraged to educate, "especially on topics related to the moral and religious aspects." Thus, the 1863 education law limited the primary education that all Afro-descendants should receive, regardless of whether they were enslaved or free. Schools for children of color were to be for both boys and girls, although they should be separated within the school appropriately, whereas schools for White children would be single-sex only unless they were incomplete schools, a category reserved for schools that did not meet the criteria set out by educational laws.[7]

In this period, the developing public education system became an important site for debate over the Spanish colonial government and White Creole elites' concerns about the intertwined issues of Spanish imperial control and race in Cuba. In the 1870s and 1880s, during the process of the abolition of slavery and in the aftermath of an anticolonial war, the debate over race and imperial-Creole disputes moved forcefully into the schoolhouses. The discussions took shape around the question of Black access to the public school system and whether this expanding public space should be racially segregated or integrated. The Spanish colonial administration's 1878 expansion of public education for Black children and the possibility of racial integration drew it into a sharp debate with Creoles in local government. During these years, public schools multiplied significantly; in 1859 there were 285 public schools paid for by municipalities, in 1867 that number had grown to 418, and by 1888 it had increased to 777.[8]

In 1878, in the aftermath of the Ten Years War and the Pact of Zanjón, the *gobierno general*, the central government of Cuba, ruled that every town should build public primary schools for children of color.[9] In providing education for Black and mulato children within the public school system, this order followed suit on but also significantly expanded earlier provisions in the 1844 and 1863 public school laws. Though the earlier laws provided for some degree of public education for children of color, they had been considerably more limited than the 1878 order. The 1844 education plan stipulated that the island's captain general would decide which towns needed schools of color, and the 1863 plan allowed towns to build racially separate schools according to their populations.[10] The 1878 order, on the other hand, mandated that *every* town should have a separate school for children of color, thus significantly expanding the access to the public education system available to Afro-descended children.

The 1878 order was also more expansive and more confrontational toward Creoles than the earlier school laws in its design to incentivize local governments to comply. The order "warned, at the same time, that if a school could not be created within a very short time frame, for economic or other reasons, it is indispensable to admit Blacks in the municipal schools for Whites."[11] In other words, if the towns did not build segregated schools for children of color, they would have to integrate their existing schools. Such a stipulation was predicated on a shared understanding of racism by the Whites in the colonial government and in the municipal governments; Spanish colonial officials presumably understood that many Creole-controlled local governments in Cuba would prefer to spend the money to build schools for children of color than to introduce racial integration in the schools.

The 1878 order strongly affirmed a commitment on the part of the Spanish colonial government to educating Black people in Cuba, even if it meant getting rid of the practice, well established in some regions, of racial segregation in the public school system. The order stated that the government was motivated by "moral and political considerations" and that it had to be implemented because "above all [racial] preoccupations is the sacred obligation to teach."[12]

Despite claims of lofty moral motives, the 1878 order by the Spanish colonial government was likely primarily driven by the particular mix of historical factors on the ground in Cuba in 1878, the year that Cuba's first bid for independence ended. The aftermath of the 1878 order revealed a great deal of contention between the Spanish colonial government and Cuban Creoles at the municipal level, namely in the ayuntamientos, who were tasked with providing schools for children of color as required in the educational order of the same year. The Pact of Zanjón and Spain's efforts to hold onto its colony required it to grant Creoles more political rights, but the Spanish colonial government also attempted to exert more control over Cubans in the aftermath of the war.[13] In debating racial segregation in the public school system, Whites on the Spanish and Cuban Creole sides revealed not only their anxiety about a multiracial population on the island but also about the relationship between Cuba and the Spanish empire.

Two years later, Article 135 of the 1880 Plan de Estudios, an updated law of public education implemented by the Spanish government, again required each municipality to provide public schools for children of color but left out the clause "according to its size" from the 1863 law that had allowed towns to evade compliance. Despite repeating earlier language that education for children of color should focus on morality and religion, the 1880 law also included a clause, perhaps intentionally vague, that suggested that the *content* of the teaching provided in segregated schools should be "on the same terms as the schools for White children."[14] The 1880 law also added an article regarding the education of *patrocinados,* the African and African-descended people who had been enslaved and were now gradually being freed while working as apprentices for the former slaveholders.

These two laws, the 1878 order and the 1880 Plan de Estudios, were important because in them the Spanish colonial government for the first time required that children of color be able to access the public primary education system. However, the default mode in the laws remained racial segregation in schools. In post-Zanjón period, as civic life in Cuba expanded, public schools represented an important public arena. The 1878 law may have opened an opportunity for integrating the primary schools, but the baseline assumption was that segregated schools would be the norm.

Still, the subsequent debates over the 1878 order with Cuban Creoles would push the Spanish colonial government and people of color themselves to be more insistent on racial integration; the seeds of that conflict were already evident in the stipulations of the 1878 order. The order was less equivocal when it came to secondary and postsecondary education. It allowed people of color to matriculate in *institutos de segunda enseñanza* (secondary-level institutes), in professional schools, and in the University of Havana as long as they met the qualifications for admission.[15] Thus, Afro-descended Cubans' access to education expanded considerably after the 1878 order and the 1880 law.

Schools for Children of Color in the Aftermath of the 1878 Order

The 1878 order would generate considerable resistance from Whites in charge of the local governments, as the years in which the central government tried to enforce the order were the very same years as the gradual abolition of slavery led to significant demographic shifts in urban areas. Though the on-the-ground fact of racial segregation in the schools varied, the Creole-run municipalities appear to have been resentful of being pushed into a corner by the colonial authorities. Most towns refused to provide schools for children of color; most of them also refused to admit children of color into the existing municipal schools for White children, as had been a contingency written into the 1878 order. In the records that list municipal schools from the 1880s, the vast majority of towns did not have schools for children of color.[16]

Nonetheless, many towns did comply with the order, representing a significant shift from the past. In the decade prior to the war, there had been only a handful of municipal schools for children of color. From at least 1859–1861, there was a boys' school in Matanzas funded by the town for pardos and morenos.[17] Bayamo also had a public school for boys of color from 1862 to 1867.[18] From 1865 to 1867, there was one public school for boys of color in Trinidad called Nuestra Senora de la Caridad and a public school for boys of color in Sancti Spíritus called San Antonio de Pádua. Aside from these four public schools for Afro-descended boys, there do not appear to have been any other municipally funded schools for Afro-descendants on the island in the decade prior to the war. The municipal schools were closed by the captain general during the Ten Years War, and when they reopened in 1873, there do not appear to have been any municipal schools for children of color.[19]

By 1880, however, there had been an explosion of municipally funded schools for Afro-descended children, likely in response to the 1878 order. Havana created eight new schools for children of color in 1880. Bejucal and Nueva Paz also created two new schools each, one for each sex, in the fall of 1879.[20] By the early years of the 1880s, it is clear that many towns had established schools for children of color to comply with the order. The schools showed up for the first time in Alfonso XII, Baracoa, Bejucal, Cabezas, Camajuani, Cardenas, Cimarrones, Esperanza, Guanajay, Guines, Havana, Macagua, (Corral Falso de) Macuriges, Matanzas, Marianao, Palmira, Paso Real San Diego, Perico, Ranchuelo, Sabanilla del Encomendador, San Diego de los Baños, San José de las Lajas, Sagua la Grande, Santa Ana, Santa Clara, and Santiago de Cuba.[21] In the 1883 Guía de forasteros, an annual report on colonial administration published by the Spanish government, the towns that had new schools for children of color listed them in neat parity: one school for boys, one school for boys of color, one school for girls, and one school for girls of color, for a total of four municipal schools in the town. This was the case, for example, in Sagua la Grande in 1883. Other towns in this period listed a great many schools for White boys and girls but also had at least one school for girls of color and one school for boys of color; among these towns were Baracoa, Guanajay, and Santa Ana.[22]

Other towns appear to have complied with the order by opening racially integrated schools. In other words, they may have allowed children of color into existing municipal schools that had previously only served White children, the backup plan written into the 1878 order for town officials who did not want to provide new schools for children of color. San José de las Lajas had a mixed-race school for each sex in lieu of a dedicated school for boys or girls of color. This suggests that the town was taking the alternative offered by the 1878 order; unable or unwilling to provide a separate, segregated school for children of color, the town integrated at least one school for each sex. There were also mixed-race schools in Baja, Alonso Rojas, Consolación del Sur, San Luis, Bahía Honda, San Diego de Núñez, Macagua, Mariel, Palmira, and Perico.[23]

Several other towns had both segregated schools and mixed-race schools. The town of Alfonso XII had one school for boys of color, one school for girls of color, and one school for White and Black boys; Macuriges had a boys' school for children of color, a girls' school for children of color, and two mixed-race boys' schools.[24] There were also schools for Whites, schools for children of color, and mixed-race schools in the towns of Cabezas and Matanzas.

The 1878 order, therefore, did appear to have a substantial effect on the availability of municipal schools for children of color. In 1881–1882 there were at least thirty-five municipal schools for children of color. If this was still a miniscule number compared to the overall number of municipal schools and the needs of children of color, it was nonetheless a significant expansion from the period before the 1878 order and before the war.

The cities of Havana, Santiago, and Cienfuegos all had substantial Afro-descended populations but different relationships to the colonial compact; the reactions of the local governments in these three cities to the 1878 order varied widely. Like Havana, Cienfuegos is in the western part of the island, the bastion of sugar production that ramped up production even as gradual abolition occurred.[25] Santiago, on the other hand, is in the eastern part of the island, where the sugar economy stagnated in the early nineteenth century. The lack of a sugar economy meant that the racial hierarchy was not as important in the east as it was in the west, nor was the colonial compact as necessary to keep the racial order intact. But Santiago also had a substantial Black population, including the island's largest proportion of free Blacks (reaching one third of the province's total population by the beginning of the nineteenth century), with a long tradition of manumission through self-purchase and of freedom claims on the state.[26] Despite their differences, in Cienfuegos and Santiago, municipal authorities resisted the 1878 order to provide schools for children of color but also refused to desegregate their municipal schools, which had been the alternative option in the 1878 order.

Despite White Creole resistance, in Cienfuegos and Santiago people of color took the lead in pressing the municipal government to comply with the order, often by appealing to the provincial or central government. Afro-descended Cubans in these locations pushed for equal school rights, that is, equal access to the developing public school system during the 1870s, 1880s, and 1890s. This was a new development in the Black educational tradition that had begun with the maestras amigas a century before.

In the late nineteenth century, Black Cubans pressing for the inchoate public education system to serve their children were part of a much wider Black push for equal school rights. By the 1860s in the United States, African American parents, students, and educational activists had won access to the public schools in most of the northern states, but most school districts limited them to segregated classrooms and schools. In the 1870s and 1880s, Black people in the US North pushed hard for more complete integration and access to the school system, precisely in the same period when the issues of access and desegregation were being debated in Cuba.[27]

Municipal Resistance to the 1878 Order: The Case of Santiago

The Santiago municipal archives from the 1880s reveal great flux in the educational situation in that city during the gradual process of the abolition of slavery. As local leaders explored how to manage the transition from slavery to freedom, education played an integral role. And it wasn't only the central and local governments that were involved in this issue; free people of color, too, petitioned governments to comply with the 1878 order.

After the order was issued, the general government sent directions to all the town councils of Cuba, via the provincial governments, about the specifications of the order and ordering them to enforce it. Upon receiving these instructions from the central government, the Santiago town council responded that there were already four schools for children of color in the city (one for girls and three for boys), a number the council considered to be sufficient for the time being. Although complete records of the Santiago schools are hard to find, there was likely at least one school for boys of color that had been converted from a school for White boys in 1875 and taught by Antonio Viosca.[28] The Santiago council acknowledged that new schools would likely have to be built in the future for children of color and assured the government that its "laudable goals" would be communicated to the school inspector.[29]

But Santiago's town council would give different reports on what was happening regarding schooling for children of color in the following few years. Six months after the 1878 order, in reaction to public and local government resistance to the order, the general government again sent out instructions, this time directly to all the municipalities in Cuba, instructing them to enforce the law. They noted that after sending the directions directly to the provincial governors, many people and the press had objected to the order and ignored it. The central government therefore decided to instruct the town councils directly and to communicate "the displeasure with which the governor [captain] general has seen that it has not been enforced."[30]

The Santiago town council responded promptly, saying that there were already schools of color for children of color in that city, that it did not object to admitting children of color into White schools if necessary, and that it was planning to augment the number of schools for children of color in that year's budget. Therefore, the council members did not consider themselves to be part of the displeasure expressed by the central government.[31] Though the Santiago town council was expressing obedience in its letters to the government, it did not seem to be as willing to actually take the steps required by these authorities. There was at least one school for Afro-descended girls likely created in response to the 1878 order, in 1880, taught by Elvira Martínez Acosta.[32]

Eight years later, in 1886, the year slavery was fully abolished in Cuba, Santiago local officials seemed less certain about their desire to educate people of color. Their tone in response to the central government's inquiries was markedly different by this point. There was a general "poverty of education" in the provincial capital, wrote the local Santiago school board to the provincial governor. Since the municipality was behind on its rent for schoolhouses, they could not find new buildings for schools. Further, although Santiago had enough public schools to cover the requirements set out by the Plan de Estudios, those schools were all for White children. The school board acknowledged that free children of color had increased in number, presumably because of the long trajectory of emancipation leading up to 1886, and yet the city only had four incomplete schools. The town council agreed with the school board's recommendation to build two more schools, one for children of each race, and both the town council and school board considered that this would satisfy the concerns of the provincial government over the education of children of color. The local school board explicitly attributed the newfound concerns for Black education, after almost a decade of dismissing the central government's concerns, to the end of the patronato, which had liberated all the slaves. The board reported that the "necessity for schools for children of color increases every day as patrocinados get full liberty and we should educate them as much as possible in moral and religious instruction which they generally lack because of their condition."[33] Also in 1886, public schoolteachers proposed building a night school for artisans, likely also a nod to the newly freed laborers who might need an education.[34]

These records reveal that the local governments reacted to the end of legal slavery with significant apprehension and that their members were thinking of the public education system as a way to control the newly freed laboring Black population, providing them only the moral and religious education that might regulate their behavior as Whites desired, and the kind of vocational education that would allow them to do certain kinds of jobs. Providing a more fulsome academic education was apparently not a priority for the local authorities in Santiago, and avoiding such an education for children of color may have been part of what made them drag their feet in response to the general government's orders.

The central government continued to admonish the local government in Santiago. In 1887 the Santiago city council was again warned by the national school board to "increase, by whatever means necessary, the number of public schools for boys and girls of color" in Santiago.[35] Then, in 1889, the provincial school board for Santiago de Cuba prompted the central government to decree, again, that children of color could be admitted into the municipal public schools.[36]

In 1890 the Santiago school board again changed its story. When the central government asked for a report on whether new schools for children of color should be built, the Santiago school board claimed that the city's schools had long been integrated.[37] This claim was inaccurate based on the board's letters from previous years in which members defended themselves against the claim of not providing children of color an adequate education by pointing out that there were enough schools for children of color. Now they claimed to have integrated the schools long before. The constant sparring between levels of governments and different defenses employed by

Santiago authorities suggests that they were, in fact, not adequately providing an education for children of color and that they were resistant to being pushed on the issue.

It was not only the central government pushing local governments to spend municipal resources on children of color and to comply with the 1878 order. Free people of color, long involved in the educational sphere and accustomed to a mode of political participation that depended on loyal subjectivity to the Spanish colonial government, also pushed the municipalities on the issue of schools for children of color. In 1890, more than a decade after the 1878 order, Manuel Campo and Antonio Ferraro, two Afro-Cuban members of a Santiago *sociedad de color* (mutual aid group for people of color) called El Progreso, petitioned the government to provide two public schools for children of color in Santiago de Cuba, one for boys and one for girls. The men addressed their petition directly to the governor general of the island, skillfully taking advantage of the antagonism that existed between the central and municipal governments in the aftermath of the 1878 order and the Ten Years War. Bypassing the local government also suggests that these Afro-descended men did not have faith in the local government of Creole Whites that had already spent a decade resisting the 1878 order to build public schools for children of color. It also demonstrated their continued use of the political strategy of loyal subjectivity to the Spanish colonial government.

In response to the petition by Campo and Ferraro, the central government requested a report from the Santiago school board. The school board objected to the two men's requests, pointing out that since 1878, Santiago municipal schools had been open to children of both races, as was its Secondary Education Institute, which meant that the claim that the clase de color was being deprived of primary education was erroneous. The Santiago school board pointed out that it would prefer to build new schools in rural areas, where they were really needed. The central government, on receiving the report from the local school board, agreed with the board and vacated the complaint of the two men.[38]

Santiago local officials resisted the central government's mandates to build public schools for children of color or face school integration as a consequence for noncompliance by first saying that the city had a sufficient number of schools for children of color and later, when it became clear that the rising number of free children of color due to abolition belied that claim, by saying that the schools had always been integrated.

Municipal Resistance to the 1878 Order in Cienfuegos

The town council in Cienfuegos took a different approach than its counterpart in Santiago, justifying its resistance primarily on financial constraints. The Cienfuegos council members were no more interested in willingly complying with the central government's 1878 and 1880 laws regarding public education for children of color than were the officials in Santiago. But the records of the Cienfuegos town council and local school board show a division of opinion on how to proceed even within the local level of government, thus complicating the dispute with the central government even further.

As in Santiago, the Cienfuegos town council received, via the governor of Cienfuegos province, news of the 1878 decision to order all municipalities to provide separate public schools for children of color and if that could not be done in all haste for whatever reason, to admit children of color into the schools already established for White children in that municipality. The Cienfuegos town council's immediate reaction was to forward the issue along to the local school board, asking it to study the issue. But in its letter to the school board, the town council preemptively asserted that the current municipal budget would not allow for increases in its outlay. Therefore, the Cienfuegos town council instructed the local school board to find a way to implement the central government's regulation while reconciling it with the constraints of the budget. The town council suggested to the school board that perhaps two of the existing municipal schools for Whites could be converted into schools for children of color and that the board pick two schools in a central location so as to be of use for children of color coming from all neighborhoods. But this recommendation was never implemented.[39]

In February 1879, a group identifying themselves as taxpayers of color from the city of Cienfuegos petitioned the governor of the province for the immediate creation of two schools for children of color, as the 1878 order had mandated. In response, the governor ordered the town to do so, but the town council requested that it instead be allowed to convert two out of twelve existing municipal schools for Whites, again pointing to budget constraints. The governor refused the council's request, answering that if the town didn't have the funds to provide new schools, then it should admit children of color to all municipal schools, as had been ordered.[40]

In the years that followed, the Cienfuegos town council responded to the central government's urgings regarding schools for children of color with similar concerns about the budget. It may be that the Cienfuegos budget was particularly limited or that the town council was made up of a group of particularly fiscally conservative men. But their budget concerns may also have simply served as an excuse to avoid implementing the 1878 order. Even though by the 1870s the Spanish colonial government had accepted the eventuality of abolition, the post-Zanjón era saw the Cienfuegos sugar planters moving in the opposite direction.[41] In Cienfuegos, the sugar industry after 1877 continued to expand as planters updated their technological capacity and efficiency while at the same time expanding their use of slave labor.[42] Therefore, the Spanish colonial government's efforts at increasing educational access for children of color was likely not high on the priority list of Cienfuegos's local leaders, who were experiencing an increase in sugar-related activity.

In January 1880, when it was again prompted by the provincial governor to implement the 1878 order, the Cienfuegos town council once again passed the issue on to the local school board to study and advise about.[43] This time, the school board responded with an extensive report, which was read and discussed at a town council meeting a few months later, in April 1880. The school board responded to the town council's original proposal that two existing public schools be converted into schools for children of color. But the school board's report deviated from this suggestion, arguing instead that rather than undertaking the cost of building any new separate schools, children of color should just be admitted into the existing schools for White children, as the 1878 order suggested should be done in case segregated schools could not be built. The rest of the school board's report was dedicated to budget issues, stating that new schools and therefore new expenses could not be pursued without accounting for the cost.

In other words, the Cienfuegos school board recommended that the city integrate the public schools rather than add a further strain on the budget by making new schools for children of color. But despite their earlier stated concerns about the budget, the town council did not agree with the school board's proposal to integrate the schools in order to save money. Instead, the president of the town council and two deputies requested that their opposition to the school board's plan be recorded. In particular, the president wanted to express his opposition to the admission of Black children into schools intended for the White race, a move he "did not consider to be convenient."⁴⁴ The fiscal concerns that made the town council hesitant to open new schools for children of color came to a screeching halt when faced with the real possibility of racial integration in the schools, demonstrating that the Cienfuegos town council had been motivated not by fiscal concerns but rather was simply unwilling to extend public education to Black children and even less willing to integrate the schools.

In January 1882, the Cienfuegos town council finally informed the provincial government that it would provide two schools for children of color by converting two existing schools for White children. But in its notice, the council struck a defensive note, emphasizing that "the municipal schools that exist in this city have been established in perfect proportion with the number of residents of the White race and the race of color." The town council also emphasized that the schools for children of color could only be provided by closing two schools for White children but that it could not be helped due to budget constraints.⁴⁵ In 1882, four years after the central government's orders to provide schools for children of color, the council responded that it was finally going to comply. Seven years later, in 1889, the local school board had to again direct the town council to open two schools for children of color, one for each sex. This time, the town council immediately agreed to fulfill the project and budget accordingly.⁴⁶

After several decades of resistance on the part of White municipal and school authorities, the 1878 order and the Spanish colonial authorities' insistence that the municipal governments build schools for children of color finally had its desired effects. Cienfuegos was forced to build some schools, and children of color apparently flocked to them. By 1892, the school board had advised the Cienfuegos town council that, given the increased number of students in the schools for children of color, the council should improve the condition of those schools and add more such schools in different neighborhoods.⁴⁷ This notice suggests that Afro-descended children and their families had taken advantage of the racially segregated schools for children of color.

As in Santiago, the back and forth about the 1878 order and the unevenness of local implementation underscores that the Spanish colonial central government was more willing to grant rights and concessions to people of color in the Cuban colony than were the Creoles who controlled the municipal governments. Although the local school boards attempted to enforce the 1878 order, the town councils resisted it. Still, the municipal governments in Santiago and Cienfuegos were ultimately forced to provide some public schools for children of color over the next decade, as they were faced with not only central government pressure but also with the numerical reality of abolition.

The conflict between the central government's attempt to provide for Black education and the Creole town councils and local school boards' resistance to those efforts reveals a society and its racial system in flux in the aftermath of a failed independence war that nonetheless changed the terms of colonial rule significantly. Everywhere in Cuba, anticolonial elements grew stronger in the 1880s, especially at the level of local government, which the Spanish authorities could no longer control in the same way as they once had.[48] Despite these changes, the central questions that had fueled the Ten Years War continued to animate politics in Cuba after it ended; among those questions was the place of Afro-descendants in Cuban society.[49] Spanish authorities, desperate to court loyalty from any segment of Cubans and eager to divide Cubans along racial lines, expanded access to the national education system to Afro-descended children with the 1878 order and the subsequent school law of 1880. In their confrontation with Creoles over this issue, Spanish colonial authorities were even willing to occasionally jettison the principle of de jure racial segregation in the schools, which had been the bedrock of Spanish colonial educational policy since the 1844 Plan de Instrucción Pública.

White Creoles in local governments, on the other hand, used the national education system to resist Spanish colonial authority over municipal schools as well as to double down on the anti-Black racism that had long informed White Creole political and social decisions. During the Ten Years War for independence (1868–1878), White Creole separatists had based their claims to sovereignty on a discourse of political unity born of racial harmony. But their commitment to the abolition of slavery, let alone to racial equality, was always tepid at best, as the historical scholarship has clearly demonstrated. The uneasy coalition of Cuban Creoles that had supported the separatist war fractured in the aftermath of the failed bid for independence. Many White Creole elites, such as those in local governments, found that the political reforms put in place by the Pact of Zanjón allowed for the kind of confrontation over local control that allowed them to wrest some power back from Spain. They stood in contrast to the Cuban separatist movement that continued to organize in exile. White Creoles in local governments in Cuba in the 1880s used the developing public education system to exert racial control over the Afro-descended population during the process of gradual abolition, attempting to block their access to municipal schools where possible and insisting on racial segregation when they were forced to admit Black children into the schools. Their continued efforts to institutionalize White supremacy speaks to the shallowness of the Cuban commitment to racial democracy despite the Cuban separatists' insistence that the Cuban nation would be "neither white nor black."

The 1878 Order: White Teachers for Black Schools

Though the limited and delayed 1878 order led to a modest increase in municipal schooling options for Afro-descended children, it does not appear to have helped Afro-descended teachers gain positions in these municipal schools. In the aftermath of the 1878 order, while some towns and cities resisted and delayed compliance, other towns appear to have promptly arranged new schools for children of color. However, most of the teachers for the new municipal schools for children of color appear to have been White.

In September 1879, aware that schools were to be established for students of color, twenty-two-year-old Isabel Moreno applied to become a teacher at one of those schools.[50] Despite her last name meaning "Black," the use of the honorific "Doña" in her files strongly suggests that she was a White woman, as the honorifics "Don" and "Doña" were usually reserved for White people in Cuba until the early 1890s.[51] Doña Isabel Moreno taught at a school for children of color in Regla, an area of Havana, for more than ten years. In 1897, though, she was teaching in a different town, at an elementary school for White girls, further suggesting that she was White, since it is unlikely that an Afro-descended woman could have taught in a public school for White children.[52]

Similarly, all of the teachers listed for the eight schools in Havana and Nueva Paz that were established after the 1878 decree appear to have been White.[53] Almost every teacher listed for the schools for children of color in the Guía de forasteros of the 1880s also appears to have been White. The teacher of the girls of color school in San José de las Lajas was Leocadia Llorente, a White woman who was the town's first licensed public schoolteacher. She had been teaching in Lajas since at least 1857 and was still teaching during the US occupation of Cuba.[54]

For some White teachers, the new schools for children of color presented their first opportunity to teach. That appears to have been the case for Isabel Moreno and for Josefa Reol, who got her teaching license in 1879 and was the first teacher at one of the schools for children of color that opened in Havana in the fall of 1880.[55] Reol and Manuela Galindo, another White teacher for children of color in the town of Alfonso XII, both went on to long teaching careers and were part of the Cuban expedition of teachers to Harvard's summer school at the turn of the century.[56] The teacher for a new school for girls of color in Santiago in 1880 also appears to have been a White woman, named Elvira Martínez Acosta.[57] In 1868 she was an assistant teacher at another school for White children. The school for girls of color that opened in 1880 appears to have been her first opportunity to be the head teacher.

The new municipal schools for children of color in the town of Bejucal did have Afro-descended teachers, though. Gumersindo Franquis Arango, the teacher of a school for boys of color, is listed as a pardo; his wife, Caridad Gispert de Franquis, who taught in the school for girls of color, was identified as morena.[58] They appear to have been the only licensed Afro-descended public schoolteachers in the early 1880s. Interestingly, in the town of Bejucal, a brother and sister with the surname Gispert taught school in the 1860s, but all indications are that they were White.

This may have been a continuation of an older pattern despite José Moreno's successful teaching application and the debate over the benefits of adhering to strict racial segregation by having children of color taught by Afro-descended teachers versus the dangers of allowing Afro-descendants to access the magisterio. Insofar as towns in Cuba created municipal schools for children of color, the teachers appear to have been mostly White. A school that opened in 1872, before the 1878 order, in Guanabacoa had a White man teacher.[59] In the mid-1860s, the *Guía de Forasteros* listed two schools in Trinidad, one in Sancti Spíritus, and one in Bayamo, all for free boys of color and all appearing to have had White men as teachers.[60]

That White municipal and school authorities preferred White teachers even for Black schools was not unique to Cuba. In Boston in the 1830s, after the city took control of a Black private school, it fired all the Black teachers and replaced them with White teachers.[61] In the nineteenth century, White Creoles in local governments in Cuba as well as in other places sought to deny Afro-descendants the social status, dignity, and authority over students that the teaching profession could provide, even as they were required to allow Afro-descended children into some of their public schools. Having White teachers for Afro-descended children may also have been a way for Whites in Cuba to maintain social control and oversight of Black schools.

Conclusion

In the shaky postwar and gradual abolition period of the 1870s and 1880s, the public education system became a site for conflict over the issue of imperial control and citizenship in Cuba. Beginning with the 1878 order, the Spanish colonial government demonstrated a willingness to jettison formal racial segregation in an effort to court Black Cuban loyalty. In doing so, the Spanish colonial government took a stance against White Creoles in local governments. This was likely an attempt to stem the tide of Afro-Cubans who, as Creole separatists planned for the next war for independence, might have found their rights best represented in the independence movement that would culminate in the war of 1895.

The effect of the 1878 order was to chip away at the security of racial segregation in the public sphere by beginning in one of Cuba's most important public institutions: the public education system. Most towns ignored the order altogether, and Cuba still did not provide enough schools for children of color or enough schools for any children, for that matter. But several towns did have municipal schools for children of color, maintaining racial segregation but expanding access for children of color. Still other towns established racially integrated schools. White Creoles in local governments and on school boards were often reticent to embrace the 1878 order requiring every town to have a school for Afro-descended children or desegregate their municipal schools, expressing nominal obedience while refusing to actually comply before finally either providing racially segregated schools or sometimes desegregating their existing schools. White Creoles in local governments continued to see the developing school system as a tool of racial control rather than a way to court Black loyalty, as the Spanish colonial government evidently did.

In 1885 and 1887, the Spanish colonial government extended the rights of Afro-descendants into other parts of the public sphere, issuing rulings that people of color had to be admitted into public spaces and served at public establishments such as parks, cafés, and theaters. In 1885 the government decree was prompted by the petition of a free Black man who had been denied service at a café. In 1887 the Spanish colonial government doubled down on its 1885 ruling that people of color could not be denied service in public places by requiring railroad companies to allow people of color to travel in first-class cars.[62] While in 1878 the government's recommendations had acknowledged that public opinion might resist government laws, the 1885 rulings explicitly stated that the government should change laws specifically to effect a change in societal norms: "Considering that custom is the fruit of the ideas inspired by law, and jealously guarding its own laws, it is the responsibility of the Authority to change the preoccupations rooted in the spirit of the public."[63] After the 1878 school order, the Spanish government experienced firsthand just how entrenched popular and local governmental opposition could be, perhaps leading it to deal more aggressively in the later rulings. The 1885 decree also reflected the abolition of slavery, which was scheduled to happen in 1888 but took effect two years early. The 1885 government decree identified free people of color as citizens with rights: "All Spaniards are guaranteed rights under the Constitution of the Monarchy, which are based in principles of equality, all classes having the same right to equal protection of the law."[64] In the same years, while Cuban separatists were also advocating for racial equality as a way to draw Whites and Blacks together in support of a new independence movement, many other White Creoles continued to support racial segregation, demonstrating the uphill battle faced by Cuban independentistas who supported the vision of José Martí and Rafael Serra. The attempts to use the public education system as a way to maintain White supremacy would continue long after Cuba became an independent republic.

The 1878 order on public education and Black children and the 1885 and 1887 government decrees arose from decades of Afro-descendants' efforts to spur the central government to accept some degree of desegregation of the public sphere and to recognize Cubans of color as citizens. The Black Cuban educational tradition had been forged in the early nineteenth century by the mostly Black and mulata maestras amigas, by militiamen who extended the tradition of loyal subjectivity into the magisterio, and by militiamen who chose to rebel against the colonial government and/or against racial slavery. In the 1880s, Afro-descendants seized on the 1878 order requiring every town to provide a school for children of color or desegregate the existing municipal schools. They sent their children to the racially segregated municipal schools where they were built or to the mixed-race schools if towns decided to desegregate their schools. Where towns resisted the order, Afro-descended families petitioned the central government, forcing the hand of local White residents who preferred to exclude Afro-descendants from their schools.

This was a period of deepening engagement with the official school system on the part of Afro-descended parents and educational activists; it also was a time of significant development of the equal school rights movement that flourished in the 1880s and 1890s in Cuba. Afro-descended

Cubans simultaneously pursued inclusion and racial desegregation in the public school system while also establishing racially separate, Black-controlled schools through their sociedades de color. Sometimes these two strands of the developing Black Cuban educational tradition combined. Afro-descended Cubans sometimes convinced municipalities to fund the schools they had founded within their mutual aid societies, effectively turning those private schools into public ones. Doing so was an example of Black Cubans using their race-based organizing strategies to expand the public sector to be more inclusive.

5

Black Teachers, Sociedades de Color, and Separate Schools

In addition to the moderate increase in access for children of color to municipal schools in the aftermath of the 1878 order, the Black Cuban educational tradition underwent a parallel significant transformation beginning in the 1870s. Since the early colonial period, enslaved and free Afro-descendants had possessed a strong organizational tradition, gathering in cabildos de nación, cofradías, militias, and escuelitas de amigas. Schools developed by Afro-descendants in the earlier part of the century were for children of color, but they often also educated White children and adults in more mixed settings than the schools established by White Creoles. The Black educational tradition that developed over the course of the nineteenth century therefore expressed a certain political vision for Cuban society and expansive ideas of Black freedom.

At the same time, Spain had ruled Cuba under martial law for much of the nineteenth century, severely curtailing options for publication, assembly, and the development of a public sphere. During the 1820s to the 1850s, the Spanish colonial government had repressed both White and non-White Creole associations in Cuba. In Cienfuegos in the 1850s, only three White sociedades existed.[1] The Black and mulato militias were abolished after the Escalera rebellion, and though they were briefly reestablished in the 1850s, they never regained their prominent place in Cuban life.[2] But despite the early to mid-nineteenth-century suppression of civic organizations, Afro-descendants continued to center education as a priority, operating schools, acquiring licenses from the educational authorities where possible, and establishing separate or private schools that were not funded by the municipal governments and were run by Black teachers or organizations where necessary.

That situation changed dramatically after the 1878 Pact of Zanjón that ended the Ten Years War. In the aftermath of the peace treaty, the Spanish constitution of 1876 and peninsular administrative laws began to be applied to the island, thereby granting Cubans significantly more freedom of the press and freedom of assembly.[3] Ten years later, an 1888 law liberalizing assembly rights in Cuba forced all associations to register with the government and led to the former cabildos being reorganized as legally acceptable *sociedades de instrucción y recreo*, societies for education and recreation. Though some Black associations may have simply changed their names and rules to reflect what the new law required, many of them were truly sociedades de instrucción, coming out of the rich tradition of salons, *tertulias* (literary or artistic gatherings), and *lectores* (readers in a workplace, as in cigar factories) of the mid- to late-nineteenth-century world. More importantly, the sociedades de color and their Black educators also stemmed directly from the nineteenth-century Black Cuban educational tradition of the maestras amigas and militiamen-teachers.[4]

The tradition of Afro-descended Cubans funding and administering separate Black schools expanded significantly in the last quarter of the nineteenth century with the many schools developed by the sociedades de color and other private schools for children of color run by people of color. These schools, like the escuelitas de amigas before them, were not funded by the municipalities and were not considered public schools. Like the militiamen-teachers, though, the Afro-descended teachers of private schools in the late nineteenth century were often able to procure teaching licenses. Black-run private or separate schools provided employment for Black teachers and spaces for Afro-descended children and adults to learn free of the White-supremacist logic that dominated the development of the public school system in Cuba.

This rich tradition of separate Black schools among the sociedades de color would prove essential to Afro-descended Cubans' educational strategies in the last quarter of the nineteenth century. It was an important part of a multipronged approach that Black Cubans used to expand primary education in Cuba and their own children's access to it. Most of the schools established by Afro-descendants in Cuba were designed to make up for the lack of educational access for Black children. But many of them were also racially integrated, educating White children, Black adults, and anyone else who needed access to schooling. In addition, Black Cubans pressed the government to provide municipal schools for children of color, particularly after the 1878 order. Thus, Afro-descended Cubans combined strategies of creating separate educational institutions, on the one hand, with pushing for equal school rights within the expanding public school system, on the other. By the 1890s these strategies would overlap, as some schools founded by Black educational societies would receive municipal funding, and some would become a de facto part of the developing public school system. For Black Cubans developing strategies of freedom at the tail end of slavery, therefore, education would be an expansive and flexible political tool.

Black Teachers in Black Schools

The 1878 order to provide schools for children of color or risk having to integrate the municipal schools prompted significant resistance from White Creoles in the town councils and school boards, but many towns did provide real schools for children of color. This modest expansion of educational access for children of color, however, did not translate to employment opportunities for teachers of color, since most of the teachers for the schools for children of color were White. Not only were the racially segregated municipal schools of the public education system taught by White teachers, but Spanish colonial educational policy still mandated fewer subjects for children of color, focusing instead on the teaching of morality and religion.

In parallel, however, the 1870s and 1880s saw an expansion of schools established and taught by Afro-descended educators. It was in these private schools that Black and mulato Cubans were able to exert control over their children's education. Though many Afro-descendants in Cuba pressed municipal schools to admit children of color, there was also a long tradition of Afro-Cubans working within the magisterio and establishing separate schools to fill the gaps in educational access left by the racist administration of the developing public school system. These schools were essential places to foster what was increasingly coming to be understood as a Black community in Cuba.

Throughout the Americas in the late 1800s, the race of the teacher and the matter of who would control the schools where Black children were taught were of paramount importance to Afro-descendants as well as to White educational authorities. In contrast to the public schools for children of color in Cuba in this period, in most parts of the northeastern United States many of the segregated Black public schools had Black teachers.[5] Not trusting White educational authorities in the public school system, African Americans in the US North established separate schools. Kabria Baumgartner writes that the separate Black schools in Brooklyn, New York, allowed Afro-descendants to "express self-determination through their own institutions."[6]

Srta. Eloisa Piñeiro.

Esta discreta y aventajada afisionada en el difícil arte de la declamación, en su corta estancia en Nueva York, nos ha proporcionado momentos de regocijo y de felicidad, con los hechizos de sus gracias naturales, con la ternura de su carácter modesto y comunicativo como por su talento revelado en lo más trivial de sus manifestaciones. Eloisa Piñeiro, es una esperanza de la patria.

Figure 2. Teacher Eloisa Piñeiro, 1899. In the caption, Piñeiro is lauded for her artful public speaking during a short stay in New York as well as personal qualities that make her "a hope of the nation." In Rafael Serra, *Ensayos políticos, sociales y económicos* (New York: A. W. Howes, 1899). Schomburg Center for Research in Black Culture, Manuscripts, Archives, and Rare Books Division, New York Public Library Digital Collections. https://digitalcollections.nypl.org/items/510d47da-713c-a3d9-e040-e00a18064a99.

Having Black teachers and administrators who controlled the schools and the curricular content was essential to such a project of self-expression. In Cuba, Black and mulato Cubans entered the magisterio in larger numbers than ever before and established separate Black schools within their mutual aid societies. Afro-descended women especially seem to have entered the magisterio in this period; many of them appear to have been able to procure licenses to teach in their private schools. Cuban historian Raquel Vinat de la Mata lists eighteen Afro-descended women teachers licensed between 1878 and the outbreak of the war in 1895; among them were Juana Pastor from Sancti Spíritus, Florencia Torres in Havana, Elena Basilio Rodríguez in Punta Brava, María de Jesus Díaz and Eloisa Piñeiro in Santiago, Petrona Labalette in Placetas, and María de Jesus Pimentel (figure 2).[7]

Some of these women represented a bridge between the maestras amigas and the licensed women teachers of the late nineteenth century. Juana Pastor had been teaching, presumably without a license, since the 1830s. Eulogia or Eduviges Pérez served as a helper to her teacher Felicia Coaffar de Marquez before she began teaching school herself in Cienfuegos in 1867 at age fifteen. Like the maestras amigas of the early nineteenth century, Pérez was "moved more by the desire to educate children than by the income that she could have gotten from them," according to an article in 1903.[8] Her school only lasted until 1868, presumably because of the outbreak of war that year, and she was married in 1871. After the war, she studied for two and a half years under the direction of Luis A. Ramos before taking and passing her teaching exam before the local school board in March 1881. She was the first licensed teacher of color in Cienfuegos, an accomplishment that led to her being feted by other residents of color in Cienfuegos following her exam. In October 1881 she opened a private school for girls, Nuestra Señora de Lourdes, which a Cienfuegos newspaper described as being "the fulfillment of the work begun in 1867."[9] By December of that year she had sixty students. By 1883 there were four private schools for children of color in Cienfuegos, but Pérez's was the only one for girls.[10] Pérez had gone from a maestra amiga, a young woman using her education to teach children informally, to a licensed teacher of a private school (figure 3). Escuelitas de amigas continued into the 1880s; a Cienfuegos count of 1,500 students in 1881 included 200 students in the different escuelitas of the city.[11]

In Guanajay in the 1880s, a teacher named Beatriz Arjona was identified as parda, a free mulata woman. She taught in a girls' school that was *mixta*, with White, Black, and mulata students. She had been taught to read by a priest friend of her family, and she taught her son, Vicente Silveira Arjona, to read. In the 1860s and 1870s they taught school together; she taught the girls, he the boys, in a school that was free to students and authorized by the mayor of Guanajay, though the school does not appear in the official records of the central government.[12] It is unclear whether she was ever granted a teaching license, but she taught in private schools, and her schools were open to children of color and White children in the tradition of the maestras amigas.

Pérez and Arjona represented not only a connection to the Black educational past but also to the future of the Afro-descended magisterio in Cuba. In the 1880s Pérez participated in the newly reinvigorated associational life of Cienfuegos, becoming a member of the Sociedad El Progreso. She was later licensed under the US occupying government and attended Harvard

Figure 3. Article on teacher Eulogia Pérez of Cienfuegos, 1903. The biographical piece appears in *El Album Cenfoguense: Revista Quincenal* of April 12, 1903. Biblioteca Provincial de Cienfuegos Roberto García Valde, Cienfuegos, Cuba.

summer school. Similarly, Arjona and her son became members of various sociedades that proliferated in the 1880s; her son would go on to become a mason, renowned poet, and during the US occupation, a licensed schoolteacher.[13]

Other Afro-descended teachers taught in private schools in the 1860s and 1870s. The famous Black teacher Antonio Medina ran his school, Nuestra Señora de los Desamparados, in Havana in those years after receiving his teaching license in 1850. His students included Miguel Gualba and Juan Gualberto Gómez, men who would become involved in journalism, politics, and the independence movement in the 1890s. In Guanabacoa in the early 1860s there was a private school for Black boys ("varones morenos") taught by Juan Hernández, whose lack of honorific in the official documents suggests that he was not White.[14] The schoolteacher José Jiménez Zúñiga is identified as pardo in Placetas in 1884 teaching at a school for boys of color.[15]

The proliferation of licensed Afro-descended teachers continued in the 1880s, and Cienfuegos seemed to lead the way. By 1889 the magazine *Minerva* congratulated no fewer than ten Black women who had become teachers in the city of Cienfuegos: "Hurray for Cienfuegos! So should we say, all those of us who desire that the progress and well-being of our race be fulfilled, when we see that in such a short time we have made so much progress in this city that we can now count these as teachers: Sras Eduviges Pérez de Rosa, Ursula Coimbra de Valverde, Dorotea Almedia de Soriano, Señoritas Filmena Berrayarza, Flora and Ana Ventura Olivera, Natividad G. González, Angela Cuartero, Ramona Sosa and Dionisia D'Wolf."[16] In addition to Pérez's school for girls were boys' schools; José Isaac García taught boys of color at San Fernando school, and Pedro Tellería taught at San Pedro school.[17]

In 1888 the Black newspaper *La Fraternidad* defended what it called the "escuelitas" in response to an article in the Spanish newspaper *El País* that blamed private schools for the poor state of education. *La Fraternidad*'s writer stated, "It matters much to the Black race, abandoned to its own efforts and to its own propaganda, that their only route to exit the tyranny of Africa that subjugates them not be obstructed."[18] This was a clear allusion to Cuban elites having made every attempt to exclude Afro-descended children from the national public school system in the nineteenth century even while blaming their lack of formal education on racist ideas of their African heritage instead of on White society, where such blame belonged. Indeed, it was precisely the descendants of people of Africa in Cuba who had taken charge of disseminating primary education among children of color and White children as well. Besides educating children of color, Black educators associated with separate schools in Cuba were looking out to the wider Cuban society and seeing education as affecting all Cubans; they participated in educating White children and later advocating for equal school rights.

Afro-Descended Cubans' Sociedades de Instrucción, Education, and Politics

The 1870s and 1880s saw a flourishing of publications and mutual aid clubs on the island, an expansion of associational life in which Afro-descendants actively participated.[19] As had been the case decades earlier for African American mutual aid societies in the northeastern United States, these societies allowed people of color to imagine themselves as a community, and their use of written reglamentos (bylaws) was a way of granting themselves recognition and authority.[20] A major focus of these organizations and publications was education. The sociedades de color, as Black mutual aid societies were called, created libraries, salons, and schools for children and adults and published newspapers that covered the educational efforts of their communities extensively.

The reglamentos of the sociedades de color reflect that for many of them, education and schooling were of paramount importance. La Bella Unión in Aguacate, Havana, was "constituted by and for individuals of la raza de color" but would also "accept the registration of Whites"; when it was registered in 1886, it informed the government of its intentions to open "Centros de Instrucción y Recreo" as soon as it had the funding to do so.[21] La Unión Fraternal, in Santa María, Havana, was a described as a "sociedad de instrucción y recreo." Article 1 of its 1890 reglamento declared the dissemination of education to be its first priority, with promotion of meetings of a recreational nature a secondary priority: "Of these goals, the first is recognized as being the most important."[22] The 1893 reglamento of the Havana club Unión y Fraternidad Centro Social de Jesús del Monte stipulated that the principal mission and object of the organization was to be the instruction of children of both sexes. The club would establish primary schools and assist in defraying costs of superior education of the children of its members.[23] Many other clubs also asserted the importance of education in their founding or registration documents; La Igualdad in Havana intended to provide a school for children and adults of both sexes.[24] La

Igualdad of Cienfuegos opened in 1888; Article 1 of its bylaws said the club had "the object of serving as a meeting place for members, giving them the means to foment education." A Black club in Cienfuegos, La Amistad, included similar language in article 1 of its own reglamento.[25] The sociedad de color El Progreso was founded in 1888 in Santiago de Cuba with the motto "For the school."[26]

It is unlikely that all the clubs that asserted the importance of education were able to establish schools. But many did. El Progreso in Santiago de Cuba received permission from the town council to open a school for children of color in 1891.[27] El Progreso in Havana opened a lay school for girls of all races on January 6, 1889. It was run by a young woman named Elena Basilio Rodríguez, a licensed teacher.[28] In July of that year, exams were administered and prizes awarded for the highest scores. Its exams were witnessed by the students' families as well as journalists from important Black newspapers such as *Minerva* and *Fraternidad* and other important members of the Black community.[29] The records of La Divina Caridad, a sociedad de color headed by the Black Cuban journalist Miguel Gualba, testify to the actual creation of its intended school in March 1889, when its expenditures include payments to the teacher.[30] El Buen Suceso, established in 1892, also appears to have had a real school, given that its 1900 reglamento laid out the daily school schedule along with the responsibilities of the education director of the sociedad.[31] In Matanzas, the sociedad La Unión established a school for boys of color and one for girls of color, taught by Felipe Bataller and Teresa Pérez de Castro, respectively.

The clubs' interest in education was further demonstrated by the many clubs' rulebooks requiring that in case of the dissolution of the club, the remaining funds and properties would be distributed to other educational programs. The Unión Fraternal reglamento stipulated that if the organization were to be dissolved, its remaining funds should be distributed among other Black clubs that maintained schools.[32] Similarly, the Bella Unión Habanera would leave its funds to free schools run by other sociedades de color.[33] Rules of La Igualdad in Havana stated that funds would go to lay schools.[34] Cienfuegos clubs La Amistad, La Igualdad, and El Progreso had similar measures in their rulebooks, providing for remaining funds to go to educational endeavors in the case of dissolution of the clubs.[35] Though the specific instructions varied, the interest in leaving remaining funds to schools pointed to the widespread interest of Black clubs in using their collective financial power to fund primary education.

The sociedades de color represented a shift in racial categories and organizing by racialized people in late-nineteenth-century Cuba. While the cabildos of the earlier colonial period had been more specifically organized around nations or ethnic groups from different parts of Africa, the sociedades de color tended to admit both pardos and morenos. In fact, the documentation of the clubs generally eschewed that terminology in favor of the terms la raza de color and la clase de color, a category that encompassed all Afro-descendants. Some groups resisted this new identification. The African-descended people in Santiago de Cuba's Casino Popular objected to the term *de color* and preferred to have separate groups for pardos and morenos. But the new clubs and schools for la raza de color largely represented a consolidation of Blackness as identity for Cubans of color.[36]

Crucially, the schools within the sociedades de color employed Black teachers. Cienfuegos seems to have been at the forefront of developing schools in their sociedades. There, the sociedad El Progreso established a school that had thirty students by 1882 and employed a teacher named Félix Madrigal; the Cienfuegos sociedad La Igualdad's school had fifty students taught by Pedro Zerquera. Cienfuegos also had a Black women's club called Hijas del Progreso, which started a school for girls run by an Afro-descended teacher and journalist, Ana Joaquina Sosa.[37] A Black man named Julian Escalera taught school through the Centro de Cocineros in Havana.[38] The existence of schools within these groups demonstrates not only that education was an important priority for people of color but also that in the face of local Creole resistance to the 1878 peninsular desegregation order, Afro-descended parents and caregivers were determined to teach their children themselves, within their own communities, employing Afro-descended teachers and in racially separate schools if necessary.

The schools of the sociedades played an important role in employing Afro-descended teachers, valorizing Afro-descended students by giving them a fuller education than the segregated public schools would, and consolidating a Black identity and community. However, the records of these schools also demonstrate that Afro-descendants in this period continued to play an important role in disseminating primary education for all Cuban children, not just Black children. This was a clear continuation of the Black Cuban educational tradition. Black educators and educational activists in this period were pursuing freedom for Afro-descendants, but in so doing, they were advancing a larger civil rights project that forced the state to serve all children.

Specifically, many of the schools of the sociedades in the 1870s, 1880s, and 1890s admitted White children as well as children of color, just as the schools of the maestras amigas and militiamen-teachers had done in the earlier part of the century. La Unión Fraternal's classes were open "to anyone who applies, without distinguishing by race."[39] La Bella Unión Habanera stated in 1888 that its principal object was to establish a school for children of both races.[40] La Divina Caridad's reglamento provided that its school for toddlers would be open to people without distinction to race.[41] In 1889, El Progreso of Havana opened a lay school for girls of both races.[42] Afro-descendants who owned property in Cuba paid taxes but were barred from government-funded schools, first by law, then by resistance to the 1878 order.[43] In response, they created schools in their sociedades, thus experiencing the same double taxation as African Americans who were denied entry to public schools and then built their own. But in their racially integrated schools, Afro-descended Cubans also used their own funds to educate White children who were not being served by the municipal schools.[44]

The schools of the Cuban sociedades represented a continuation of a longer Black educational tradition in another way as well. Like the maestras amigas, who in the 1830s were at the forefront of the movement for tuition-free education, the sociedades emphasized that their schools should be free to their students. Article 2 of the Unión y Fraternidad bylaws stated that its school's students would receive free instruction, and article 74 in the education section of its lengthy bylaws reiterated that primary education will be free. The group would also establish night classes for adults.[45] A similarly named but separate organization, Unión Fraternal, established in 1886, stated in article 1 of its 1890 reglamento, "The object of this society is to disseminate education freely; to hold recreational meetings, and the mutual protection of its members in case of sickness or death. Of these goals, free education is recognized as the most important." In article 3 its reglamento reiterated that Unión Fraternal would "establish, therefore, different classes for free education to all those who sought it."[46] El Liceo's principal object was likewise "to offer free primary education."[47] The Bella Unión Habanera's records don't specify that its own school would be free but required that in case of the group's dissolution, any remaining funds would go to "sustaining *free* schools run by similar sociedades" (emphasis mine).[48] The sociedades in Cienfuegos allowed members to send their children to school without paying tuition.

The schools established by some of the sociedades de instrucción also educated adults.[49] Night schools for adults were open even to adults who were not members of the sociedad, demonstrating their commitment to making education more broadly accessible.[50] Nonmembers' children were also accepted into the schools of the sociedades. Article 77 of the Unión y Fraternidad reglamento stipulated that "members and nonmembers who desire to matriculate a child should present him or her to the general board of the center so that they can record their name, last name, address, and the information of their parents."[51] Another of the groups said it would provide free education to anyone who sought it. Again, the schools of the sociedades de color appear to have adhered to a democratizing principle in that they were often available for boys and girls, children and adults, members and nonmembers.

The sociedades de instrucción y recreo, like the schools of the maestras amigas, demonstrated a capacious understanding of who should receive an education. They educated Black and White children. They also often educated adults. And the schools were not just for members. Thus, although the tuition-free schools of the sociedades were paid for by their members, the beneficiaries of that education were not only the members. Many children and adults were educated without having paid tuition or membership dues.

Afro-descended members of sociedades de color pushed Cuba's leaders to expand access to education for all Cubans in other ways as well. In an 1888 article in the Black newspaper *La Fraternidad*, reprinted from *El País*, a teacher from Havana province insisted that Cuban society needed to prioritize education more. Teacher pay needed to be regulated, and more schools were needed to train teachers. "Until all the social classes, without distinguishing by race, receive an education that is expansive, rational, concrete, and disseminated to the four winds and in all directions, we will not have a country, nor order, nor morality, nor true progress."[52] The Black newspaper's reprinting of an article from a Spanish newspaper by a likely White Cuban teacher suggests that, for Black activists in Cuba, education was not only a racial issue but a wider social priority.

Black Cuban educators in the 1870s, 1880s, and 1890s were continuing in the Black Cuban educational tradition of providing Afro-descended children access to education, providing employment for Black and mulato teachers, educating girls and Black adults and White children, all of whom were being underserved or not served at all by the official public education system, and disseminating education for free while doubly shouldering the cost of schooling. In so doing, they were participating in the social and political life of Cuba although several of their reglamentos specifically prohibited discussion of politics within the clubs, an apparent requirement of the registration laws for the sociedades. Article 2 of the reglamento of Bella Unión Habanera prohibited "the treatment of political, economic, and religious questions."[53] Others had similar language. But in pursuing a particular kind of educational agenda, Afro-Cuban educators, parents, and students were in fact treating political issues. The struggle for Black schools to educate boys and girls, Whites and Blacks and mulatos, children and adults, members and nonmembers was a form of Black political protest against the existing system.[54] By their very existence and because of the merging of separate private Black schools and municipal funds that would come soon, Black educators forced an expansion of the developing national education system in Cuba.

From Separate Schools to Municipal Funding

Afro-descended Cubans' educational work and activism was central to the development of the Cuban educational system in the nineteenth century. In many aspects, the Black Cuban educational tradition was at the vanguard of what would soon become progressive, liberal aspirations for school systems throughout the Americas. Black and mulato men and women teachers often taught students of all races, often in the same classrooms; they provided tuition-free education at a time that it was not readily available on the island; and they taught a wider range of students, providing crucial schooling to populations the official education system disdained, particularly girls and formerly enslaved adults. Black-run schools were not insular spaces set apart from the larger educational context in Cuba but rather avant-garde institutions that contributed crucially to the development of educational ideologies and systems on the island.

That Afro-descended educators and their schools were central in the nineteenth-century development of the public school system in Cuba becomes even clearer in the fate of some of the private schools founded by Afro-descended Cubans, such as those that were part of the sociedades de color. At the request of the Black educators associated with them, some of these schools eventually were funded in part or in full by the municipalities, essentially becoming part of the public school system.

This pattern echoed that of Black schools throughout the United States that sometimes also received funding from the municipalities or were otherwise absorbed into the public school system. In Boston at the beginning of the nineteenth century, Black children were excluded from the new public schools, so African Americans established their own separate schools. But by 1812, the city was providing "modest financial support."[55] The Colored School in Brooklyn also received some funding and administrative oversight from the city in the 1820s and 1830s, until it was made part of the Brooklyn public school system. A similar phenomenon occurred in Nantucket, Massachusetts.[56]

In Cuba, an example of this occurs with various schools of sociedades de color in Cienfuegos in the late nineteenth century. Cienfuegos's major sociedades de color, namely El Progreso and La Amistad, were founded in 1879, followed by La Igualdad in 1882 and several others in the 1890s. Many of these clubs' schools subsequently were subsidized by the local government.[57] In the 1880s, as the sociedades de color flourished in Cienfuegos, several of them asked the town council to subsidize their schools. In October 1883, the town council agreed that beginning in January 1884 and at the request of the Black clubs La Amistad and El Progreso, it would pay for a teacher of primary education to work in each of the two clubs' schools.[58] It was not so amenable to La Igualdad's request, for some reason; in 1886, the president of the Black club La Igualdad also spoke to the town council, requesting that his club's school be subsidized like those the town council was already subsidizing, but this time the council refused.[59]

At the end of 1884, one of the deputy mayors of Cienfuegos proposed that, given that the council was subsidizing the schools for boys of color of two sociedades, it would be natural and just to also fund Nuestra Señora de Lourdes, the school for girls of color run by Eulogia Pérez, the first licensed Afro-descended woman teacher in Cienfuegos. The deputy mayor referred to the "brilliant results" of the school's students in recent exams.[60] The school did receive municipal funding. In 1886 the town subsidized it with seventeen pesos, and by 1889 it gave the school thirty-four pesos. By 1889 the school had "99 students, divided into three sections: free, subsidized by the municipality, and private."[61]

The description of this school as a private, racially separate school taught by an Afro-descended woman who had received a teaching license from the government speaks to the lack of clear distinctions between private and public, White and Black, tuition-free and tuition-based schools in this period and to the way Afro-descended educational activists and families took advantage of the situation. Pérez's school educated girls of color, some of whom seem to have paid tuition, others whose education was paid for by the town council, and still others who attended for free, meaning that Pérez herself bore the costs of educating many girls, in the manner that the maestras amigas had before her. Still, by charging tuition to some students, she was able to make a living. And by insisting that the municipality bear some costs for the education of Afro-descended children, Pérez was exerting pressure on the Cuban public education system to make room for children of color.

This interest on the part of the Black clubs in having town councils subsidize their schools and some town councils' apparent willingness to do so was happening at the same time that the Cienfuegos town council was resisting the 1878 order's directive to build new schools for children of color and the gradual process of abolition was coming to an end. The Cienfuegos town council had reacted to the 1878 order by declaring that the municipal budget could not afford to build new schools for children of color and had ordered the local school board to solve the issue. The school board, in turn, had suggested that the town proceed as the colonial government suggested in such cases, to allow children of color to enter the existing municipal school. But the council balked at the specter of racial integration in the municipal schools and prevaricated, avoiding taking any steps to comply with the 1878 order for more than a decade.

In this context, the town council somehow found funds to subsidize a few of the schools of Cienfuegos's sociedades de color. Perhaps it considered the separate Black schools a useful safety valve that appropriately preserved the racial segregation council members desired. And paying for these teachers was surely cheaper than opening two new schools, which might have involved not only hiring teachers but also renting or building space and furnishing the supplies. In convincing town councils to fund Black schools, Afro-descended educators picked up where the Spanish colonial government's 1878 order and 1880 school law left off. The Black clubs seem to have had more success than the Spanish colonial government, perhaps because the years of pressure by the central government had eased the way but also perhaps because local Afro-descendants were able to collaborate more productively with White local governments than the Spanish colonial authorities with whom Creoles were in a prolonged confrontation over political reform.

By 1887 La Amistad club asked to convert its already subsidized school into a municipal school financed entirely by the town council. The council passed the request on to the local school board, which quickly declined it.[62] The club, one year after the end of the process of gradual abolition, might have found itself enrolling more students than it had the resources to support. By the late 1880s, residents from neighborhoods throughout Cienfuegos and rural districts around it were flooding the town council for requests to subsidize their schools or add schools in their districts.[63]

Conclusion

Though the sociedades de color had mixed results in securing municipal funding for their schools, their limited success and their interaction with the town councils shows how essential Black educational institutions were to the development and expansion of public education on the island. In the absence of the central government's ability to force local governments to build schools for children of color and in the face of local White resistance to efforts to spend public resources on growing numbers of free children of color, Afro-descended educators financed, founded, and populated their own schools. Then they savvily tried to find a back door into the public education system, with mixed results. In the case of Pérez's school, tuition-paying students overlapped with Pérez providing her services for free and with some degree of town funding, all at the same time. In this strategy, her work and other Cubans' paralleled the efforts of African American educators who also established their own separate Black schools in the early nineteenth century in the US North and in the second half of the century in the South, taking on the financial burden that the state refused to meet and later finding ways to secure public funding.

The schools created by the Black clubs represented a clear interest in racial-separatist organizing by Afro-descendants on the island, all of whom would be free from slavery by 1886, and especially a valorizing of Black teachers. But in requesting and sometimes obtaining municipal funding for these schools, educators were also working outside of their own schools, pushing the government to improve educational options for Black children in creative ways. The two members of the Santiago sociedad de color El Progreso, Manuel Campo and Antonio Ferraro, petitioned the central government in 1890 to have Santiago build schools for children of color. In Cienfuegos, too, the 1878 order was met by a petition in February 1879 by Black inhabitants requesting that the city council comply with the order and urging the council to integrate the existing schools if they couldn't finance separate schools.[64] People of color started their own schools for children of color, showing a commitment to racial-separatist organizing when necessary but also demonstrating their commitment to education for Cuban society writ large, as they often accepted White children as well. And they pushed for the state to spend resources on their children equally, advancing what in the US context is often called the struggle for equal school rights. In the 1890s the educators and activists involved in the sociedades de color would make equal school rights a central piece of their civil rights struggle. Lawsuits made by people of color against the Spanish government and the colonial government's concessions produced drastic results in the world of education, race, and segregation.

6

The Directorio Central de las Sociedades de la Raza de Color and the 1890s Campaign for Equal School Rights

In the last quarter of the nineteenth century, in the midst of the lengthy and contested struggles over the abolition of slavery and the end of colonial rule, Afro-descended thinkers and activists in Cuba made equal school rights a centerpiece of their civil rights campaign. Members of the Black clubs organized under an umbrella organization called the Directorio Central de las Sociedades de la Raza de Color and petitioned the Spanish colonial authorities over a host of civil rights issues including the problem of racial segregation in the public school system in the 1880s and 1890s.

In 1893 the directorio achieved something remarkable: the Spanish colonial authorities ordered that Afro-descended children should be admitted into all municipal schools on the island of Cuba, thus desegregating the Cuban public school system. Afro-descended Cubans associated with the directorio used race-based organizing to achieve racial integration in the school system, thereby decisively shaping one of the most important Cuban public institutions of the day. This strategy of using Black organizations to affect the wider Cuban society was a continuation of the Black educational tradition that had previously used educational activism and Afro-descended organizations to broaden tuition-free primary schooling for all children and provide more public schools for children of color, among many examples.

In the records of the directorio and its constituent clubs in meetings leading up to the legal confrontation with the Spanish colonial government, the Black leaders and members of the directorio insisted that education was their foremost priority. "We have to insist especially about the municipal schools," proclaimed the newspaper *La Igualdad*.[1] They articulated expansive reasoning for the prioritization of education in their racial justice struggles. Education could help Afro-descendants in Cuba, all of whom were now free from slavery, by improving their occupational status and their morality, they claimed. Integrating the public schools would also lead to harmonious race relations, which would help cohere Cuban society, especially in a period of crisis and disunity. In the records of the directorio's meetings, education is used as a flexible and multipurpose political and social tool.

By the 1890s, in the aftermath of the abolition of slavery, Afro-Cuban political activists were also using education to talk about freedom in terms of citizenship, rights, and the state's obligation to its people. In so doing, they were responding to the evolving terms of Spanish colonial rule but also to the notions of cubanidad, Cuban nationhood, that were finding new purchase in the independence movement being organized from New York and Florida and that would erupt into war in 1895.

Despite a long tradition of loyal subjectivity to the Spanish empire, many Black Cubans by the 1890s were either separatists looking for some degree of autonomy from Spain or others who had embraced full legal independence as a political goal. Some had been censured or exiled for their political activities or speech against the Spanish colonial government in Cuba, among them the president of the directorio, Black intellectual Juan Gualberto Gómez. The liberating rhetoric of the independence movement and the imagined Cuban nation, along with the concessions granted to people of color by White Creole independentistas looking to win supporters, were attractive to many people of color. In addition, many Black Cuban intellectuals strongly contended that ideas of republicanism and modernity were better reflected in the independence movement than in the Spanish empire.[2] Still, even as the liberating rhetoric of the possible Cuban nationalism was attracting followers, Black Cubans were able to achieve significant concessions from the Spanish colonial government.

Black Cuban leaders involved in educational efforts in this period were more often than before members of the educated Black bourgeoisie who had aspirations of political power and of leadership among Afro-descendants. They prioritized equal school rights because they desired access to Cuban public institutions and the integration of Cubans of color into Cuban society. In pursuing those ends, many members of the directorio disdained the African cultural practices of some members of the clase de color; they positioned themselves as leaders of a larger group of Afro-descendants who needed schooling in part to learn Western, bourgeois, and patriarchal customs.[3] The directorio also avoided the alternative political strategy of creating a separate Black political party, although that was a strategy Gómez had considered and the directorio was itself a form of race-based political organizing.[4] The strategy of creating race-based organizations would continue, however, and in 1908 the Cuban Partido Independiente de Color, a Black political party, would be formed.

The Afro-descendants involved in the directorio's suit for equal school rights, therefore, were different than the Black and mulata maestras amigas who had worked outside of the official school system and the militiamen-teachers who had rebelled against slavery and the colonial state. They were of a higher socioeconomic class, had more political access and aspirations, and imagined themselves to be citizens to whom the government owed equal school rights. Still, in their campaign for equal school rights, the members of the Black clubs associated with the directorio and the students and parents who supported the school integration campaign were drawing on the long nineteenth-century history of the Black Cuban educational tradition.

The Year 1886: The Directorio's Formation

Educational efforts found purchase in the many sociedades de color that proliferated in this period. In 1886 the directorio was formed as an umbrella organization to coordinate the political activities of these Black clubs under the direction of Juan Gualberto Gómez. Gómez was born free to enslaved parents in Cuba, studied with the renowned Afro-descended Cuban teacher Antonio Medina, and later became a prominent journalist and an activist for the causes of racial democracy and Cuban independence. The directorio was an effective presence in Cuba, pooling the energy and resources of Black clubs throughout Cuba to support its work, particularly when it came to schooling. In 1892, an Episcopalian missionary wrote to Gómez asking if the directorio clubs could put some money together to fund the higher education of a particularly talented boy of color in his school; the request suggests that within a few years of its founding, even non-Cuban Whites understood the directorio to have some mobilizing power.[5]

The directorio's most significant accomplishments took the form of a civil rights campaign in the early 1890s that particularly focused on education.[6] Earlier government decisions on segregation in schools and public spaces were on the books, but their most progressive measures were not enforced. In addition, the 1878 ruling required municipalities to provide schooling for children of color by providing racially segregated municipal schools, suggesting that segregated schools were perfectly legal options for educating children of color. The directorio undertook to engage with the Spanish colonial government for the recognition and expansion of these earlier decisions regarding people of color and for the mandated racial integration of all public schools.

As the campaign progressed, the directorio's constituent clubs continued to operate their own schools, host evening lectures and concerts to perform and share music and literature, and otherwise organize separately from Whites. In 1894 the directorio opened a boarding school in Havana for girls of color, particularly for those from the provinces who wanted an opportunity to study in the capital.[7] But though the directorio performed its own racially separate activities, its members were also interested in creating official pathways for people of color to assert their rights vis-à-vis the government. And the directorio was insistent on the importance of integration in the public sphere, most of all in public education.

The directorio had to be careful to emphasize Black Cubans' desire for integration into Cuban society and to defend Black political mobilization from Whites who feared another Haiti in the long aftermath of the Haitian revolution. In 1892 Juan Bonilla, a Black Cuban journalist who was in exile in New York, wrote that the directorio did "not seek to create a separate Black party, or to interrupt the march of the country."[8] The member clubs and the directorio itself may have constituted a racial organization with separatist organizing, but its supporters were careful to remind everyone that the aims of the directorio were strictly integrationist. Its support of an integrated public education system reflected that position.

The 1892 Meeting of the Directorio Central de la Raza de Color

In March 1892, six years after slavery was abolished in Cuba and three years before another separatist war would begin, the call went out for a meeting of the sociedades de color. A July 7 circular solicited reports from each club on the status of Afro-Cubans in their area and what the problems, necessities, and aspirations of people of color were.[9] In August 1892, the Directorio Central de las Sociedades de la Raza de Color met with its constituent groups to restructure the organization and set an agenda.

In the records of this meeting, it is clear that the directorio was in the midst of promoting a large and far-reaching civil rights movement. The most striking part of these records, however, is how central education was to the push for racial equality and racial justice on the part of these Black

Cuban activists. This is made evident in the minutes of the assembly of the directorio and repeatedly addressed by the constituent clubs in their reports. After reading all the reports, the working groups assigned by the directorio's assembly concluded that "the first and most generally felt of all our necessities consists of finding effective methods of developing Instruction."[10] The groups determined that in order to do so, they would have to push for the racial desegregation of the public schools of Cuba.

The directorio noted that the municipalities were making it difficult for Afro-descended Cuban children to access education by establishing segregated schools for Black children in compliance with the 1878 ruling rather than integrating the existing schools. Further, some municipalities had not even taken the step of providing separate schools for children of color while continuing to bar their admission into the existing municipal schools. The result, according to the directorio's report, was slowness in the development of educational access for all Cubans but especially for Afro-descended children.

In their own reports, the member clubs overwhelmingly agreed that access to education was the most important priority for Afro-descendants. This was the case even though clubs described different situations on the ground. Some towns allowed Blacks to attend any of the municipal public schools; others did not. In Trinidad the complaints were that the schools were legally segregated, which meant that there were not enough educational opportunities for Black people, especially for the grand majority who lived in rural areas. Juan Tranquilino Lapatier, writing on behalf of some of the Black clubs in Santiago de Cuba wrote that although Black children were not explicitly or legally barred from the municipal schools, people demonstrated certain scruples that produced the same result of barring entry to children of color. There were not enough schools, and those that existed were incomplete, in contradiction to the laws governing provincial capitals. In Santiago, the fault was understood to lie not with laws or policies but with their enforcement.[11]

In singling out education as their most important political priority, the sociedades de color were extending the work of earlier teachers and activists in the Black Cuban educational tradition. All of the member clubs as well as the directorio's working group acknowledged that Black people had created many educational opportunities and that the level of education among Afro-descended Cubans was due primarily to their own schools and teachers. Black Cubans who had gotten education had done so through their own efforts. Some pointed to individuals' efforts to learn, and others pointed to private schools sustained almost entirely by Blacks.[12]

But the Black clubs of the 1890s were working in a new context. Slavery had only been abolished in 1886, and most of the recently freed Afro-descendants on the island had not had an opportunity for schooling. The Holguín club representative noted that people of color made up half of the population of that region, and of those, 70 percent had been enslaved and part of the gradual abolition apprenticeship system.[13] The directorio working group echoed this concern when it wrote, "There has been significant progress on this path in recent years, but the legacy of slavery has been so great that nobody can or should be surprised that the intellectual state of the class we belong to is not satisfactory yet."[14] The long Black educational tradition of nineteenth-century Cuba had not penetrated the plantations, and now that all Afro-descendants in Cuba were free from slavery, the educational system had to adapt to accommodate them. It was to this expanded need for Black access to education that the directorio and its members now turned their attention.

Black Cuban activists associated with the directorio wanted the municipal schools to be desegregated primarily to increase educational access. But desegregation would have other benefits as well, they claimed. For example, desegregation would serve to lessen racial animosity. "In various parts of the island, [municipal schools] are shared between White and Black students. And we can affirm that wherever this is the case, there is greater harmony between classes," claimed an 1893 article in the Black newspaper *La Igualdad*.[15] Directorio members expressed concern that what they called "caste distinctions" were taking root under the segregated public education system.[16] Here, its Afro-descended members echoed US abolitionist Frederick Douglass, who just a few decades earlier had asserted that integrating public schools, where children could experience "contact on equal terms, is the best means to abolish caste."[17]

Such a call for racial harmony had clear political ramifications for the Cuban independence movement's democratic principles. Many Black Cuban political leaders supported the Cuban separatist movement, and conversely, many Black supporters of the independence movement were committed to racial democracy and to greater access to education. The Casino de Artesanos in Holguín referred to Whites and Blacks as "citizens of one nation" who were "part of a free and democratic America."[18] The report of the directorio was published almost in full by independence activist and

Afro-descended Cuban Juan Bonilla, who wrote from exile in New York in the pro-independence newspaper *Patria*.[19] Black Cuban educational activists' desire to desegregate the schools thus served to support the ideas of cubanidad undergirding the independence movement that was heating up in the 1890s.

Racial desegregation would also benefit the broader Cuban society by leading to an improvement of the public education system overall, which was still underdeveloped in the 1890s. Valuable municipal resources were wasted on maintaining segregated schools, if they provided schools for children of color at all. Lapatier, writing on behalf of the Black clubs in Santiago de Cuba, referred to all of the public schools as "few, and poorly attended."[20] The representative of a different club in Santiago de Cuba said the schools were in hands of the teachers who did not have enough knowledge and were incompetent. Schooling needed a "complete transformation," wrote this representative. "It is not only the raza de color that suffers its effects, . . . it is everyone, but since it affects us directly, I present the question nakedly, so that the Directorio may advocate for measures that would end this painful question."[21] Here we see that Black Cubans were once again at the forefront of developing the educational system in Cuba for the benefit of Cuban children of all races.

The use of education as a multivalent political tool extended in other directions as well, as is reflected in the clubs' reports and the directorio's concluding report at their meeting. Education was also prioritized because it could be used to repudiate the White-supremacist arguments used to justify discrimination. Most Black intellectuals and activists in turn-of-the-century Cuba firmly disavowed the principles of biological race that asserted that Blacks were biologically different from and inferior to Whites. Lapatier, writing on behalf of El Club de Oriente and Alcázar Antillano, both in Santiago de Cuba, denounced the practice of inscribing sacraments in the parochial records by race, "as if a natural difference existed between White and Black children."[22] For their part, Whites across the Americas had a well-established set of ideas to justify slavery that were mobilized to also justify inequality and oppression after the abolition of slavery. Whites pointed to what they perceived as Black Cubans' lack of education, preparation, and culture. Afro-Cuban leaders rejected this argument, commenting on its hypocrisy. At the 1892 directorio meeting, the delegate of El Fénix de Trinidad wrote bluntly, "It is clear that those who held one class in slavery, abjection, and misery cannot on redemption day claim that the consequences of these evils are a reason to curtail the rights of the redeemed man, or to isolate him from society."[23]

However, once the justification for oppression was exposed, it could be remedied, theoretically. Extending educational access to Blacks would serve to undercut White supremacists' arguments by giving Black Cubans academic instruction while also fostering morality, culture, and good social habits. Antonio Moro González, the president of the club from Trinidad, wrote that educating la raza de color in this manner would be "the first steps to obtain our desires, shared by a majority of the White race who want unity and to live in a modern society."[24] Education could advance those interests by undercutting White-supremacist justifications for oppression.

Education was also a means of criticizing and making claims on a government that Black Cubans felt had a responsibility toward them as citizens. The Constitution of 1876, which established in Spain a constitutional monarchy, had been extended to Cuba in 1881, granting Cubans all the rights of Spanish citizenship. Black Cubans were aware of these rights and mobilized around them.[25] And yet, the members of the directorio complained that the government was acting as a hindrance to racial equality in Cuba rather than helping Black Cubans. They complained that interracial relations would have been better, thus allowing Cubans of color to advance, if it weren't for government obstructionism. And repeatedly referring to both Black and White Cubans as "citizens of one nation," the delegates from Holguín contended that Blacks' civil and political rights had not been fully recognized. Once again, this report from Holguín proposed that education was the solution; it would get rid of "irritating inequality," therefore allowing the entire nation of Cuba, still a colony, to take its rightful place, "encased in free and democratic America."[26] The report ties various strands of thought together. Afro-Cubans used education as a way to remind the government of its obligations to them as citizens; this was a new relation to the Spanish colonial government that overlapped with prior relations of subjectivity. At the same time, they alluded to their interests in the developing ideas of the Cuban nation espoused by the separatist movement, even while the report was urging the Spanish government to recognize Black Cubans as citizens of Spain.

Education could also serve as a tool of liberation, according to members of the directorio. Being "instruido e ilustrado," educated and enlightened, meant that a person wouldn't tolerate subordination, claimed the delegate from Holguín:

Education, as you all know, is the fountain from which man drinks the fruitful and life-giving wisdom of freedom; no educated and enlightened man easily tolerates the anomalies that the capricious fate of a fellow man, shielded by the accumulation of circumstances that favor him, establishes as an irrefutable principle the subordination of one over another. With enlightenment, fear disappears, the possibility disappears that, no matter how powerful, no matter how protected... a man or a people, will try to dominate, deny the right to freedom to that same man, his equal.[27]

The records of the 1892 meeting reflect that for Afro-descended Cubans, education and more specifically a campaign for equal school rights could respond to multiple problems. Opening municipal schools to all children would expand educational access to children of color while elevating the quality of education for all Cuban children, since resources could be spent more efficiently. It would also enhance social harmony and unity, potentially bolstering the project of national independence. And it would promote personal liberation, encouraging people to resist domination by others.

The directorio concluded,

In all the [club] reports we have examined, there is a unanimous desire that we petition until accomplishing education in common, the official declaration that municipal schools are for all children of a region without distinction of color; this is a desire that this Commission agrees with and recommends not only because it is just, but because we understand that it responds to the needs of the patria, which today suffers seeing its children separated and differentiated in education and position according to the color of their skin.[28]

By listening to the members of Black clubs around the island, the directorio determined that its political campaign had to focus on equal school rights.

La Igualdad, the newspaper that served as the mouthpiece of the directorio, reiterated after the directorio's claim was filed that "we must insist especially on the municipal schools." Like Gómez and the directorio, the newspaper cited the earlier measures as precedent, in this case considered to be both good and bad:

The more we examine this problem, the less justifiable we find segregation. This distinction is not established in any law. The law of public education only requires that for every certain number of inhabitants there will be a school.... The most important law regarding this is the 1879 circular by then Governor General Arsenio Martínez Campos, in which he recommends that great attention should be paid to the education of children of color. It is true that General Campos, though he was inclined to integrated education, let the municipalities make separate schools for children of color, but only if they had enough money to do so. If they didn't have funds, they had to admit children of color into the existing schools for Whites.[29]

The newspaper also recapped several of the other issues raised by the directorio and likely to be raised by its opponents. These issues spanned social as well as political spheres. First came the issue of the possibility of social discord arising from extending the rights of people of color. *La Igualdad* asserted that school integration would lead to racial harmony and not to race wars. It supported this claim by pointing out that in Cuban cities, children of all races lived in close proximity and played together in the streets peacefully. If they could play together, asked the newspaper, why would they object to going to school together? The paper also pointed out that the upper levels of education, the secondary education institutes and the university, had long been officially integrated without protest from the elites who attended them, and it proposed that if the elites didn't mind integration, then the lower classes, who already lived in close quarters in the island's cities, should not object either. Social concerns blended into political ones at the end of the article. The newspaper asserted that society and the government owed a debt to people of color after maintaining them in slavery and ignorance and therefore an obligation to educate them. The progress of people of color would benefit them and also the wider society. "Equality and culture, consideration and knowledge: this is what the Cuban clase de color wants, to be a factor of progress in this country. The privileged classes and the State can do a lot about this. If they do this, they'll be the first in reaping the benefits of this initiative, at the same time as fulfilling their social obligation."[30]

The Year 1893: The Directorio's Instancia and the Spanish Colonial Government's Response

After the 1892 meeting, the directorio submitted petitions to the Spanish colonial government of Cuba. Juan Gualberto Gómez, as head of the directorio, cited 1885 and 1887 rulings on the rights of Black people in the public sphere as precedent and asserted that the point of these rulings had been to "make the preoccupation of castes disappear" and that they didn't "allow for distinction of any sort to be made in public places on the basis of color."[31] The petitions asked that the government enforce the earlier rulings. More importantly, the directorio's petition requested that the law be changed to require all the municipal schools in the country to accept children of all races rather than allowing towns to provide segregated schools, as the 1878 ruling had done. The directorio wanted the government to issue new decrees not only clarifying the letter of the law and adding penalties for noncompliance but also identifying the spirit and goal of these measures, to achieve desegregation and to promote equality before the law.[32]

In considering the directorio's request, the Consejo General de Administración of the Spanish colonial government made note of the 1878, 1885, and 1887 rulings, commenting that the government had earlier "realized the glorious act of declaring everyone equal before the law." The government asserted that social hierarchies were important but that these should not be based on race. The consejo's order agreed with members of the directorio that barring discrimination based on race would not cause upheaval to the social order: "In all civilizations there are categories within the social order, and people surround themselves with people from their own social category. But these categories are not organized by reason of color, rather by their social position that is recognized generally, founded in their education, culture, and other circumstances that create distinctions."[33] By recognizing class distinctions within Cuba's population of color, the consejo made clear that its concern was only about elite people of color's rights being violated. It was not, in other words, particularly concerned with all members of the Afro-descended population. It asserted that the owner of an establishment had a right to make rules about that establishment, but those couldn't be based on color. The raza de color in Cuba was, according to the consejo, characterized by a love of order, respect for social institutions, and consideration and respect toward the White race. Since the government had already recognized these tendencies by abolishing slavery and declaring everyone to be equal before the law, the government should, according to its abilities, enable the "suffering and loyal" clase de color to enter the social order.[34]

Therefore, advised the consejo, the government should enable Afro-descendants to enter into social life "as feasible, according to their present circumstances." Again, the class implications in this statement are clear. Those people of color who had already achieved a certain level of education and refinement, their present circumstances, were to be allowed into the social order. This was not a sweepingly progressive statement about social equality, but it did begin to address race-based discrimination.[35]

In addition to submitting petitions to the government, the directorio was actively involved in negotiating with the government. During the government's consideration of the directorio's claims, Gómez met several times with the captain general and other top officials.[36] In consultation with Gómez, the central government reached a compromise position regarding the directorio's demands, agreeing to some of the more substantial ones and letting others fall by the wayside, such as specifically issuing written documents and warnings to the town mayors and implementing a fine system for noncompliance with the rulings.[37] In other words, the directorio had a hand in formulating and elevating the demands but also was involved in the government's consideration of them.

The directorio prevailed. In December 1893, the Spanish colonial government, considering the directorio's request, ruled that children of color should be admitted to municipal schools, explicitly extending to primary instruction the 1878 ruling that had only applied to upper-level education. The central government intended to promote "not perfect legal equality, by nobody negated or argued, but rather a real, positive, and practical equality in the order of general relations of social life"; continuing inequality in schools did not fit with that governmental aim. It further declared that schools were "fertile ground for the birth and establishment of spontaneous, natural, noble, and frank feelings of equality in children of different races throughout the course of their lives."[38]

The rulings were published in the *Gaceta de la Habana* immediately, and in the same month, the rector of the University of Havana sent a copy of it to the provincial boards of public education and instructed them and the local primary school boards to comply with the order.[39] The following month, the governor of Matanzas province, Bravo y Joven, sent every mayor in the province a circular advising them to exactly comply with the central government's resolutions. In this circular the governor praised the captain general's "noble and elevated attitude" and said the mayors should undertake whatever measures were necessary to prevent the government's goals from becoming "illusory or sterile" because of "apathy or indifference." He instructed mayors and local officials to take seriously and respond to the complaints of people of color.[40] Months later, in August 1894, the rector followed up on the new law by requesting that the provincial school boards inquire from the local school boards whether the order had been fulfilled and to respond with a report on this issue. In the two responses in the records, from the provincial school boards of Santa Clara and Puerto Principe, they both claimed to have taken action by, for example, publishing the order in the local official bulletins and having the local school boards comply with the order. Both also claimed, however, that they had been admitting students without distinction as to race for years.[41]

The letter circulated by the Matanzas governor as well as the steps taken by the university rector in charge of education on the island suggest that there was official support for the central government's resolutions, despite the recognition that the measures had been first introduced by the directorio, and support for enforcing the law.

Reactions to the Rulings

The 1893 ruling by the Spanish colonial government was celebrated as a victory by Afro-Cubans, and the members of the directorio were credited with its accomplishment. On December 14, 1893, *La Igualdad* published the news, writing that the "General Government resolved yesterday the petitions that the directorio had elevated. The resolution of the Government is favorable to the rights and interests of [la clase de color]." The newspaper described the event as a "repair of justice, a testimony of sympathy . . . the realization of a generous effort in favor of progress and culture and of the dignity of one part of our people, whose path to moral freedom and intellectual redemption is now facilitated."[42]

La Igualdad pointed out that the directorio and its members and supporters deserved a great deal of credit, especially given how much opposition they had faced. The paper praised government officials for their action, attributing the success of the claim to the righteousness of the cause, the progressive spirit of Cuban society, and lastly to the "excellent dispositions of the public power" and the "spirit of justice of General Calleja, backed up by the goodwill of the Secretary of the General Government, Estanislao de Antonio."[43] The paper highlighted the ruling that would open up all eight hundred municipal schools to children of color.[44]

For several months, *La Igualdad* published letters of congratulations to the directorio and its leader, Juan Gualberto Gómez. The letters came from all parts of Cuba, from Cubans in exile, and notably, one from Spain. Rafael María Labra, the famous Spanish abolitionist and president of the Sociedad Abolicionista Española, wrote to Gómez and the directorio; the letter was reprinted in full, with extensive commentary, in *La Igualdad*.

Labra referred to the campaign and lawsuit executed by the directorio as the "natural conclusion of the abolition campaign," though he also wrote that he did not think that "our campaign with the laws of 1873, 1881, and 1886" was finished. Here, Labra connected the abolition of slavery with the movement for racial justice a few years later in Cuba. Labra also directly commented on the educational efforts of people of color. Although the 1892–1893 campaign affected public schooling options for Blacks, which Labra praised, he also applauded their separate schooling projects. In a phrase that communicated his disdain for African traditions, he looked "with great interest in the efforts of people of color to educate themselves, to transform African cabildos into mutual aid and instruction clubs."

In keeping with such an assimilationist posture, Labra stressed the importance of exercising caution and moderation, praising the directorio's campaign as "reasonable and respectful." He also wrote, "It would be criminal to forget human solidarity and turn rehabilitation efforts into exclusionary tactics," asserting that such an effort would deserve the condemnation, not the praise, of abolitionists. "Luckily," he continued, "this is the feeling of the men of color in the Antilles. I congratulate you for that, since I see in the harmony of Whites and Blacks the first guarantee of redemption and prosperity."[45] Labra was urging the directorio to maintain, in its civil rights campaign, a focus on racial integration and to avoid any racial tensions.

The newspaper stressed that although Labra was not an independentista, he was a "liberal and egalitarian" autonomist. Although many Black Cubans who supported this movement were also supporters of the independence movement, they valued the support they received from autonomists like Labra and the concessions they received from the Spanish colonial government on issues of racial justice.

Years 1893–1894: White Resistance to the General Government's Order

The order to integrate schools and the other rulings resulting from the directorio's campaign were met with resistance by Whites. Newspapers of the period were flooded by reports of discrimination against Black Cubans.[46] In 1894, Gómez toured various provinces with the island's captain general, focusing on those where resistance to the 1893 ruling had been reported.[47]

White backlash to the resolutions seemed to occur predominantly in Havana, Matanzas, Cienfuegos, and Sagua la Grande. These western provinces were important sugar regions where there had been many slaves and where there were consequently large Black populations. Segregation in public establishments had long been a concern; the 1880s rulings had been based on suits about segregation in cafés and theaters, and these continued to be focal points of resistance after the 1893 ruling. As early as a few days after the 1893 ruling, newspapers including *El Regional* were already publishing reports of episodes in which café owners had not served Black patrons.[48] After the rulings, the Havana union of café owners met to discuss how to proceed. The union as whole did not take any action, though owners of three or four cafés decided to refuse service to people of color.[49] In Matanzas, Le Louvre café refused service to a person of color on at least one occasion.[50] In January 1894, a prominent Black family was barred from entering El Teatro Tacón in Havana.[51] Resistance, having occurred in the public spheres such as cafés and theaters that were explicitly mentioned in the 1893 rulings, extended to the other major public site referred to in the rulings: the municipal public schools.

In July 1894, *La Nueva Era* newspaper, edited by Afro-Cuban journalist Martín Morúa Delgado, complained that a school in the Havana neighborhood of Punta y Colón was not admitting children of color more than six months after the 1893 ruling had desegregated all municipal schools.[52] Thereafter, Morúa Delgado filed a suit or petition with the general government. In response to the government's inquiries a year later, the university rector asserted that although the school was still displaying a sign that designated it as a municipal school for White boys, the teacher-director of that school was not barring admission to boys of color. On the contrary, stated the rector, the teacher had been admitting boys of color for years before the 1893 order, and out of seventy-eight students matriculated, twenty of them were of color, and thirteen children of color were present on the day that there had been an inspection of the school. Therefore, the rector contended that the problem had to do with the school's sign, as the 1893 ruling had not specified that schools had to change their signs. The rector suggested that the government adopt a general standard for signs in the schools. As a consequence of the rector's report and the response of the Junta Superior de Instrucción Pública, the government dismissed Morúa Delgado's suit against the school in September 1895 and adopted a law specifying the shape, dimensions, and content of municipal school signs.[53]

In Morúa Delgado's suit against the school, we see that, though the 1893 ruling gave rise to instances of White people's refusal to comply with the new law and to continue to deny service to people of color, it also provided people of color a new justification and platform with which to complain about grievances and claim their rights.

"Patience and Tenacity": The Response from the Directorio and Its Supporters

In the face of White resistance to the integration of public spaces including the public schools, Afro-Cuban intellectuals had to craft a practical strategy to attain their goals. They had convinced the general government to support their cause, and they had to work to make sure their support continued. They also had to convince racists among the White public whose preoccupations lingered, those who feared that Black people taking full possession of their rights would erode the rights of White people, and those who feared that racial integration would cause social disturbances. Therefore, the directorio and its supporters preached nonviolence, patience, and moderation; at the same time, they confronted government officials, filed complaints with authorities and registered them in Black newspapers, and crafted an ideology meant to achieve equal rights for Black people within the structures of the Spanish constitution and state while preserving the harmony of Cuban society and perhaps their hopes for an independent Cuba.

Black Cubans insisted on their commitment to the health of the wider society and on their patriotism while moving forward on the issues that affected Black people in Cuba. This balancing act is reflected in an article in *La Igualdad* noting that people of color would continue moving forward with "our faith in our patriotism, our love of our race, and our constant devotion to the interests of our country and the exaltation of all our brothers."[54] Another such article urged people to prove to Cuba that "we are her beloved sons, and far from provoking social danger, we want to protect her from such disturbances."[55]

In response to White-supremacist accusations of disorder and race wars, the directorio and *La Igualdad* as its mouthpiece urged Black people toward moderation, prudence, and caution. Invoking history, they responded first by pointing to the peaceful transition from slavery to freedom. During the struggle for abolition, White people asserted that the freedom of Black people would cause ruin, but in the aftermath of freedom, everyone could agree that Blacks had "made legitimate and prudent use of their freedom. . . . Let's do the same with the rights we just achieved." Such an approach would prove that "our wish to develop and grow reconciles perfectly with the legitimate rights of the White class."[56] "Have patience, friends; continue each day being more prudent and measured," the paper advised on one occasion.[57] On another, it wrote, "We advise to our friends calm and prudence. We have to keep in mind the reality and not put into doubt for one moment the sanity and common sense of the raza de color. People who expect conflicts are our enemies. Let's not satisfy them."[58]

Black activists in the 1890s discredited those who resisted the desegregation orders by pointing out that they perpetrated a small, isolated set of incidents and not widespread resistance.[59] They also argued that White resisters were largely from the lower classes and that colonial authorities, upper-class Whites, and elite institutions actually supported Black civil rights activists. This affirmed the racial uplift idea that race was separate from class or culture and that Blacks could achieve a high level of class and culture. This argument was mobilized to support school integration despite any existing popular opposition; the secondary education institutes and the university had been desegregated in 1878, and there had not been any instances of racist tension in those places. An article in *La Igualdad* asked, "If the most enlightened institutions don't experience quarrels or repugnance [due to racial integration], why should the institutions of the lower classes?"[60] Black Cuban defenders of the 1893 resolutions also brought up class differences among Whites in response to concerns that lower-class Black and mulato Cubans were uneducated and therefore undeserving of equal rights. In response, Black Cuban activists pointed out that not all Whites were at the same intellectual and moral levels but still received rights, so why should Black people not receive the same treatment?[61]

More specifically, in the face of White resistance, the directorio insisted on a mechanism for remedying wrongs, through legal means. It issued a circular with specific instructions. People of color who experienced any wrongdoing should go to the governing authorities, not the judicial authorities. The governing authorities were committed to implementing the regulations and could impose fines on public institutions that refused to serve or admit people of color. In some cases, if violations of government resolutions were accompanied by other issues such as physical assault, then those might also be brought to the attention of the judicial authorities.[62] *La Igualdad* emphasized, "The law is our weapon. The authorities should be the keepers of our rights."[63] In another article about school enrollment, now that all municipal schools were required to accept children of color, *La Igualdad* instructed people of color on the process by which they could matriculate their children in schools. It also urged parents and tutors to report any violations or cases in which children were not admitted because of racism to the mayor or provincial government "immediately . . . to prevent the right just given to a third of the population from becoming illusory."[64]

In first submitting claims through legal channels to the government and then responding to violations of the new rulings through legal channels, Afro-Cuban activists in the directorio and beyond were pursuing a practical strategy that ideologically affirmed a commitment to the legal structures of the Spanish state and Cuban colony. Their faith in the Spanish constitution being applied equally to Afro-descendants as citizens was reflected in their continued use of legal channels to redress grievances and in their rhetorical allusions to the Spanish constitution and their use of the language of rights. *La Protesta* newspaper celebrated the 1893 rulings by declaring that action along these lines should have been taken a long time ago, given that people of color were citizens under the Spanish constitution and were therefore entitled to full civil and political rights. Furthermore, the reference to the Spanish constitution played into political issues that were affecting Cuba and Spain and the position of people of color in the liberal versus conservative tendencies in Spanish politics. The rights allowed to Blacks under the Spanish constitution were finally being extended to them because the liberal reformers were now in power.[65] *La Igualdad* also turned to the law when it came to the matter of racial segregation in the public schools: "The more we examine this problem, the less justifiable we find segregation. This distinction is not established in any law." The newspaper reviewed the public school law, all the laws passed since the Pact of Zanjón, and the 1878 decree by Governor General Martínez Campos.[66]

Supporters from abroad also referred to the language of rights and laws. Puerto Rican poet Lola Rodríguez de Tío wrote an open letter to a Black Cuban newspaper saying that the issues brought by the directorio were "not a question of races. It's a question of rights and justice." She connected the question to larger global trends: "Those who respect democracy and ideas of progress and fraternity seek to resolve [this issue] in an elevated and generous way."[67]

La Igualdad, the directorio's primary mouthpiece, was a little slower in making assertive claims about rights, perhaps because Gómez was in charge and did not want to offend the officials from whom he had successfully exacted concessions. But by April 1894, with patience wearing thin, *La Igualdad* forcefully made a case that the validity of the 1893 rulings was not based on charity or wisdom of the authorities but rather based in Spanish law and the rights of Black men as Spanish citizens: "The measures taken by the General Government in favor of la raza de color conform to the fundamental document of the State which recognizes equal rights for all Spaniards."[68] Here, the writer was making much more fundamental claims about the rights granted to people of color, moving beyond the authority of the general government and captain general to the constitution of Spain. Sartorius points out that as Spain incorporated some aspects of a liberal democratic project in the late nineteenth century, its people experienced overlapping modes of belonging in the Spanish empire, as subjects and as citizens.[69] In the absence of voting rights, Black Cubans were left to petition the government rather than vote, but they called on the language of citizenship and rights to back their claims.

Pushing la Raza de Color toward the Schoolroom

The directorio's dual approach to the results of the rulings—to urge patience and moderation on the one hand and to insist on legal remedies from the authorities on the other—was largely abandoned in its approach to the ruling on the racial integration of municipal schools. When it came to the most important priority, education, Afro-Cuban members of the directorio took a much more aggressive stance.

In early January 1894, right before municipal schools reopened after the holidays, *La Igualdad* published an article about the effects of the new ruling on municipal schools, which would now all be open to all children of color, thus effectively instantly opening 820 schools, all the municipal schools in the country, to children of color. Widening educational access had been a major priority for Afro-descendants in Cuba, so the ruling was an important victory. *La Igualdad* wrote that it was "indispensable" that people of color take advantage of this newly won right: "Just as we recommend caution and measure regarding our right to enter cafés, etc., we are inclined to push la raza de color toward the school desks. On this issue, we will be intransigent with everyone; with the authorities, with the teachers, and with the parents of families."[70]

The column reiterated the importance of education for the Black community in Cuba and asserted that it would not take a great effort to get children of color into the school desks of the municipal schools: "The raza de color in this country has always demonstrated a great attachment to instruction" and had always deeply felt the lack of schools available to them. Furthermore, the lack of education among Black people in Cuba was "not due to laziness or lack of real desire on their part"; rather, it was due to their oppression during slavery and a lack of support for education from Cuban society after abolition. Despite these obstacles, the article continued, Black people had prioritized education. It gave credit to the Black community exclusively for the relatively good state of Black education in Cuba and reaffirmed a commitment to education as a personal, community, and social tool for improvement. The article concluded that the wider access to education was a "saving measure . . . upon which the future of our people rests."[71]

The column in *La Igualdad* also emphasized the utility of education in keeping the government accountable to people of color. In the aftermath of the 1893 ruling, for the first time, the state and society were going to fulfill their obligation to Black Cubans by guaranteeing them access to the public education system as the state should have been educating people of color long before.[72] Education was framed as a right and equal school rights as the logical extension of those rights.

Beyond focusing on education as a claims-making tool, the directorio again used education to debunk fears that racial integration would lead to social disorder or violence. A September 1893 article in *La Igualdad* argued that in the places in Cuba where the municipal schools had already been integrated, "there is greater harmony between classes and there is superior social advancement." Those examples of integrated schooling demonstrated that "preoccupations have been spent," in other words, the social, racist objections to racial integration in schooling were not going to be a barrier to the 1893 government resolutions, and that was evident from earlier examples of integrated schooling:

> If it is mandated that all schools be for all children of all races, nothing will happen. The sky won't fall; there won't even be the slightest protest. Here, where people have wanted to make the most of "preoccupations" to maintain separate schools, it should be known that in municipalities with separate schools, the teachers have accepted children of color when the parents PAID, and nobody gets alarmed, or worried, nor do they rebel against presence of a Black child. What does this mean, if not that the argument about preoccupation is false?[73]

The January 1894 article continued the theme, contending that if racist preoccupations did linger in White society, then racial integration in the schools would get rid of what remained: "There, at the school desks, there is no room for supremacies besides application and intelligence." Integrated education would educate White people as to what were the ideas of morality and justice held by cultured people throughout the world.[74] Education would benefit Black people and the larger society by presenting a more educated and cultured clase de color to society. But integrated education would also work on White people; it would teach them to put their racist ideas behind, therefore contributing to social harmony in another way as well.

In various articles from late 1893 and into 1895, *La Igualdad*, as the mouthpiece for the directorio, used ideas of racial integration in the public education system to confront several layers of problems. The articles affirmed the importance of education for the Black community and considered the education of people of color through the sociedades de instrucción to be a credit to the community. They also used examples of previous racial integration in schools to argue that education was not going to cause social disturbances, as Whites feared, but that it would instead foster racial harmony and social unity. And the articles used education to enhance the directorio's negotiations with and obtaining rights from the Spanish colonial government. The strategy of using education to make all these claims at various levels was effective because of the wider importance of education. In the nineteenth century, modernizing Latin American nations were developing lay, obligatory, and public education paid for by the government. The common school movement was taking off in the United States. Thus, education was a widely recognized symbol of what governments owed their citizens within a liberal republican framework and of what a modern and progressive society would do.

Directorio members understood how education could work to legitimize their various claims, which is why they were able to leverage it effectively. *La Igualdad* connected education for Blacks and the health of the society to their ideas about education in a more universal sense. The newspaper's editors and writers asserted that education was a fundamental social function. Articles proclaimed a "deep conviction" that primary education should be obligatory and free in Cuba.[75] In discussing many aspects of educational philosophy, Afro-Cubans made clear that their interest in education was fundamentally tied into what they thought about their goals for racial justice and the needs of Black people in Cuba; they saw education as an integral part of how they envisioned a broader Cuban society.

Conclusion

For Cubans of color involved in the civil rights campaign of the Directorio Central de las Sociedades de la Raza de Color, 1894 was spent struggling over the 1893 government resolutions requiring that the public sphere be racially integrated, particularly the schools. Though the governor general supported the cause promoted by the directorio, many local authorities refused to enforce the rulings, and some popular opposition surfaced. In response, the directorio and its Black Cuban supporters articulated a discourse about racial justice that was tailored to respond to multiple arguments. Education was one of the most important aspects of the new regulations, and Afro-Cubans continued to use it as an important political tool in responding to racial discrimination and opposition to its civil rights campaign.

By early 1895, the third and final war of independence in Cuba had begun. Many Afro-descended supporters of the Cuban separatist movement hoped, despite recent concessions of the Spanish colonial government to people of color, that an independent, republican Cuba would better protect the rights of people of color. Still, in the resistance of many White Creoles and local authorities to the school desegregation order prompted by the Directorio's equal school rights campaign and in the longer history of White Cuban Creole opposition to Black schooling, a tradition of anti-Black racism would continue to plague ideas of Cuban nationhood well into the republican period and beyond.

Despite the inconclusive state of affairs over the recently issued regulations when the war began in 1895, the concerted efforts by Black sociedades to get civil rights concessions from the Spanish colonial government and the Spanish government's rulings would have significant effects on the new Cuban republic. In the activism of the directorio and its supporters during the 1890s, the elaboration emerges of a Black educational ideology that informed their larger political thinking. Black Cuban educational activists were both on the offensive and on the defensive; they generated the discussion, and they responded to their interlocutors, constantly trying to diminish fears of racial warfare and to guarantee the health of their society while still staying true to the cause of racial justice that the Black community needed. The experience of being in a position to demand rights from the government would shape the way Afro-Cubans approached their position within an independent Cuba. Their insistence on the importance of greater racial harmony for the sake of social unity reflected how they interacted with Whites in Cuba and how they understood themselves to be part of Cuban society. In rejecting the strategies of armed rebellion against the government (undertaken by many Afro-descendants in Cuba in the first half of the nineteenth century, including the militiamen-teachers) and of separatist political organizing (which would be embraced in the early twentieth century by the Partido Independiente de Color), in trying to calm the fears of social disturbance, and in advocating for the racial integration of the schools, the leaders of the directorio demonstrated their commitment to improving the situation of Black people within the society and the polity and not outside of them. But the many sociedad de color members and the leaders of the directorio were also using education as a way to continue the project of personal and collective emancipation for Afro-descendants in the aftermath of slavery, drawing on traditions of race-based organizing that allowed them to create common cause with other people of color as well as looking to the broader society. The varied approaches and goals of the Black Cuban educational tradition would shape how Afro-descendants approached social and political issues during the US intervention and in the Cuban republic.

7

"No Division by Color"

US School Inspectors and the Aftermath of the War of Independence

Black Cuban educators and activists were able to make critical advancements in educational access for Black children in Cuba in the last quarter of the nineteenth century. During the waning days of colonial rule, Cubans of color pushed the Spanish colonial government to desegregate the public schools, thereby improving educational options for Black children while also racially integrating a significant part of the public sphere. This successful campaign for equal school rights was one culmination of the Black Cuban educational tradition developed over the course of the nineteenth century. The main goal of this educational ideology was to expand schooling options for children of color. Other characteristics of the Black educational tradition that existed in many but not all of the schools established by Afro-descended educators or advocated for by Afro-descended activists were offering tuition-free education, educating both Black and White children, providing schooling for both boys and girls, and having classrooms that were often integrated by sex and/or race. The desegregation of municipal schools represented an important leap forward in many of those goals.

The colonial government's order integrating public schools was still being hotly debated and unevenly enforced just one year later, in 1895, when the final separatist war began. This last Cuban war of independence (1895–1898) decimated the island. The theater of war stretched from Oriente, the easternmost part of the island, into the sugar-producing western part. The island's economy was ruined, the countryside was destroyed, towns and plantations were leveled, and under a reconcentration policy of Spanish general Valeriano Weyler, entire populations were moved into newly created population centers. The upheaval of the war ensured that the public school system and everything else was left in shambles. Just as the Cubans were on the verge of winning the war, the US military invaded and occupied the island, setting up a military government that would rule the island for four years (1898–1902).[1] Racism against Afro-descendants was not a North American import to Cuba, but the pressures of US military occupation pushed racial tensions on the island in a new direction. The once racially inclusive Cuba Libre movement became more conservative in the aftermath of the war, under pressure from the US government to prove that Cubans were capable of self-government.[2]

The war of independence, the US occupation, and the attendant changes in Cuban society deeply affected the lives of Afro-descended Cubans. But the legacy of Black educational activism in Cuba was such that not even the racist assumptions of the southern-dominated US military government could fully derail the progress made by Black educators, parents, students, and politicians in the realm of schooling. Just as much as the effects of war and neo-imperial rule, the legacy of the Black educational tradition shaped the Cuban school system as it continued to develop under the occupation and in the early republic.

The continued impact of the Black Cuban educational tradition is perhaps most evident in the reports of the US school inspectors after the war. Importantly, US school inspectors found that many of Cuba's public schools were not segregated by race. This was likely due to the directorio's successful campaign to desegregate the schools and to the work of earlier generations of Black and mulato teachers and educational activists.

The US Occupation and the Connections between Race, Education, and Suffrage

One of the United States' central projects during the military occupation was the overhaul of the public school system. Cuba had been devastated by the war of independence, and the public school system had also suffered. In a report on education in Cuba, Puerto Rico, and the Philippines written for the US commissioner of education, Robert Lawrence Packard praised the public school system begun by the Spanish in 1842 as excellent in theory, while criticizing the poor administration and lack of funding under colonial rule. Packard pointed out that "the ten years war was a serious interruption to the schools, and during the last war they were all closed by Captain-General Weyler, except in the provincial capitals and garrisoned towns," and that "even many of these schools were slimly attended or abandoned by the teachers" because they were not getting paid. Although the schools were ostensibly reopened in February 1898, the war had taken its toll, and schools remained in bad condition until the American occupation. He further emphasized that it "must be borne in mind that the school system of Cuba, while always, according to American standards, imperfect, has suffered, along with all other institutions, from the war, and that its condition in 1899 was not fairly representative of its condition five or ten years earlier."[3]

Packard's nuanced observations notwithstanding, the US government frequently portrayed the public education system in Cuba as underdeveloped to justify its invasion of Cuba as a civilizing mission. For the United States, the educational system was key to advancing the US administration's long-term goal to annex Cuba. Schools could be used to assimilate Cubans in a civilizing and imperial project in hopes of building a consensual annexationist movement.[4]

This goal of neo-imperial expansion to annex Cuba and the use of schools to cultivate conditions that would advance that goal were driven by ideas of what Cubans were and what they could become. The US discourses of progress, civilization, and readiness for republican government that shaped how the neo-imperial government approached the public school system in Cuba were deeply racialized. Not only did US officials fear giving political power to Cuba's large Afro-descended population, but they also understood all Cubans—as presumed products of racial mixing between Spaniards, Africans, and Indians—to be less than White. For the US occupiers, Cubans' lack of Whiteness cast into doubt their ability to self-govern. At the turn of the twentieth century, scientific racism informed national projects throughout the Americas and helped determine who would be recognized as citizens.[5]

Soldiers of the US military government were coming from a post–Civil War context in the United States in which Reconstruction had been abandoned and the federal government had pulled the military out of the southern states, leaving the vast majority of the United States' African American population in the hands of Southern White supremacists who used extrajudicial violence to overturn state governments and to terrorize and disenfranchise African Americans. Along with violence, education and suffrage were used successfully to control the Afro-descended population in the United States. For example, White supremacists in the US South used literacy tests to disenfranchise African Americans.

Convinced of the racial inferiority of all Cubans and especially of Afro-descended Cubans, US military officials in Cuba prepared to use the two tools they had successfully used to marginalize African Americans in their own country: suffrage and education. Leonard Wood, then US military governor of Cuba, began efforts to restrict suffrage "to such of the citizens of Cuba as are able to read and write," according to the 1899 census. The report drew explicit comparisons between Afro-descendants in both countries. It stated that Black Cubans were "somewhat superior to the colored population of our Southern States, being more self-reliant, temperate, frugal, and intelligent, and since the abolition of slavery showing a strong desire to own their homes, to educate their children, and to improve their condition." The report deemed relations between Whites and Blacks in Cuba to be better than in the United States, attributing the difference to the lack of a "hard and fast color line" which in turn was due to "the common struggle in which they were engaged against Spain." It stated that there were many people of color in the Cuban army of liberation from 1895 to 1898, and some of them held high ranks: "The laws made no discrimination between them."[6]

The 1899 census determined that the "colored" population of Cuba (which for the US census organizers included Chinese, who in Spanish censuses had been recorded as White) was about 32 percent of the population in 1899 and that their distribution was uneven throughout the island. Puerto Principe had the lowest percentage of the "colored element, including negro and mixed races," with 20 percent. In Havana province they made up 26 percent of the population, 30 percent in Santa Clara, and 40 percent in Matanzas; Santiago had the highest proportion of people of color, with 46 percent of the population being counted as such. The report noted that the early nineteenth-century increase in the number of people of color had to do with the transatlantic slave trade and that the decrease since the middle of the century was evidence of "the inability of an inferior race to hold its own in competition with a superior one, a truth which is being demonstrated on a much larger scale in the United States."[7] Rather than focusing on slavery-related mortality, the end of the slave trade, and a rise in white immigration, US officials attributed demographic shifts to racist social Darwinist ideas about fitness and survival.

Focusing on suffrage, the census report noted that out of the potential voters in Cuba (males over the age of twenty-one), "44.9% were Whites, born in Cuba, . . . 30.5% were colored, and . . . nearly all the colored were born in the island."[8] Lastly, the report moved on to education and literacy rates. Literacy in Cuba had risen steadily in the second half of the nineteenth century, which is evident in comparisons of the 1861 census (19.2 percent literacy), 1887 census (27.7 percent of the population able to read), and 1899 census (36 percent literacy). By 1899 the literacy rate in Cuba was higher than the average literacy rate in much of the rest of Latin America.[9]

Breaking down literacy by racial categories, the census reported that among White Cuban citizens who were natives of the island, 51 percent were unable to read, while 74 percent of "Colored" Cuban citizens were unable to read. The illiteracy rate was significantly higher among people of color, but it was also very high among the White Cuban population. "One half of Whites (50.8 percent) and rather more than one fourth (28 percent) of colored were able to read," the report stated. Among people of color, women had higher literacy rates than men, but the opposite was true in the White population. Women of color also worked at much higher rates (five times) than White women. Whites and people of color of school age (5–17 years) attended school at roughly the same low rate: 16.5 percent for Whites and 13.8 percent for people of color.[10] A literacy test in Cuba, therefore, would disenfranchise many potential voters of all races but would disproportionately disenfranchise Black and mulato Cubans.

Although the US government attempted to impose a limited suffrage, veterans of the liberation army mounted a campaign against the policy. In 1901 Cuban veterans and separatists in the constitutional assembly ultimately insisted on including universal manhood suffrage in the constitution of the Republic of Cuba.[11]

Cubans and Public Education during the Occupation

Armed with the census data on race, literacy, and suffrage and drawing on their own experiences with African Americans in the United States, the US military government in Cuba undertook a major public education project that was openly modeled "as far as practicable to the public school system of the United States."[12] In December 1899, the US military government in Cuba ordered the schools to be reopened. In June 1900, military order 368 reorganized the administration of schools. It created a commissioner of public schools, superintendent of schools, and provincial superintendents for each of the provinces. These officials would be in charge of pedagogy and curricular development as well as implementing courses of study and choosing texts. The occupying government also created local school boards that would be in charge of hiring teachers and inspecting schools.[13] During the first year of Wood's administration, enrollment increased from 20,000

Figure 4. Cuban municipal school building, 1899. The photograph is filed in the *US Report on the Census of Cuba*, 1899 (Washington, DC: US Government Printing Office, 1900), 566, available in the Government Information and Maps Department, University of South Carolina, https://digital.library.sc.edu/collections/report-on-the-census-of-cuba-1899/.

at the end of the war to 100,000.[14] In 1900, despite a 10 percent decrease in the population due to the last war of independence (from 1.67 to 1.57 million from 1894 to 1900), there were 3,313 schools in operation on the island, with 3,553 teachers and 143,120 students (figure 4).[15]

Race was an important concern for American officials involved in the public school overhaul. US school officials explicitly connected their experiences with race in US public schools to their mission in Cuba. In response to the solicitation of recommendations for a superintendent of Cuban schools by General James H. Wilson, head of the Department of Matanzas and Santa Clara in Cuba, an American colleague wrote,

> Thinking that it may be that in some of the provinces of Cuba the colored people largely outnumber the Whites, I take the liberty to mention that I know of a colored teacher in St. Louis, Missouri, who has shown for many years a remarkable power of organization in colored schools. . . . His name is O.M. Wood, he is Principal of L'Ouverture School. . . . I know he would make a great success in the work of or-

ganizing for colored people. Should General Wilson see his way to appoint one superintendent of the White schools of the two provinces and one for the colored schools of the same.[16]

Notably, the writer assumed that the schools of the province of Matanzas and Santa Clara would be segregated by race and that the teaching and administrative force would need to be similarly segregated. Moreover, he assumed that the experience of an educator in the segregated US South would be relevant to the administration of segregated schools in Cuba. Assuredly, many US officials, coming from a context in which the areas with large Black populations had segregated school systems, assumed that the schools in Cuba would also be racially segregated.

But the development of the public education system was not just imposed from the top down, and US officials were not the only ones involved in this overhaul of the public education system. Cubans, too, participated in the rebuilding of the public school system by collaborating with the US school officials but also by reopening schools, teaching, and sending their children to school.

For some Cubans, the intervention government's efforts in the public school system were a beneficial and welcome change from their understanding of the dysfunction of the system under Spanish colonial laws and from the devastation of the war, and they actively joined in the educational project imposed by the US military government. Many Cuban elites were employed by the US military government. Esteban Borrero Echavarría had been exiled in Key West, Florida, and had been the director of a school there. During his exile, he was a strong supporter of the independence of Cuba and of the separatist movement. His hopes for Cuban sovereignty notwithstanding, the US government appointed him subsecretary of the Department of Public Education in 1899–1900, during which time he publicly and enthusiastically supported the US military government's overhaul of the public education system in Cuba.[17] The first secretary of education and justice, José Antonio González Lanuza, was also a former exiled member of the Cuban independence movement.[18]

Aside from Cuban elites being hired by the occupation government, it quickly became apparent that Cubans on the ground were not waiting for US permission to move forward with their educational plans. Many teachers, principals, and other Cuban school administrators at the local level wrote letters to the US military government in the early years of the occupation requesting funding from the occupation government. Even though these educators found themselves in need of money, they were interested in restarting Cuban schools, at least on local and regional levels, even without the US initiative. In February 1899, José Monte from the town of Santo Domingo in Matanzas province proposed an education plan for that town's schools based on the existing educational structure; his unsolicited proposal was forwarded to the provincial governor of Matanzas and Santa Clara.[19]

In October 1899, the secretary of the Department of Justice and Public Instruction, González Lanuza, acknowledged that Cubans were not waiting for US action on the schools. He wrote that it was not practical to delay opening schools until the US occupiers' school system was set up. First, he said, it would take too long. And anyway, Cubans had schools up and running: "Throughout the interior of the island, schools are open, either under the old system or under that which certain town councils have adopted for themselves, as in other provinces there are town councils that have done what they please in this matter, opening and closing schools, appointing and discharging teachers, increasing and reducing salaries, even modifying the general plan of studies." He advised Major General John Brooke to leave public instruction in the hands of the town councils provisionally, giving them some general rules and allowing them to make provisional appointments. They could be reorganized later according to US recommendations.[20] Though the United States is often depicted as the bastion of decentralized schooling, in González Lanuza's report Cubans had a strong sense of local schooling and local government initiative and did not wait for the occupation government to set up a national system before sending their children to local schools.

As the census report and many other documents show, US officials and occupying forces viewed Cubans as a racialized population, disdained Afro-descendants, and attempted to limit power to the better classes of Cubans, in their view. Education was an important consideration in these machinations. US military officials in Cuba were mindful of the links between race and education in their own country. Their ideas about race affected how they confronted the public school system they were trying to set up. And yet, Cubans were also very involved in the public education system even during the occupation, and they brought their own ideas of the connections between race and education to bear.

The public education system set up by the US occupation government did not spontaneously appear; rather, it was built on the foundations of a century of progress toward a national public education system during the colonial period. The US military government kept many colonial laws; even though it used a discourse that portrayed Spain as backward, it simultaneously used the structures of Spanish colonialism to construct a US neocolony.[21] Furthermore, the school system was built on Cuban teachers in schools that had either not shut down during the war or started back up again on their own after the war without waiting for directions from the occupying forces.

During the colonial period there had been a real if modest expansion of Black access to the public education system and a decisive move away from racial segregation in the public schools. In addition, the break between the colonial and the ostensible modern of the US occupation and imagined independent future was a messily lived encounter, as Marial Iglesias Utset has pointed out.[22] There were many continuities in terms of racial constructs and public institutions from the colonial period through the wars of independence. It was this landscape that US administrators were now facing.

Race and the School Inspection Reports

Military order 368 that set up the public school system required that the schools be inspected, and the US administrators began inspection immediately, in 1899. As US military government officials began to survey the schools, they were confronted with a racial reality that was radically different from what they had been expecting. The school inspectors were sent into the schools with printed forms that they were expected to fill out based on their observations, their discussions with school administrators and teachers, and school records. These printed forms specified that inspectors should take note of enrollment and attendance, divided by race and sex.

School inspection reports have survived from three key departments under the US occupation: Havana province, the Department of Matanzas and Santa Clara (initially one department and later split), and the Department of Santiago de Cuba. The capital city of Havana and its surroundings were highly populated and had become more populated during the last war of independence as people fled the warfare of total attrition in the countryside. The city had long had a large Black population. Not only that, but the province of Havana, along with the province of Santa Clara and Matanzas, was where the bulk of the sugar plantations were; they had large slave populations, and many descendants of the enslaved lived in the area. In Matanzas especially, slavery was stubbornly clung to since the plantations were technologically advanced and heavily capitalized and the enslaved outnumbered free people of color. Emancipation proceeded very slowly in Matanzas, and planters worked hard to maintain the now-free wage workers under their control and on their plantations. Santiago de Cuba, far removed from sugar production and from the capital, had its own unique history of race relations. Its free population of color had grown significantly in the nineteenth century as planters fled Saint Domingue with their slaves. In 1862, 33 percent of the population of the province of Santiago were free Blacks and mulatos, a population that increased further with rapid emancipation during the Ten Years War (1868–1878). In all of these areas, orders for school inspections went out in 1899 and 1900.

In February 1899, the chief ordinance officer for the Department of Matanzas, a man from the United States, submitted a report on the state of schools in the city of Matanzas. He was assisted in his ten-day inspection of the city schools by the Cuban Claudio Dumas, a school principal; Dumas is described in the report as "a superior educator and refined and cultured gentleman." The report was critical of much of the public school system in the city of Matanzas. It said the eighteen schools were not well distributed among the population, serving the nicer areas of town more than the poor areas. It described the situation under Spain as placing pro-Spanish teachers in schools who had little sympathy among the population and a curriculum that magnified the importance of Spain. Lastly, the report focused on the students, finding them in "bad physical condition" and plagued by poverty and a lack of cleanliness. The enrollment in schools (926) was less than 12 percent of the school-age population, and only 474 of them were present on the days of the inspections. However, the report also praised the teachers who kept schools running under difficult conditions and without getting paid. When it came to race in Matanzas public schools, the 1899 report observed that "no distinction of color is made in the schools, but there is a tendency to separate Whites from the others. Only a few colored children were found in the schools viz:—66 out of 474."[23] Presumably, this meant that although de jure racial segregation had been struck down in the schools, some White Cubans still excluded Afro-descended children from municipal schools (figure 5).

As a province, Matanzas had a 42 percent population of color and a relatively large number of small landholders. In contrast to the school in-

Figure 5. Students and teachers of a public school for girls in Matanzas, 1899. The photograph is filed in the *US Report on the Census of Cuba*, 1899 (Washington, DC: US Government Printing Office, 1900), 570, held in the Government Information and Maps Department, University of South Carolina.

spection reports for the city of Matanzas, a series of inspection reports in 1900 for other towns within Matanzas province revealed a high level of enrollment and attendance among children of color and almost complete integration of the schools. As in other forms used by US inspectors, the preprinted form required the inspectors to list enrollment and attendance numbers by sex and by race. Some of the schools in these towns in Matanzas province were of mixed gender, although most of them were separated by sex.[24] Schools inspected by American officials in the towns in Matanzas province were racially integrated, and children of color made up nearly half of the enrolled students and those in attendance at inspection time (figure 6). Given that the non-White population of Matanzas was almost half, this suggests that children of color were proportionally represented in Matanzas province's public schools, at least in the countryside.

School inspection records exist for the same period (June 1900) for Santiago de Cuba province as well. For the schools in that province, the local inspector, a US military man named George M. Brooke, was tasked with

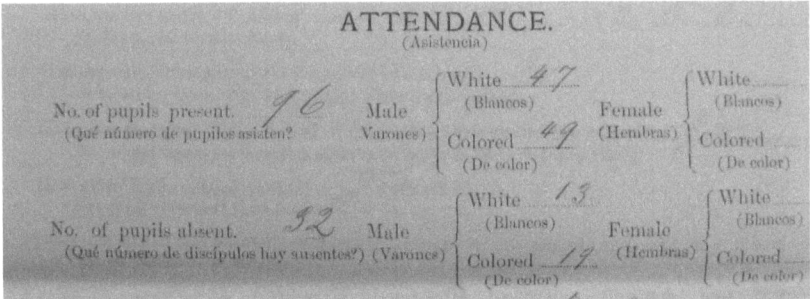

Figure 6. Inspection report for Céspedes School 4 in Recreo, Matanzas, 1899. This boys' school had more "Colored (De Color)" students than "White (Blancos)" students. Record group 140, entry 3, box 87, US National Archives and Records Administration, College Park, MD.

filling out preprinted forms that likewise assumed enrollment and attendance could be divided by sex and by race. Although the assumption was correct when it came to gender, given that the Spanish practice of dividing schools by sex was maintained in many schools (although not in all of them, as the Matanzas records show), the US officials' assumption that primary public schools would be segregated by race was mistaken. The Santiago school inspection forms for 1900 reflect one US official's on-the-ground realization of this phenomenon. Inspector Brooke wrote notes on almost every inspection form that he submitted for the towns of San Luis, Alto Songo, and Palma Soriano in the province of Santiago. They stated, "no division by color; considered impracticable" or "claimed to be impracticable" (figure 7).[25] Not only were the schools of mixed races, so were the pupils, to Brooke's eyes. He wrote on one form, "division between races is not reliable. Many intermediate types, some indeterminable" (figure 8).[26]

Brooke's brief notes are very revealing about the racial situation in these classrooms in Oriente. First, they suggest that in the towns of Santiago province, the schools were largely racially integrated. This corresponds to reports by Santiago's sociedades de color to the directorio in their 1892 meeting. In some schools, children of color may have even outnumbered White children. It is also possible that inspector Brooke counted many more students as "colored" than Cubans might have done, thus presenting a skewed perception of racial integration. However, his phrasing, "consid-

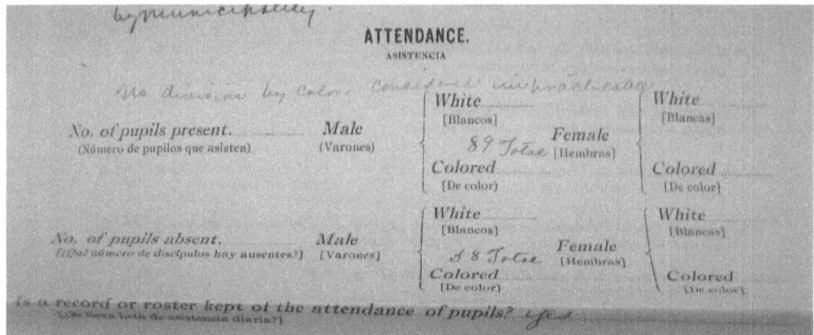

Figure 7. Inspection report for School 1 in San Luis, Santiago de Cuba province, 1900. A handwritten note in red ink says, "No division by color, considered impracticable." The school's female students are counted as present or absent, but the information is not broken down by race. Record group 140, entry 3, box 62, US National Archives and Records Administration, College Park, MD.

ered impracticable," suggests that the decision not to racially segregate the schools belonged to the Cubans. It also reveals much about the inspector's own understandings of race. US officials who created the form evidently expected racial segregation, and Brooke himself revealed that he anticipated a clearer and more identifiable racial binary in terms of phenotype in the students he was seeing. Instead, he made note of the effects of racial miscegenation that seemed to surprise him. On some forms he skipped writing down how many students of each race there were, instead providing a total and claiming the schools were integrated. On others he attempted to distinguish between the races but found himself unable to do so based on his own understanding of what the racial categories were.

In the Department of Havana, records exist for a 1900 inspection of schools. In some neighborhoods, race is not mentioned. In Regla, a traditionally Black and Indigenous neighborhood on the outskirts of Havana, the American school inspector, 1st Lieutenant Dwight Aultman, commented on the racial integration in the schools. In his description of the schools in Regla he commented on race, describing them as "a primary school for small boys; negroes and Whites mixed indiscriminately" and "a primary school for small girls, negroes and Whites not separated," and "White and colored children not separated."[27] As an American, his idea of who was not White might have been different than a Cuban's, but his notes

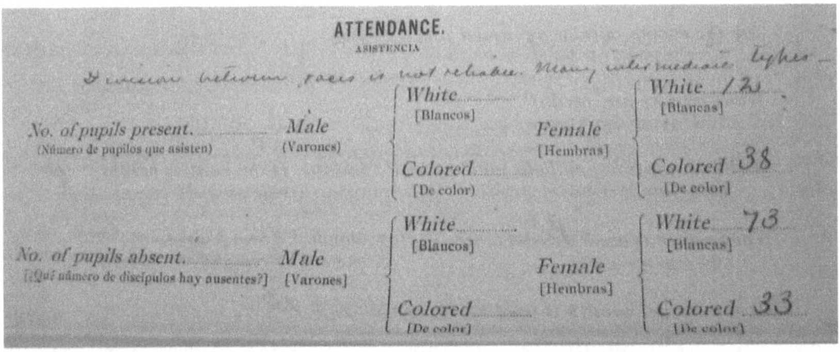
ATTENDANCE.
ASISTENCIA

No. of pupils present. (Número de pupilos que asisten)	Male (Varones)	White [Blancos] ... Colored [De color] ...	Female [Hembras]	White [Blancas] 12 Colored [De color] 38
No. of pupils absent. [¿Qué número de discípulos hay ausentes?]	Male [Varones]	White [Blancos] ... Colored [De color] ...	Female [Hembras]	White [Blancas] 73 Colored [De color] 33

Figure 8. Inspection report for School 2 in San Luis, Santiago de Cuba province, 1900. The report counts 85 female "white" students and 71 "colored" students, and a handwritten note at the top cautions, "Division between races is not reliable. Many intermediate types." Record group 140, entry 3, box 62, US National Archives and Records Administration, College Park, MD.

make clear that there was a lack of separation between what he perceived to be different races.

The first inspections done by US military officials in charge of primary public education, then, suggest that the primary schools in the Cuban public education system were, at least in many places, racially integrated and proportionally attended by children of color. This suggests that the push for the integration of the public schools at the end of the nineteenth century undertaken by the Directorio Central de las Sociedades de la Raza de Color carried through the war years and into the first year of the new century.

Perhaps learning from their failure to restrict Afro-Cubans' voting rights, or perhaps because they were faced with so much racial integration in the schools they inspected, US officials did not attempt to impose legal segregation in the public schools in Cuba. But as historian Bonnie Lucero argues, the tacit US approval of discriminatory actions by some schoolteachers and administrators constituted "a policy of inaction" that supported US efforts to use the public school system to reestablish social and racial hierarchies.[28] Still, the public schools remained relatively well integrated in the first decade of Cuban self-rule, acting perhaps as the last bastion of the Cuba Libre project that had once at least paid lip service to racial inclusion but was rapidly becoming more conservative.

Race in the Early Republican Public School System, 1902–1910

In 1902 the United States pulled out of Cuba after a military occupation that had implemented drastic overhauls in many institutions, notably the public school system. The newly established Secretaría de Instrucción Pública, the national Department of Public Education, continued the system implemented by the US military occupying government, with the school calendar, the teaching-school system, and the system of licensing teachers. For several years after the American intervening government withdrew from Cuba, when discussing school laws and regulations Cuban public education administrators would often cite the military orders published by the US government.[29] Cuban elites' understanding of the function of education for modernity lined up with the prevailing US ideas on education, so it is not surprising that the structures of education should be so closely adhered to. Still, those Cubans involved in the public education system were also often nationalists who saw it as a way to prepare Cubans for republican life and instill patriotism for the Cuban, not American, nation.[30] As White and Black Cubans considered the future of their schools and their democracy, racial concerns were paramount. Cuba's democracy was "constituted by two races, of different aspirations, both dominated by stubborn prejudices," wrote Eduardo Pla, director of Havana's secondary schooling institution.[31]

Most importantly for Afro-Cubans, the public school system in the early republic appears to have been racially integrated legally but also largely in practice. Even in the short time between the Spanish colonial government's desegregation order and the beginning of the war, the long history of Black Cuban educational activism had ensured that racial desegregation in Cuban public schools was a given. In the lengthy conversations about the public school system in the Cuban constitutional convention, the issue of race in the public schools did not arise. There was no attempt to reimpose de jure racial segregation, even as US officials and some Cubans tried seriously to restrict the voting rights of Afro-descended Cubans.[32]

Because school surveys and statistics, especially those in *La Instrucción Primaria* published by the new Department of Public Education, were broken down by race, we know that throughout the early years of the Cuban republic, Black children, who made up about one-third of the school-age population, also made up one-third of the matriculated students across the country. Therefore, Afro-Cuban children were fully represented in the public school system in the first few years of the republic.[33] In many towns, particularly those in the province of Santiago, Black children outnumbered Whites in schools.[34] What's more, they generally attended school at the same rates as White children.[35]

The racially integrated education that had been a shock to the US military administrators was also likely still surprising for some White Cubans for whom racial segregation in the public school system had been the focus of decades of debate. White Cuban opposition to public school integration is evident in the large numbers of White Cubans who began to send their children to private schools, which largely remained racially segregated. But in the early years of the republic, many more students still attended public schools than private ones. In 1902 only 10 percent of school-age children were matriculated in private schools, while 44 percent were matriculated in public schools. Neither public nor private institutions provided enough educational options for Cuban children, however, since almost half of them were not enrolled in school at all.[36]

Aside from the *La Instrucción Primaria*'s careful statistics being broken down by racial category as well as by gender, race was mentioned in the magazine only rarely.[37] Early republican Cuba was rife with racial tension and with the failures of Cuban nationalism to alleviate racial discrimination and inequality. The public education system was clearly bearing witness to these social phenomena, but little mention is made of them in the Department of Education's few surviving records.

In one rare instance, a school inspection report did mention the issue of racial integration in the public schools. The inspector for the town of Guanabacoa near Havana noted that a sharp decrease in matriculated students in that school district over the previous several years was not due to White children dropping out "despite attending with children of color." Rather, children of color tended to drop out after the third year for reasons that were "difficult to determine."[38] Thus, according to this inspector, there was no racial animus driving White children out of the schools but rather what might now be called a student retention issue. This was likely due to the continued racial discrimination in Cuban society, which affected not only education but also health and employment outcomes in republican Cuba. Children of color from poorer families may have had to go to work at younger ages.

Although Black children were surprisingly well represented in the early years of republican Cuba's public schools, Black teachers were notably absent. In 1902 more than 96 percent of all Cuban teachers were White; only 3.4 percent, 119 out of 3,458, were classified as "de color." By 1906,

5.8 percent of Cuban teachers were Black, still a startlingly small proportion.[39] During the nineteenth century, even an expansion of public school access for children of color did not translate to more employment for Afro-descended teachers. As some towns provided public schools for children of color, they might even have drawn students from the escuelitas de casa or other private schools run by Black educators, thereby limiting employment options for their teachers. Black and mulato teachers were able to teach in the private schools such as the escuelitas that continued to function and other private schools, little documented, that existed throughout the republican period.[40]

But under the occupation and early republic, as the importance of patronage networks to disperse public administration positions and funds increased, White men crowded into the teaching profession.[41] Battles for control between the local school boards and the centralized Department of Education may also have affected Black teacher employment. The editorial board of *La Instrucción Primaria* complained that the local school boards were not abiding by the rules set by the centralized Department of Education. The ongoing tension centered to some extent on the issues of testing, certifying, and appointing teachers for the public schools. The local school boards continued to appoint teachers who weren't on the certified list or fire those who were. According to the Department of Education, local school boards operated out of personal animus, not from professional considerations.[42] Cuba's public sector in the early twentieth century, like that in the United States, was very dependent on a patronage system that often excluded Afro-descendants from public-sector jobs; the public sector had become practically the only industry in Cuban hands since Americans and Europeans had come to dominate the agricultural sector.[43] It is possible that, had it been adhered to, the more meritocratic system promoted by the central Department of Education might have served to help Black teachers, who were otherwise discriminated against by or unable to access the patronage networks of the local school board system.

But a centralized system may have also had the effect of overlooking traditional or informal ways of accessing jobs that may have existed for Afro-Cuban teachers. If the teacher-qualifying system did not take into account the historical lack of access to schooling among Afro-Cubans, then Black teachers might not have had any way to enter the normal schools (teachers' colleges) or pass the qualifying tests. In addition, the expansion of Black children's access to the public school system itself, while benefiting Black children, may have harmed Black access to the teaching profession.

Reyita Castillo Bueno, a Black maestra amiga, noted in her autobiography that she ran her school until a public school was opened in her town.[44] The formal school system that had the potential to be a liberating force for Black students also may have shut down traditional opportunities for Black teachers.

Conclusion

Though the Spanish colonial order desegregating Cuba's municipal schools was short-lived, the political and educational activism that led to the order had been long. The Black Cuban educational tradition led by Afro-descended educators, students, their families, and activists had prioritized education as a tool of personal, communal, and social liberation throughout the nineteenth century. They forged educational opportunities to meet the demand of free Black and mulato Cuban children, educating them for free in their homes when necessary. They often educated poor White children who were not receiving an education. Through the educational activities of Black teachers, a Black Cuban educational tradition developed whose contours featured Black-run schools that often educated children of both sexes and races in racially integrated settings. Black Cubans established separate schools due to the discrimination they faced from White Creole Cuban educational officials; these schools allowed Afro-descended teachers to find employment and Afro-descendants to valorize themselves and their children away from the White-supremacist gaze. But Black teachers and activists also pursued licensing for themselves and entrance to the municipal schools for children of color. Their dedication culminated in the successful 1894 desegregation order whose tenure was nonetheless cut short by war and military occupation. Despite such a significant rupture, the Black Cuban educational legacy continued to shape the Cuban public school system during the occupation and in the first decade of the twentieth century, as US military officials found, to their surprise, that racially integrated schools were the norm in many parts of Cuba.

Epilogue
Race in Cuba's Schools, 1910 and Beyond

The resilience of Afro-descended Cubans' successful efforts to secure equal school rights shone through war, military occupation, and the early years of the republic, yet by 1910, the public school system in Cuba was facing significant challenges. Corruption was rampant as patronage networks distributed public-sector jobs, usually excluding Black and mulato Cubans. Many White families fled the public school system for private schools, which proliferated in the republican period (1902–1959). Catholic schools, long a staple of Cuban education, continued to function despite some Cuban nationalists' concerns that the Spanish clergy was supported by the United States in their efforts to maintain social order. Furthermore, Protestant missionaries entering the island often partnered with US corporations to build schools in sugar-company towns that would train the workers as well as providing business education for elite Cubans.[1]

In 1908 an autonomous Black political party was formed in Cuba. The Partido Independiente de Color (PIC) broke with the discourse of raceless nationalism that required Afro-descended Cubans to limit their organizing to existing political parties and to foreground their Cubanness instead of their Blackness. The breach prompted a backlash in which thousands of Black Cubans were massacred in 1912. One of the PIC's central concerns was the educational system in Cuba, which it viewed through a racial justice lens. In addition to criticizing the antipatriotic nature of the education received at private schools, the PIC also portrayed private schools as discriminatory and elitist. Private schools attracted those who were disappointed by the public schools' lack of resources, they pointed out, but that was not an option for poor and Black children. In so doing, PIC activists called for the equality of schooling for all Cuban children, a clear continuation of the directorio's accomplishments in the late nineteenth century. Furthermore, the PIC, continuing the Black Cuban educational tradition, called for free, obligatory education at all levels for all children.[2] During much of the history of the Black Cuban educational tradition, racially separate social and political organizations such as schools and sociedades were used to advance the educational lives of all children while simultaneously calling for racial integration. In a continuation of that tradition, the PIC again used race-based organizing to improve major public institutions for all Cubans, not just Black Cubans.

From the 1920s to the 1950s, enrollment in private schools mushroomed: 25,000 in 1934; 71,000 in 1943; 80,000 by 1949.[3] As Whites fled the public schools, Black Cubans were left with a neglected public school system, and Cuban society became more segregated. In the face of re-entrenched racial segregation and discrimination, Afro-descended Cubans drew on their long educational tradition. They pursued schooling through various settings; maestras amigas continued to run escuelitas from their homes, the Oblate Sisters of Charity educated Black girls, and other private schools taught Black children in the first half of the twentieth century.[4] White flight from the public school system betrayed many White Cubans' opposition to the racial democracy that had been envisioned by the most progressive elements of the Cuban nationalist movement. Nowhere was this more visible than in their response to the public school system as it had been decisively shaped by the Black educational tradition.

The 1959 Revolution in Cuba was in large part a response to the "republic's failure to build the *patria* with all and for all envisioned by Martí."[5] Afro-descended Cuban activists and communities pressed the Castro regime to act on racial inequality, and the Revolution took decisive action when it came to education. In 1961 the private schools, which had been mostly segregated, were nationalized, and a literacy campaign extended into the most disadvantaged parts of Cuban society. By the early 1980s the Revolution had virtually eliminated racial inequality in literacy as well as in primary, secondary, and university-level education. But as scholar Devyn Spence Benson notes, racism persisted in Cuba during the Revolution and its aftermath, coexisting with state measures to eliminate it. The 1990s economic reforms that followed the collapse of the Soviet Union further increased racial inequality.[6]

The story of Afro-descended Cubans in shaping educational systems on the island to the benefit of Cubans of all races has been repeatedly buried. The Black Cuban educational tradition has been silenced in the official narratives even as it was emerging, as in the case of the White Creole members of the education section of the Sociedad Económica vilifying maestras amigas even though it was those Afro-descended women who advanced not only their own but also White Creoles' most important educational policies. Then too, the racial uplift focus of the 1890s equal school rights campaign by the directorio emphasized the postabolition educational activities of the men involved in the sociedades de color, ignoring a longer, more working-class, more gendered, and sometimes more radical Black Cuban educational tradition.

The Cuban Revolution pointed to its 1961 literacy campaign as the successful culmination of its short-lived antiracist campaign, presenting the literacy campaign and racially integrated classrooms as a sign that justice for Afro-descendants had been delivered through the field of education "thanks to the Revolution."[7] But the revolutionary government ignored Black Cubans' own endeavors in the field of education, shutting down the Black sociedades de color, nationalizing all the private schools including Black-led ones, and foreclosing many of the educational options Afro-descended Cubans had painstakingly built for themselves over the course of more than a century and a half.[8]

As the struggle for Black freedom in Cuba has shifted over time, Black activists, Cuban governments, and social discourses have borrowed from old strategies and created new ones under changing circumstances. In recent years, Afro-Cuban activists have pointed to continued racial discrimination on the island, and the Cuban public school system today is experiencing greater inequality, often along racial lines. Tutors have become legal in Cuba, as have private classes, suggesting that Cubans may again face unequal access to education with a racial dimension.[9] In the United States, the Supreme Court decision in *Brown v. Board of Education of Topeka* to desegregate schools, coming sixty years after the Cuban desegregation order, was not enforced. Although the Civil Rights Act of 1964 finally achieved some school desegregation, its effects were limited to the South, and northern schools escaped mandated desegregation. Today, many schools in the United States are more racially segregated than they were in the 1950s.[10] The renewed urgency of the issue of racial segregation in education in Cuba and the United States necessitates a closer look at the strategies, ideologies, and successes of and the challenges facing the Black Cuban educational tradition of the nineteenth century. Afro-descended Cubans were central in developing the educational systems in Cuba in order to advance the cause of Black freedom and of freedom for all Cubans. As questions of racial justice and Black freedom become more explicitly posed in Cuba today, the legacy of the Black Cuban educational tradition must be remembered.

NOTES

Introduction

1 I follow Kabria Baumgartner and Zoë Burkholder in using the term "equal school rights" here to signal that, for Afro-descended Cubans, access to education and in particular to the developing national public school system was part of a broader campaign for equality and rights. Baumgartner, *In Pursuit of Knowledge: Black Women and Educational Activism in Antebellum America* (New York: New York University Press, 2019); Burkholder, *An African American Dilemma: A History of School Integration and Civil Rights in the North* (New York: Oxford University Press, 2021).
2 "Escuelas municipales," *La Igualdad,* January 4, 1894. *La Igualdad* issues are archived at the Biblioteca Nacional José Martí in Havana. All translations are mine unless otherwise indicated.
3 Matt D. Childs, "'Sewing' Civilization: Cuban Female Education in the Context of Africanization, 1800–1860," *The Americas* 54, no. 1 (1997): 87. See also Kenneth F. Kiple, *Blacks in Colonial Cuba, 1774–1899* (Gainesville: University Presses of Florida, 1976).
4 Alejandro de la Fuente, *Havana and the Atlantic in the Sixteenth Century* (Chapel Hill: University of North Carolina Press, 2008), 174.
5 Michael Zeuske, "Two Stories of Gender and Slave Emancipation in Cienfuegos and Santa Clara, Central Cuba," *Gender and Slave Emancipation in the Atlantic World,* ed. Pamela Scully and Diana Paton (Durham, NC: Duke University Press, 2005), 181–198.
6 Robert Paquette estimates that 20 to 30 percent of the island's enslaved population resided in cities. Though it is clear that in Havana, there was increasing residential segregation that pushed Afro-descendants into neighborhoods just outside the city walls, the colonial cities would have also been places where Spaniards, enslaved people, and free people of color interacted in the streets. Robert L. Paquette, *Sugar Is Made with Blood: The Conspiracy of La Escalera and the Conflict between Empires over Slavery in Cuba* (Middletown, CT: Wesleyan University Press, 1988), 33–39. See also Guadalupe García, *Beyond the Walled City: Colonial Exclusion in Havana* (Oakland: University of California Press, 2016).
7 Chira, *Patchwork Freedoms*; Camila Cowling, "Gendered Geographies: Motherhood, Slavery, Law, and Space in Mid-Nineteenth-Century Cuba," *Women's History Review* 27, no. 6 (June 2017), 939–953; Claudia Varella and Manuel Barcia, *Wage-*

Earning Slaves: Coartación in Nineteenth-Century Cuba (Gainesville: University of Florida Press, 2020).

8 On Cuba's free Black population, see Childs, *The 1812 Aponte Rebellion in Cuba*; Chira, *Patchwork Freedoms*; Pedro Deschamps Chapeaux, *El negro en la economía habanera del siglo XIX* (Havana: Unión de Escritores y Artistas de Cuba, 1971); de la Fuente, *Havana and the Atlantic in the Sixteenth Century*, 147–185; Rafael Duharte Jimenez, *El negro en la sociedad colonial* (Santiago, Cuba: Oriente, 1988); Sherry Johnson, *The Social Transformation of Eighteenth-Century Cuba* (Gainesville: University Press of Florida, 2001), 184–186; Kiple, *Blacks in Colonial Cuba*; Herbert S. Klein, "The Colored Militia of Cuba: 1568–1868," *Caribbean Studies* 6, no. 2 (July 1966): 17–27; Jane G. Landers, *Atlantic Creoles in the Age of Revolutions* (Cambridge, MA: Harvard University Press, 2010); Verena Martínez-Alier, *Marriage, Class, and Color in Nineteenth-Century Cuba: A Study of Racial Attitudes and Sexual Values in a Slave Society* (Ann Arbor: University of Michigan Press, 1974); Paquette, *Sugar Is Made with Blood*, chapter 4; Reid-Vazquez, *Year of the Lash*; David Sartorius, *Ever Faithful: Race, Loyalty, and the Ends of Empire in Spanish Cuba* (Durham, NC: Duke University Press, 2013).

9 Laws against enslaved people achieving literacy were enacted in many southern states. In Cuba and most of the Caribbean and Latin America, there were no legal proscriptions to teaching enslaved people to read and write. The Iberian legal tradition suggested that the enslaved were supposed to be taught Christian doctrine by their owners, but slaveholders in Cuba during the nineteenth-century expansion of slavery and the sugar plantations appear to have ignored this mandate. Frank Tannenbaum famously argues in *Slave and Citizen* (Boston: Beacon, 1946) that the Catholic Church mitigated some of the worst factors of plantation slavery better than the Anglican Church. The slave codes and public education laws in Cuba required that slaves be taught religious content, but by the nineteenth century in Spain and in Cuba, the Church had lost much political power and was unable or unwilling to educate enslaved people in Cuba. In contrast, on many non-Hispanic Caribbean islands, Protestant missionaries penetrated the plantation worlds in order to educate enslaved Africans and Afro-descendants. For US laws against the literacy of enslaved people, see Birgit Brander Rasmussen, "'Attended with Great Inconveniences': Slave Literacy and the 1740 South Carolina Negro Act," *PMLA* 125, no. 1 (2010): 201–203, http://www.jstor.org/stable/25614450; Smithsonian American Art Museum, "Literacy as Freedom," Washington, DC, September 2014, https://americanexperience.si.edu/wp-content/uploads/2014/09/Literacy-as-Freedom.pdf.

10 There were at least a few night academies for enslaved people. For example, Emma Pérez writes that a White teacher from Santa Clara named Carmita Gutiérrez in 1868 established the Academia Nocturna Gratuita, whose students were mostly enslaved Black people; Emma Pérez, *Historia de la pedagogía en Cuba desde los orígenes hasta la guerra de independencia* (Havana: Cultural, 1945), 286–289. There is also some evidence that enslaved people were educated by their owners. See Juan Justo Reyes, *Memoria sobre los progresos que ha hecho la instrucción pública bajo la protección de la Real Sociedad Patriótica de la Habana desde que se puso en activo*

ejercicio su clase de educación (Havana: Imprenta del Gobierno y Capitanía General, 1830), 84. Other examples appear in this book.
11 Danielle Terrazas Williams, *A Capital of Free Women: Race, Legitimacy, and Liberty in Colonial Mexico* (New Haven, CT: Yale University Press, 2022). See also Martínez-Alier, *Marriage, Class, and Color in Nineteenth-Century Cuba*; Reid-Vazquez, *Year of the Lash.*
12 Span and Sanya, "Education and the African Diaspora."
13 For midwives of color in Cuba, see Michele Reid-Vazquez, "Tensions of Race, Gender and Midwifery in Colonial Cuba," in *Africans to Colonial Spanish America: Expanding the Diaspora*, ed. Rachel O'Toole, Sherwin Bryant, and Ben Vinson III (Chicago: University of Illinois Press, 2012), 186–205. For more on the domestic labor of Black women in Cuba, see Anasa Hicks, *Hierarchies at Home: Domestic Service in Cuba from Abolition to Revolution* (New York: Cambridge University Press, 2022).
14 Laird W. Bergad, "Slavery in Cuba and Puerto Rico, 1804 to Abolition," *The Cambridge World History of Slavery*, vol. 4, ed. David Eltis, Stanley L. Engerman, Seymour Drescher, and David Richardson, 98–128 (Cambridge, England: Cambridge University Press, 2017); Laurent Dubois, *Avengers of the New World: The Story of the Haitian Revolution* (Cambridge, MA: Harvard University Press, 2004); Ada Ferrer, *Freedom's Mirror: Cuba and Haiti in the Age of Revolution* (New York: Cambridge University Press, 2014), 29, 81–103; C. L. R. James, *The Black Jacobins: Toussaint L'Ouverture and the San Domingo Revolution* (New York: Random House, 1963); Franklin Knight, *Slave Society in Cuba during the Nineteenth Century* (Madison: University of Wisconsin Press, 1974); Manuel Moreno Fraginals, *El ingenio: Complejo económico-social cubano de azúcar* (Havana: Editorial de Ciencias Sociales, 1978); Paquette, *Sugar Is Made with Blood*, chapter 2.
15 G. Antonio Espinoza, "National Education Systems: Latin America," in *The Oxford Handbook of the History of Education*, eds. John L. Rury and Eileen H. Tamura (New York: Oxford University Press, 2019), 201–203; Carlos Newland, "La educación elemental en Hispanoamerica: Desde la independencia hasta la centralización de los sistemas educativos nacionales," *Hispanic American Historical Review* 71, no. 2 (May 1991): 348–352; Ángel Huerta Martínez, *La enseñanza primaria en Cuba en el siglo XIX, 1812–1868* (Seville: Excma. Diputación Provincial de Sevilla, 1992), 29.
16 Antonio Bachiller y Morales, *Apuntes para la historia de las letras, y de la instrucción pública de la isla de Cuba*, vol. 1 (Havana: P. Massana, 1859); Childs, "'Sewing' Civilization"; José F. Martínez y Díaz, *Historia de la educación pública en Cuba desde el descubrimiento hasta nuestros días y causas de su fracaso* (Pinar del Río, Cuba: Casa Villalba, 1943).
17 For examples of histories that emphasize Spain's repressive use of education in Cuba, see José María Aguilera-Manzano, "The Role of Higher Education Reform in the Construction of Cuban Identity," *Latin Americanist* 54, no. 2 (2010): 95–111; Edward D. Fitchen, "Primary Education in Colonial Cuba: Spanish Tool for Retaining 'La Isla Siempre Leal?'" *Caribbean Studies* 14, no. 1 (April 1974), 105–120; Larry R. Jensen, *Children of Colonial Despotism: Press, Politics, and Culture in Cuba, 1790–1840*

(Tampa: University of South Florida Press, 1988). Spain was slower in developing a public education system in the peninsula than other European countries due to a sluggish economy, the Spanish political system that insulated the political elite from popular pressure, and the power of the Catholic Church, which was deeply suspicious of lay education. It was not until 1857 that the *Ley Moyano* creating a national education system was passed in Spain. See Carolyn P. Boyd, *Historia Patria: Politics, History, and National Identity in Spain, 1875–1975* (Princeton, NJ: Princeton University Press, 1997), 8–12; Stanley G. Payne, *A History of Spain and Portugal* (Madison: University of Wisconsin Press, 1973), 490.

18 For a partial list of the history of education in Cuba, see Paulino Castañeda Delgado and üJuan Marchena Fernández, "Notas sobre la educación pública en Cuba, 1816–1863," *Jahrbuch für Geschichte von Staat Lateinamerikas* 21 (1984): 264–282; Justo A. Chávez Rodríguez, *Bosquejo histórico de las ideas educativas en Cuba* (Havana: Pueblo y Educación, 1996); Childs, "'Sewing' Civilization"; Yoel Cordoví Núñez, *Magisterio y nacionalismo en las escuelas públicas de Cuba, 1899–1920* (Havana: Editorial de Ciencias Sociales, 2012); Sandra Estévez Rivero, "La instrucción pública: Forjada de la conciencia política entre negros y mulatos libres en la ciudad de Santiago de Cuba (1526–1868)," in *Por la identidad del negro cubano*, ed. Pedro Castro Monterrey, Sandra Estévez Rivero, and Olga Portuondo Zúñiga, 41–64 (Santiago, Cuba: Caserón, 2011); Fitchen, "Primary Education in Colonial Cuba"; Martínez y Díaz, *Historia de la educación pública en Cuba*; Cuba, Ministerio de Educación, *La educación en los cien años de lucha* (Havana: Pueblo y Educación, 1968); Huerta Martínez, *La enseñanza primaria en Cuba*; E. Pérez, *Historia de la pedagogía en Cuba*; Louis A. Pérez Jr., "The Imperial Design: Politics and Pedagogy in Occupied Cuba, 1899–1902," *Cuban Studies/Estudios Cubanos* 12 (July 1982): 1–19; Enrique Sosa Rodríguez and Alejandrina Penabad Félix, *Historia de la educación en Cuba*, 10 vols. (Havana: Pueblo y Educación, 2005); Raquel Vinat de la Mata, "Colores y dolores de la educación femenina en Cuba (siglo XIX)," in *Emergiendo del silencio: Mujeres negras en la historia de Cuba*, ed. Oilda Hevia Lanier and Daisy Rubiera Castillo (Havana: Editorial de Ciencias Sociales, 2016), 89–130; Raquel Vinat de la Mata, *Luces en el silencio: Educación femenina en Cuba 1648–1898* (Havana: Política, 2005).

19 On the Spanish empire in this period, see Jeremy Adelman, *Sovereignty and Revolution in the Iberian Atlantic* (Princeton, NJ: Princeton University Press, 2006); Martin Blinkhorn, "Spain: 'The Spanish Problem' and the Imperial Myth," *Journal of Contemporary History* 15, no. 1 (January 1980): 5–25; Charles Esdaile, *Spain in the Liberal Age: From Constitution to Civil War, 1808–1939* (Oxford, England: Blackwell, 2000); Stephen Jacobson, "'The Head and Heart of Spain': New Perspectives on Nationalism and Nationhood," *Social History* 29, no. 3 (August 2004): 393–407; John Lynch, *Latin American Revolutions, 1808–1826: Old and New World Origins* (Norman: University of Oklahoma Press, 1994); Sartorius, *Ever Faithful*; Francisco Scarano, "Liberal Pacts and Hierarchies of Rule: Approaching the Imperial Transition in Cuba and Puerto Rico," *Hispanic American Historical Review* 78, no. 4 (November 1998): 583–601; Christopher Schmidt-Nowara, *The Conquest of History:*

Spanish Colonialism and National Histories in the Nineteenth Century (Pittsburgh, PA: University of Pittsburgh Press, 2006).

20 Sartorius, *Ever Faithful*. See also Ferrer, *Insurgent Cuba*, 129–133; Lillian Guerra, *The Myth of José Martí: Conflicting Nationalisms in Early Twentieth-Century Cuba* (Chapel Hill: University of North Carolina Press, 2005), 10; Oilda Hevia Lanier, *El Directorio Central de las Sociedades Negras de Cuba, 1886–1894* (Havana: Editorial de Ciencias Sociales, 1996).

21 On the history and theory of public education broadly, see William J. Reese, "The Origins of Progressive Education," *History of Education Quarterly* 41, no. 1 (Spring 2001): 1–24; Henry A. Giroux, "Theories of Reproduction and Resistance in the New Sociology of Education: A Critical Analysis," *Harvard Educational Review* 53, no. 3 (August 1983): 257–293; Mary Jo Maynes, *Schooling in Western Europe: A Social History* (Albany: State University of New York Press, 1985); John W. Meyer et al., "Public Education as Nation-Building in America: Enrollments and Bureaucratization in the American States, 1870–1930," *American Journal of Sociology* 85, no. 3 (November 1979), 591–613; John L. Rury and Eileen H. Tamura, eds., *The Oxford Handbook of the History of Education* (New York: Oxford University Press, 2019), especially part 3, "The Rise of National Education Systems," 149–259.

22 Fernando Reimers, "Education and Social Progress," in *The Cambridge Economic History of Latin America*, vol. 2, ed. Victor Bulmer-Thomas, John Coatsworth, and Roberto Cortes-Conde (Cambridge, England: Cambridge University Press, 2006), 435; Newland "La educación elemental en Hispanoamerica," 345–357.

23 The development of public school systems in Latin America was a direct challenge to the power of the Catholic Church, which was conservative in its politics and in its intellectual pursuits. Liberal intellectual currents in Latin America after the wars of independence, on the other hand, prized independence of mind and empirical inquiry over the authoritarian, dogmatic approach of the Catholic Church. See Espinoza, "National Education Systems."

24 Newland, "La educación elemental en Hispanoamerica," 357.

25 For a selection of works on nineteenth-century public education in Latin America, see Marcelo Caruso, "Literacy and Suffrage: The Politicisation of Schooling in Postcolonial Hispanic America, 1810–1850," *Paedagogica Historica* 46, no. 4 (August 2010): 463–478; Brooke Larson, *The Lettered Indian: Race, Nation, and Indigenous Education in Twentieth-Century Bolivia* (Durham, NC: Duke University Press, 2024); Newland, "La educación elemental en Hispanoamerica"; Gabriela Ossenbach, "Research into the History of Education in Latin America: Balance of the Current Situation," *Paedagogica Historica* 36, no. 3 (2000): 841–867; João Paulo G. Pimenta, "Education and the Historiography of Ibero-American Independence: Elusive Presences, Many Absences," *Paedagogica Historica* 46, no. 4 (August 2010): 419–434; Reimers, "Education and Social Progress"; Mary Kay Vaughan, *The State, Education, and Social Class in Mexico, 1880–1928* (DeKalb: Northern Illinois University Press, 1982); Gregorio Weinberg, *Modelos educativos en la historia de América Latina* (Buenos Aires: A-Z, 1995).

26 Reimers, "Education and Social Progress."
27 Espinoza, "National Education Systems, Latin America," 200.
28 Ferrer, *Insurgent Cuba;* Bonnie Lucero, *Revolutionary Masculinity and Racial Inequality: Gendering War and Politics in Cuba* (Albuquerque: University of New Mexico Press, 2018); Guerra, *Myth of José Martí*. See also Benson, *Antiracism in Cuba*; Aviva Chomsky, "'Barbados or Canada?': Race, Immigration, and Nation in Early Twentieth-Century Cuba," *Hispanic American Historical Review* 80, no. 3 (2000): 415–462; de la Fuente, *A Nation for All*; Aline Helg, *Our Rightful Share: The Afro-Cuban Struggle for Equality, 1886–1912* (Chapel Hill: University of North Carolina Press, 1995).
29 Guerra, *Myth of José Martí*.
30 Conde Rodríguez, "Cultura y educación en los años iniciales de la República de Cuba."
31 Manuel Barcia, *The Great African Slave Revolt of 1825: Cuba and the Fight for Freedom in Matanzas* (Baton Rouge: Louisiana State University Press, 2012); María del Carmen Barcia, *Los ilustres apellidos*; María del Carmen Barcia, "Poder étnico y subversión social: Los batallones de pardos y morenos de Cuba." *Islas* 1, no. 1 (2005); Childs, *The 1812 Aponte Rebellion in Cuba;* Pedro Deschamps Chapeaux, *Los batallones de pardos y morenos libres* (Havana: Arte y Literatura, 1976); Aisha Finch, "'What Looks Like a Revolution': Enslaved Women and the Gendered Terrain of Slave Insurgencies in Cuba, 1843–1844," *Journal of Women's History* 26, no. 1 (2014): 112–134; Finch, *Rethinking Slave Rebellion in Cuba;* Phillip A. Howard, *Changing History: Afro-Cuban Cabildos and Societies of Color in the Nineteenth Century* (Baton Rouge: Louisiana State University Press, 1998); Henry B. Lovejoy, *Prieto: Yorùbá Kingship in Colonial Cuba during the Age of Revolution* (Chapel Hill: University of North Carolina Press, 2019); Michele Reid, "Protesting Service: Free Black Reponses to Cuba's Reestablished Militia of Color, 1854–1865," *Journal of Colonialism and Colonial History* 5, no. 2 (2004): 1–22; David Sartorius, "My Vassals: Free-Colored Militias in Cuba and the Ends of the Spanish Empire," *Journal of Colonialism and Colonial History* 5, no. 2 (2004).
32 For the myth of racial equality, see Chomsky, "Barbados or Canada?"; de la Fuente, *A Nation for All;* Ferrer, *Insurgent Cuba;* Helg, *Our Rightful Share*. On racial uplift, see Lee D. Baker, *Anthropology and the Racial Politics of Culture* (Durham, NC: Duke University Press, 2010); Kevin Gaines, *Uplifting the Race: Black Leadership, Politics, and Culture in the Twentieth Century* (Chapel Hill: University of North Carolina Press, 1996).
33 For analyses of approaches to racial organizing in Cuba, see Helg, *Our Rightful Share*; Pappademos, *Black Political Activism and the Cuban Republic*. On the Partido Independiente de Color and the ensuing massacre, see Bárbara Danzie León et al., *Apuntes cronológicos sobre el Partido Independiente de Color* (Santiago, Cuba: Santiago, 2010); Helg, *Our Rightful Share*.
34 C. L. R. James, *Black Jacobins*; Eric Williams, *Capitalism and Slavery*, 3rd ed. (Chapel Hill: University of North Carolina Press, 2021).

35 Burkholder, *African American Dilemma*, 6; Jarvis R. Givens, *Fugitive Pedagogy: Carter G. Woodson and the Art of Black Teaching*. Cambridge, MA: Harvard University Press, 2021, 10–13.
36 For an overview of the historiography on African American intellectual history, see Brandon R. Byrd, "The Rise of African American Intellectual History," *Modern Intellectual History* 18, no. 3 (2021): 833–864, doi:10.1017/S1479244320000219.
37 Ada Ferrer, "Introduction to Part II," in *Breaking the Chains: The Afro-Cuban Fight for Freedom and Equality, 1812-1912*, ed. Aisha Finch and Fannie Rushing (Baton Rouge: Louisiana State University Press, 2019), 135.
38 Cedric J. Robinson, *Black Marxism: The Making of the Black Radical Tradition*, 3rd ed. (Chapel Hill: University of North Carolina Press, 2000). See notes 5 and 6 in Finch, "What Looks Like a Revolution," 129–130.
39 Jennifer Morgan, "Partus Sequitur Ventrum: Law, Race, and Reproduction in Colonial Slavery," *Small Axe* 22, no. 1 (2018): 14–16.
40 Finch, "What Looks Like a Revolution"; see also Neil Roberts, *Freedom as Marronage* (Chicago: University of Chicago Press, 2015).
41 Walker and Rickford participated in the National Academy of Education/Spencer annual meeting, dissertation fellows mentorship session, November 2014, Washington, D.C.
42 Devyn Spence Benson, Daisy Rubiera Castillo, and Inés María Martiatu Terry, eds., *Afrocubanas: History, Thought, and Cultural Practices* (New York: Rowman and Littlefield International, 2020); Brunson, *Black Women, Citizenship, and the Making of Modern Cuba*; Hicks, *Hierarchies at Home*; Angela Crumdy, "Teaching Revolution: Women Primary School Teachers, Race, and Social Reproduction in Cuba," PhD diss., City University of New York, 2022, https://academicworks.cuny.edu/gc_etds/4927; Nancy Raquel Mirabal, *Suspect Freedoms: The Racial and Sexual Politics of Cubanidad in New York, 1823-1957* (New York: New York University Press, 2017); Vinat de la Mata, *Luces en el silencio*; Vinat de la Mata, "Colores y dolores."
43 Byrd, "Rise of African American Intellectual History," 842.
44 Cited in Byrd, "Rise of African American Intellectual History," 838. See also Burkholder, *African American Dilemma*, 6.
45 For a selection of the extensive history of African American education, see James D. Anderson, *The Education of Blacks in the South, 1860-1935* (Chapel Hill: University of North Carolina Press, 1988); Baumgartner, *In Pursuit of Knowledge: Black Women and Educational Activism in Antebellum America*; Burkholder, *African American Dilemma*; Candace Cunningham, *"I Hope They Fire Me": Black Teachers in the Fight for Equal Education* (Athens: University of Georgia Press, forthcoming); Ansley T. Erickson, *Making the Unequal Metropolis: School Desegregation and Its Limits* (Chicago: University of Chicago Press, 2016); Adam Fairclough, *Teaching Equality: Black Schools in the Age of Jim Crow* (Athens: University of Georgia Press, 2001); Glenda Gilmore, *Gender and Jim Crow: Women and the Politics of White Supremacy in North Carolina, 1896-1920* (Chapel Hill: University of North Carolina Press, 1996); Givens, *Fugitive Pedagogy*; Michael Hines, *A Worthy Piece of Work: The Untold Story of Madeline Morgan and the Fight for Black History in Schools* (Boston: Beacon Press,

2022); Brian P. Jones, *The Tuskegee Student Uprising* (New York: New York University Press, 2022); Hilary J. Moss, *Schooling Citizens: The Struggle for African American Education in Antebellum America* (Chicago: University of Chicago Press, 2009); Robert C. Morris, *Reading, 'Riting, and Reconstruction: The Education of Freedmen in the South, 1861–1870* (Chicago: University of Chicago Press, 1976); Vanessa Siddle Walker, *Their Highest Potential: An African American School Community in the Segregated South* (Chapel Hill: University of North Carolina Press, 2000); Heather Andrea Williams, *Self-Taught: African American Education in Slavery and Freedom* (Chapel Hill: University of North Carolina Press, 2005).

46 There is not yet a significant body of historical work on Black education in Latin America, although there has recently been some movement in this direction. For a few examples, see George Reid Andrews, *Afro-Argentines, 1800–2000* (New York: Oxford University Press, 2004), 45–46, 60–64; María Agustina Barrachina, "Entre la igualdad y la segregación: Las disputas por la educación de los afrodescendientes en el Buenos Aires postrosista," *Claves: Revista de Historia* 5, no. 9 (2019), 115–143; Erika Denise Edwards, *Hiding in Plain Sight: Black Women, the Law, and the Making of a White Argentine Republic* (Tuscaloosa: University of Alabama Press, 2020), chapter 6; Diana Sosa Cárdenas, *Los pardos: Caracas en las postrimerías de la colonia* (Caracas: Universidad Católica Andrés Bello, 2010), 40–41.

47 Moss, *Schooling Citizens*, 9.

48 See Edwards, *Hiding in Plain Sight*, especially chapter 6, "Lessons of Motherhood: The Beginning of Institutionalized Whitening."

49 Davarian L. Baldwin, foreword to *Ideas in Unexpected Places: Reimagining Black Intellectual History*, ed. Brandon R. Byrd, Leslie M. Alexander, and Russell Rickford (Evanston, IL: Northwestern University Press, 2022), xv.

50 Ada Ferrer, *Cuba: An American History* (New York: Scribner, 2021), 167.

51 Excellent new scholarship on Black childhood in Cuba and Puerto Rico by Anasa Hicks and by Solsiree del Moral has so far focused on the early twentieth century, not the Spanish colonial period. Anasa Hicks, "Dubious Victimhood: Labor, Race, Age and Honor in Republican Cuban Courts," in *The Global History of Black Girlhood*, ed. Corinne T. Field and LaKisha Michelle Simmons (Chicago: University of Illinois Press, 2022); Solsiree del Moral, "'Una niña humilde y de color': Sources for the History of an Afro–Puerto Rican Childhood," *Journal of Caribbean History* 53, no. 2 (2019): 192–222.

52 Fitchen, "Primary Education in Colonial Cuba"; Jesse Hoffnung-Garskof, *Racial Migrations: New York City and the Revolutionary Politics of the Spanish Caribbean* (Princeton, NJ: Princeton University Press, 2019); Lisandro Pérez, *Sugar, Cigars, and Revolution: The Making of Cuban New York* (New York: NYU Press, 2018); Alfonso W. Quiroz, "Free Association and Civil Society in Cuba, 1787–1895," *Journal of Latin American Studies* 48, no. 1 (February 2011): 33–64.

53 For Cuba's Black press, see Pedro Deschamps Chapeaux, *El negro en el periodismo cubano en el siglo xix* (Havana: Revolución, 1963). For an overview of and excerpts from the Black press throughout Latin America, see Paulina Laura Alberto, George

Reid Andrews, and Jesse Hoffnung-Garskof, eds., *Voices of the Race: Black Newspapers in Latin America, 1870-1960* (New York: Cambridge University Press, 2022).

54 Stephanie E. Smallwood, "The Politics of the Archive and History's Accountability to the Enslaved," *History of the Present* 6, no. 2 (2016): 117-132, https://doi.org/10.5406/historypresent.6.2.0117.

55 Michel-Rolph Trouillot, *Silencing the Past: Power and the Production of History* (Boston: Beacon, 1995); Brian Connolly and Marisa Fuentes, "Introduction: From Archives of Slavery to Liberated Futures?" *History of the Present* 6, no. 2 (Fall 2016): 105-116.

56 Aisha K. Finch, "The Repeating Rebellion: Slave Resistance and Political Consciousness in Nineteenth-Century Cuba, 1812-1844," in *Breaking the Chains: The Afro-Cuban Fight for Freedom and Equality, 1812-1912*, ed. Aisha K. Finch and Fannie Rushing (Baton Rouge: Louisiana State Press, 2019), 138-157; Marisa Fuentes, *Dispossessed Lives: Enslaved Women, Violence, and the Archive* (Philadelphia: University of Pennsylvania Press, 2016); Saidiya Hartman, *Lose Your Mother: A Journey along the Atlantic Slave Route* (New York: Farrar, Straus, and Giroux, 2007); Saidiya Hartman, "Venus in Two Acts," *Small Axe* 26 (June 2008): 1-14; Lisa Lowe, *The Intimacies of Four Continents* (Durham, NC: Duke University Press, 2015); Morgan, "Partus Sequitur Ventrum."

57 Brandon R. Byrd, Leslie M. Alexander, and Russell Rickford, introduction to *Ideas in Unexpected Places: Reimagining Black Intellectual History*, ed. Byrd, Alexander, and Rickford (Evanston, IL: Northwestern University Press, 2022), 4.

58 Burkholder, *African American Dilemma*, 5.

59 See Sara Vogel and Ofelia García, "Translanguaging," in *Oxford Research Encyclopedia of Education* (New York: Oxford University Press, 2017), doi:10.1093/acrefore/9780190264093.013.181.

Chapter 1. Maestras Amigas and the Shaping of a Black Cuban Educational Ideology in Early Nineteenth-Century Cuba

1 María de los Reyes Castillo Bueno, *Reyita: The Life of a Black Cuban Woman in the Twentieth Century* (Durham, NC: Duke University Press, 2000): 55-56.

2 For escuelitas de amigas in Cuba, see Bachiller y Morales, *Apuntes para la historia de las letras*, 1:66-68; Childs, "'Sewing' Civilization," 87; Estévez Rivero, "La instrucción pública; Deschamps Chapeaux," *El negro en la economía habanera*, 125-130; Sarah L. Franklin, *Women and Slavery in Nineteenth-Century Colonial Cuba* (Rochester, NY: University of Rochester Press, 2012), 91-93; Luz Mena, "Stretching the Limits of Gendered Spaces: Black and Mulato Women in 1830s Havana," *Cuban Studies* 36 (2005): 87-104; E. Pérez, *Historia de la pedagogía en Cuba*, 50-52; Salvador García Aguero, "Lorenzo Menéndez (o Meléndez), el negro en la Educación cubana," *Revista Bimestre Cubana* 39, no 3 (May-June 1937): 351-358; Cuba, Ministerio de Educación, *La educación en los cien años de lucha*, 27.

3 For the history of national public education systems in the nineteenth century, see Giroux, "Theories of Reproduction and Resistance"; Carl Kaestle, *Pillars of the Republic: Common Schools and American Society, 1780-1860* (New York: Hill and

Wang, 1983); Maynes, *Schooling in Western Europe*; Meyer et al., "Public Education as Nation-Building"; Reese, "Origins of Progressive Education"; Rury and Tamura, *Oxford Handbook*, part 3.

4 "This is the afterlife of slavery—skewed life chances, limited access to health and education, premature death, incarceration, and impoverishment." Hartman, *Lose Your Mother*, 6.

5 For competing ideologies regarding liberalism and the colonial state among planter and intellectual Creoles, see for example Aguilera-Manzano, "Role of Higher Education Reform."

6 Nineteenth-century sources refer to the women who operated informal schools in their homes as amigas (friends) or maestras amigas. In "'Sewing' Civilization," Childs uses the evocative term "mulata amigas" to refer to Afro-descended teachers of the escuelitas de casa who comprised the majority of maestras amigas.

7 Christopher Schmidt-Nowara, "The Specter of Las Casas: José Antonio Saco and the Persistence of Spanish Colonialism in Cuba," *Itinerario* 25, no. 2 (2001): 93–109, doi:10.1017/S0165115300008846; Quiroz, "Free Association and Civil Society in Cuba."

8 Domingo del Monte, *Escritos*, vol. 1 (Havana: Cultural, 1929), 71, https://ufdc.ufl.edu/UF00075391/00001.

9 Reyes, *Memoria sobre los progresos*, 4; Childs, *The 1812 Aponte Rebellion in Cuba*, 58; A. Suárez y Romero, "Educación: Enseñanza privada," *Revista de la Habana*, 1854, 209.

10 Cuba, Ministerio de Educación, *La educación en los cien años de lucha*, 10–30. On the other end of the spectrum, in the northeastern United States, where public schooling was more quickly developed, 70 percent of White males were enrolled in schools in 1840. See Meyer et al., "Public Education as Nation-Building," 595.

11 Reyes, *Memoria sobre los progresos*, 65.

12 Lucia Provencio Garrigós, "¡Mujeres a la escuela! Lo que quería ser público y resultó privado: Santiago de Cuba a principios del siglo XIX," in *Historia de las mujeres en América Latina*, ed. Sara Beatriz Guardia (Lima: Centro de Estudios la Mujer en la Historia de América Latina, 2012), 170.

13 Quiroz, "Free Association and Civil Society in Cuba," 39–41.

14 Bachiller y Morales, *Apuntes para la historia de las letras*, 1:36.

15 Reyes, *Memoria sobre los progresos*, 5–6.

16 Bachiller y Morales, *Apuntes para la historia de las letras*, 1:25–32.

17 Antonio Bachiller y Morales, "Apuntes para la historia de las letras en la isla de Cuba," *Revista de la Habana*, March 1–September 1, 1854, 34.

18 José Antonio Saco, *Memorias sobre caminos en la isla de Cuba* (New York: G. F. Bunce, 1830), 32–36; Inés Roldán de Montaud, "La carrera de un alto funcionario moderado en Cuba: Vicente Vázquez Queipo (1804–1893)," in *L'État dans ses colonies: Les administrateurs de l'empire espagnol au XIXe siècle*, ed. Jean-Phillipe Luis (Madrid: Casa de Velázquez, 2015), 137–156, https://books.openedition.org/cvz/1196?lang=en. For more on Saco and other Cuban liberal elites, see Josef Opatrny, "José

Antonio Saco's Path toward the Idea of Cubanidad," *Cuban Studies* 24 (1994): 39–56; Schmidt-Nowara, "Specter of Las Casas."
19 Childs, "'Sewing' Civilization," 83–84, 95.
20 In Bachiller y Morales, *Apuntes para la historia de las letras*, 1:6; see also 1:5–7; Deschamps Chapeaux, *El negro en la economía habanera*, 125–130; Estévez Rivero, "La instrucción pública," 54–55.
21 Reyes, *Memoria sobre los progresos*, 8.
22 Childs, "'Sewing' Civilization," 93; Louis A. Pérez Jr., *Cuba between Reform and Revolution*, 3rd ed. (New York: Oxford University Press, 2006), 52; Vinat de la Mata, "Colores y dolores," 100.
23 Havana's walls were built in the seventeenth century, using slave labor, as tools of racial exclusion and social control. See Guadalupe García, *Beyond the Walled City*, especially chapter 2.
24 Reyes, *Memoria sobre los progresos*, 83.
25 Reyes, *Memoria sobre los progresos*, 83–84.
26 "Comunicaciones relacionadas con el establecimiento de escuelas para personas de color," 1828, Coleción de Manuscritos Sociedad Económica de Amigos del País, vol. 3, no. 8, Biblioteca Nacional José Martí, Havana.
27 Franklin, *Women and Slavery*, 92.
28 Cuba, *Plan y reglamento para las escuelas gratuitas de enseñanza mutua de esta ciudad, Pueblo-Nuevo y Ceiba-Mocha* (Matanzas: Imprenta de la Real Marina, 1835); del Monte, *Escritos*, 289.
29 Bachiller y Morales, "Apuntes," *Revista de la Habana*, 34.
30 Guía de forasteros de la siempre fiel isla de Cuba (Havana: Imprenta del Gobierno y Capitanía general por S. M. etc., 1837), 177–178. The Guía de forasteros was an annual report on the administration of Cuba published by the Spanish government 1837–1884. The reports are posted by the Library of Congress at https://www.loc.gov/item/44027902/.
31 There are some minor discrepancies between the figures shown by José F. Martínez y Díaz in his history of public education of Cuba and the 1846 "Apuntes" articles by Bachiller, but they are close. Martínez y Díaz, *Historia de la educación pública en Cuba*, 43; Bachiller y Morales, "Apuntes," *Revista de la Habana*, 33–35.
32 Bachiller y Morales, "Apuntes," *Revista de la Habana*, 33. See also del Monte, *Escritos*, 273–284.
33 Guía de forasteros, 1837, 164–165.
34 Paquette, *Sugar Is Made with Blood*, 119.
35 Childs, "'Sewing' Civilization," 95–107.
36 Louis Pérez, *Cuba between Reform and Revolution*, 69–70; Deschamps Chapeaux and Pérez de la Riva, *Contribución a la historia*, 5.
37 María Cristina Hierrezuelo, "Women 'of Color' in Santiaguera Colonial Society: A Commentary," in *Afrocubanas: History, Thought, and Cultural Practices*, ed. Devyn Spence Benson, Daisy Rubiera Castillo, and Inés María Martiatu Terry (New York: Rowman and Littlefield International, 2020), 39–56.

38 In Deschamps Chapeaux, *El Negro en la economía habanera*, 11–12. See also Reid-Vazquez, *Year of the Lash*, 17–43;
39 Deschamps Chapeaux, *El negro en la economía habanera,* 121, 128; Deschamps Chapeaux and Pérez de la Riva, *Contribución a la historia,* 9.
40 Pelayo González de los Ríos, "Ensayo histórico-estadístico de la instrucción pública de la isla de Cuba, libro Segundo, de la instrucción intelectual. Primera parte de la instrucción primaria, capitulo III." In *Memorias de la Sociedad Económica de la Habana,* Anales de Fomento, series 5, vol. 9 (Havana: Tiempo, 1864), 54.
41 Vinat de la Mata, "Colores y dolores," 104.
42 Since at least the eighteenth century and around the world, there have been schools for young and sometimes poor or Indigenous children that were run by women in their own homes who usually taught the basics of reading, writing, arithmetic, and religion. In Britain and colonial New England, these were called "dame schools." In Spain and Latin America, they were known as *escuelitas*, and the women who ran them were sometimes referred to as *maestras amigas*. See Philis Barragán Goetz, *Reading, Writing, and Revolution: Escuelitas and the Emergence of a Mexican American Identity in Texas* (Austin: University of Texas Press, 2020); Peter Gordon, "Dame Schools," in *The Oxford Companion to British History* (Oxford, England: Oxford University Press, 2015); Elizabeth P. Harper, "Dame Schools," in *Encyclopedia of Educational Reform and Dissent,* ed. Thomas C. Hunt, James C. Carper, Thomas J. Lasley, and C. D. Raisch (Thousand Oaks, CA: Sage, 2010), 258–260, https://doi.org/10.4135/9781412957403; J. H. Higginson, "Dame Schools," *British Journal of Educational Studies* 22, no. 2 (1974): 166–181, https://doi.org/10.2307/3119841; Oresta López, "Las maestras en la historia de la educación en México: Contribuciones para hacerlas visibles," *Sinéctica* 3 (2006): 4–16; Olegario Negrín Fajardo, "Maestros y educadores españoles en el siglo XVIII," *Cuadernos de estudios del siglo XVIII* 15 (2017), 117–157, doi:10.17811/cesxviii.15.2005.117-157; Dorothy Tanck, "Escuelas, colegios y conventos para niñas y mujeres indígenas en el siglo XVIII," in *Obedecer, servir y resistir: La educación de las mujeres en la historia de México,* ed. Adelina Arredondo (Mexico City: Universidad Pedagógica Nacional, 2003), 45–62.
43 Lucia Provencio Garrigós, "La *Trampa* discursiva del elogio a la maternidad cubana del siglo XIX," *Americanía,* no. 1 (2011): 42–73; Franklin, *Women and Slavery*; Hicks, *Hierarchies at Home,* 29–35.
44 Ramón Zambrano Valdés, "Los niños," *Revista de la Habana* 2 (1853–1854): 53.
45 Mena, "Stretching the Limits," 98.
46 Vinat de la Mata, "Colores y dolores," 101.
47 Félix González, in vol. 6, March 1817, Memorias de la Sociedad Económica de Amigos del País (SEAP), Havana, cited in Vinat de la Mata, "Colores y dolores," 98.
48 Bachiller y Morales, *Apuntes para la historia de las letras,* 1:7–15; Deschamps Chapeaux, *El negro en la economía habanera,* 121–124.
49 In Deschamps Chapeaux, *El negro en la economía habanera,* 129.
50 *Memorias de la SEAP,* 1823–1826, cited in Deschamps Chapeaux, *El negro en la economía habanera,* 121.

51 González, in *Memorias de la SEAP*, 1817, cited in Vinat de la Mata, "Colores y dolores," 98.
52 *Memorias de la SEAP*, 1817, cited in Vinat de la Mata, "Colores y dolores," 101.
53 "Personas no solo ignorantes hasta la estupidez, sino de costumbres no limpias y de raza equívoca." Bachiller y Morales, *Apuntes para la historia de las letras*, 1:15.
54 "Dirigidas por negras y mulatas horras." Bachiller y Morales, *Apuntes para la historia de las letras*, 1:7.
55 Reyes, *Memoria sobre los progresos*, 11–12.
56 Reyes, *Memoria sobre los progresos*, 32.
57 Saco, *Memorias sobre caminos en la isla de Cuba*, 33.
58 Finding by the Provincial Commission of Primary Education, in Bachiller y Morales, "Apuntes," *Revista de la Habana*, 49.
59 Reyes, *Memoria sobre los progresos*, 29.
60 Bachiller y Morales, *Apuntes para la historia de las letras*, 1:7.
61 Martínez-Alier, *Marriage, Class, and Color in Nineteenth-Century Cuba*; Karen Morrison, *Cuba's Racial Crucible: The Sexual Economy of Sexual Identities, 1750–2000* (Indiana University Press, 2015); Reid-Vazquez, *Year of the Lash*, 32–35.
62 Del Monte, *Escritos*, 257.
63 In Deschamps Chapeaux, *El negro en la economía habanera*, 126, citing the education section of the Sociedad Económica, 1827, in legajo (leg.) 3, expediente (exp.) 159, Instrucción Pública, ANC.
64 Deschamps Chapeaux, *El negro en la economía habanera*, 122–140.
65 Bachiller y Morales, *Apuntes para la historia de las letras*, 1:7.
66 Reyes, *Memoria sobre los progresos*, 29.
67 Bachiller y Morales, *Apuntes para la historia de las letras*, 1:7.
68 For a twentieth-century example of race-based solidarity and efforts at racial integration coexisting, see Devyn Spence Benson, "Redefining Mestizaje: How Trans-Caribbean Exchanges Solidified Black Consciousness in Cuba," *Small Axe: A Caribbean Journal of Criticism* 25, no. 2 (2021): 91–108.
69 E. Pérez, *Historia de la pedagogía en Cuba*, 52; Bachiller y Morales, "Apuntes," *Revista de la Habana*, 49.
70 Vinat de la Mata, "Colores y dolores," 101.
71 García Aguero, "Lorenzo Menéndez," 360.
72 Emilio Bacardí y Moreau, *Crónicas de Santiago de Cuba* (Santiago, Cuba: Arroyo Hermanos, 1923), 2:338–339, http://ufdc.ufl.edu/AA00062763/00006.
73 Bacardí y Moreau, *Crónicas*, 2:398.
74 Reid-Vazquez, *Year of the Lash*, 107–110.
75 Rainer Schultz, "The Liberal Moment of the Revolution: Cuba's Early Educational Reforms, 1959–1961," *Cuban Studies*, no. 49 (2020): 215–236. https://www.jstor.org/stable/26983800.
76 Castillo Bueno, *Reyita*, 50–59, 123.
77 Denise F. Blum, *Cuban Youth and Revolutionary Values: Educating the New Socialist Citizen* (Austin: University of Texas Press, 2011), 147.

78 In Blum, *Cuban Youth and Revolutionary Values*, 147.
79 Blum, *Cuban Youth and Revolutionary Values*, 147–150.

Chapter 2. Rebellious Teachers, 1812–1844

1 On Cuba's militias for pardos and morenos, see María del Carmen Barcia, "Poder étnico y subversión social"; Childs, *The 1812 Aponte Rebellion in Cuba*; Deschamps Chapeaux, *El negro en la economía habanera*; Gloria García, *Conspiraciones y revueltas: La actividad política de los negros en Cuba, 1790–1845* (Santiago, Cuba: Oriente, 2003); Klein, "Colored Militia of Cuba"; Johnson, *Social Transformation of Eighteenth-Century Cuba*, 11, 64–68; Landers, *Atlantic Creoles*, 141–142; Reid, "Protesting Service"; Sartorius, "Ever Faithful"; Sartorius, "My Vassals." See also Ben Vinson III, *Bearing Arms for His Majesty: The Free-Colored Militia in Colonial Mexico* (Stanford, CA: Stanford University Press, 2002).
2 Deschamps Chapeaux, *El negro en la economía habanera*, 57–86.
3 Childs, *The 1812 Aponte Rebellion*, 97–112; Landers, *Atlantic Creoles*, chapter 4; Howard, *Changing History*; Lovejoy, *Prieto*, 78; María del Carmen Barcia, *Los ilustres apellidos*; Childs, "Gendering the African Diaspora in the Iberian Atlantic," 232, 242–244.
4 Andrews, *Afro-Latin America*, 107.
5 Sartorius, *Ever Faithful*, 61.
6 Ira Berlin, *Many Thousands Gone: The First Two Centuries of Slavery in North America* (Cambridge, MA: Harvard University Press, 1998); Childs, *The 1812 Aponte Rebellion*, 84; Klein, "Colored Militia of Cuba," 20; Landers, *Atlantic Creoles*, 1–14, 152.
7 For US examples of teachers disseminating the social capital acquired through literacy and the teaching profession to Afro-descended children, see Anderson, *Education of Blacks in the South*; Adam Fairclough, *A Class of Their Own: Black Teachers in the Segregated South* (Cambridge, MA: Belknap, 2007); Glenda Elizabeth Gilmore, *Gender and Jim Crow: Women and the Politics of White Supremacy in North Carolina, 1896–1920* (Chapel Hill: University of North Carolina Press, 1996); H. Williams, *Self-Taught*.
8 Deschamps Chapeaux, *El negro en la economía habanera*, 18, 121.
9 Deschamps Chapeaux, *El negro en la economía habanera*, 63–64, 122–125; Landers, *Atlantic Creoles*, 154.
10 Deschamps Chapeaux, *El negro en la economía habanera*, 122, 125.
11 Deschamps Chapeaux, *El negro en la economía habanera*, 122–125.
12 Deschamps Chapeaux, *El negro en la economía habanera*, 123.
13 Manuel Barcia, *Seeds of Insurrection: Domination and Resistance on Western Plantations, 1808–1848* (Baton Rouge: Louisiana State University Press, 2008); Manuel Barcia, *Great African Slave Revolt of 1825*; Manuel Barcia, *West African Warfare in Bahia and Cuba: Soldier Slaves in the Atlantic World, 1807–1844* (New York: Oxford University Press, 2014); Childs, *The 1812 Aponte Rebellion*; Finch, *Rethinking Slave Rebellion in Cuba*; Finch, "Repeating Rebellion"; Gloria García, *Conspiraciones y revueltas*; Lovejoy, *Prieto*.
14 Sartorius, *Ever Faithful*, 1.

15 C. Robinson, *Black Marxism*, xxx. See also Robin D. G. Kelley's foreword, "Why Black Marxism? Why Now?," in Cedric Robinson's *Black Marxism*, xi–xxvi.
16 Gloria García, *Conspiraciones y revueltas*, 1.
17 Finch, "Repeating Rebellion," 142.
18 Deschamps Chapeaux, *El negro en la economía habanera*, 126.
19 In reality, efforts at Black education also caused another kind of violence—White violence against Black schools, teachers, and students. See Baumgartner, *In Pursuit of Knowledge*; Tubyez Cropper, *What Could Have Been*, video (New Haven, CT: Beinecke Library, Yale University, 2022), at YouTube, https://www.youtube.com/watch?v=gmXF3N620lo. For literacy and rebellion, see Megan Callahan, "'The Dangers' of Literacy: How Literacy Laws in Early America Ensured the Continuation of Slavery and the Oppression of Enslaved Peoples," PhD diss. (State University of New York at Stony Brook, 2020); Rasmussen, "Attended with Great Inconveniences"; Smithsonian American Art Museum, "Literacy as Freedom."
20 "Education in the Southern States," *Harper's Weekly*, November 9, 1867, 706, cited in Smithsonian American Art Museum, "Literacy as Freedom."
21 Juan José Benites and José Policeto Gómez to Francisco Dionisio Vives, 1828, José Augusto Escoto Cuban History and Literature Collection, ca. 1574–1922 (MS span 52), folder 921, Houghton Library, Harvard University, Cambridge, MA.
22 Benites and Gómez to Vives, Escoto Cuban History and Literature Collection.
23 Benites and Gómez to Vives, Escoto Cuban History and Literature Collection.
24 Benites and Gómez to Vives, Escoto Cuban History and Literature Collection.
25 Carlos Manuel Trelles, *Matanzas en la independencia de Cuba* (Havana: Avisador Comercial, 1928), 14; Alain Yacou, *Essor des plantations et subversión antiesclavagiste à Cuba, 1791–1845* (Paris: Karthala, 2010), 256.
26 *Colección de los fallos pronunciados por una sección de la Comisión militar establecida en la ciudad de Matanzas para convocer de la causa de conspiración de la gente de color, etc.* (Matanzas: Imprenta de Gobierno, 1844).
27 Deschamps Chapeaux, *El negro en la economía habanera*, 130; Deschamps Chapeaux, *Los batallones de pardos y morenos libres*, 80–83; Deschamps Chapeaux and Pérez de la Riva, *Contribución a la historia*, 8; Childs, *The 1812 Aponte Rebellion*, 176; Finch, "Repeating Rebellion," 146; Gloria García, *Conspiraciones y revueltas*, 107–113; Reid-Vazquez, *Year of the Lash*, 130; Juan Felipe Risquet, *Rectificaciones: La cuestión político-social en la isla de Cuba* (Havana: Patria, 1900), 140; "Sociedades: La integración de pardos y morenos," *Cuba*, March 1968, 54, at University of Florida Digital Collection, https://ufdcimages.uflib.ufl.edu/AA/00/06/82/06/00071/03%20-%20Marzo%201968.pdf.
28 Childs, *The 1812 Aponte Rebellion*; Ferrer, *Freedom's Mirror*.
29 Lovejoy, *Prieto*; Howard, *Changing History*.
30 Gloria García, *Conspiraciones y revueltas*, 108.
31 Cited in Deschamps Chapeaux, *Los batallones de pardos y morenos libres*, 80, 83.
32 Childs, *1812 Aponte Rebellion*, 98–99.
33 Risquet, *Rectificaciones*, 140. Reid-Vazquez says they were executed (*Year of the Lash*, 46).

34 Alejandro de la Fuente and Ariela J. Gross, *Becoming Free, Becoming Black: Race, Freedom, and Law in Cuba, Virginia, and Louisiana* (New York: Cambridge University Press, 2020), 191; Deschamps Chapeaux, *El negro en la economía habanera*, 131; Risquet, *Rectificaciones*, 139; Rafael Hernández Rodríguez and Dick Cluster, *The History of Havana* (New York: Palgrave Macmillan, 2006), 57; Reid-Vazquez, *Year of the Lash*, 169. Someruelos Street has since been renamed Calle Aponte. Someruelos was the captain general during the Aponte rebellion and the person who ordered Aponte killed. Matthew Norman and Fiona McAuslan, *The Rough Guide to Havana* (London: Rough Guides, 2010), 29.

35 Givens, *Fugitive Pedagogy*, 13; Roberts, *Freedom as Marronage*.

Chapter 3. Racial Segregation in Cuba's First Law for Public Education

1 See Reid-Vazquez, *Year of the Lash*.
2 "Lifting as We Climb" was the motto adopted by the National Association for Colored Women when it was founded in the United States in 1896. Baker, *Anthropology and the Racial Politics of Culture*, 63. Historians of African American education have documented how, for African Americans, education was often a collective endeavor in which Black students and educators were concerned about their own educational and professional journey as well as of how their actions could affect the Black community with which they identified. Anderson, *Education of Blacks in the South*; Fairclough, *Class of Their Own*; Elizabeth Gilmore, *Gender and Jim Crow*; H. Williams, *Self-Taught*.
3 Reid-Vazquez, *Year of the Lash*.
4 Childs, *The 1812 Aponte Rebellion in Cuba*; Finch, *Rethinking Slave Rebellion in Cuba*; Reid-Vazquez, *Year of the Lash*, 98–116; Paquette, *Sugar Is Made with Blood*.
5 "Expediente general de la Insurrección de Cuba. Primera parte: Mando del general Lersundi, 21 de septiembre de 1868 a 4 de enero de 1869," cited in E. Pérez, *Historia de la pedagogía en Cuba*, 235.
6 E. Pérez, *Historia de la pedagogía en Cuba*, 238.
7 Bacardí y Moreau, *Crónicas de Santiago de Cuba* 2:419.
8 Expediente relativo a que se haga obligatoria la instrucción primaria para los niños de seis a diez años de edad, 1880, Instrucción Pública Junta Local de Instrucción 1889–1896, leg. 227, Instrucción Pública, Gobierno Municipal de Santiago de Cuba, Colonia, AHPSC.
9 Sosa Rodríguez and Penabad Félix, *Historia de la educación de Cuba*, 8:111–122; Fitchen, "Primary Education in Colonial Cuba"; Jensen, *Children of Colonial Despotism*; E. Pérez, *Historia de la pedagogia en Cuba*, 231–241.
10 Fitchen, "Primary Education in Colonial Cuba."
11 Gabriela Ossenbach Sauter, "Política educativa española para la isla de Cuba en el siglo XIX (1837–1868)," *Historia de la Educación* 2 (1983), 268–269.
12 Jensen, *Children of Colonial Despotism*; Gillian McGillivray, *Blazing Cane: Sugar Communities, Class, and State Formation in Cuba, 1868–1959* (Durham, NC: Duke University Press, 2009); Paquette, *Sugar Is Made with Blood*.

13 "La instrucción pública en Cuba: Su pasado, su presente," *La Instrucción Primaria: Revista Quincenal* 4, no. 21 (June 1906): 719.
14 "Cuba y Puerto-Rico. 1844-octubre 27. R.O. aprobando el plan general de Instrucción pública para las islas de Cuba y Puerto-Rico," Legislación Ultramarina (Madrid: Spain, Ministerio de Ultramar, 1865), 4:48, at University of Florida Digital Collections, https://ufdc.ufl.edu/AA00080854/00001. The plan also stipulated that slaveholders would teach their slaves, but instruction would be limited to Christian doctrine. See also Sosa Rodríguez and Penabad Félix, *Historia de la Educación en Cuba*, 8:19–22.
15 José Esteban Liras, *Resumen de la legislación de primera enseñanza vigente en la isla de Cuba, 1895* (Havana: La Propagandista, 1895), 13–15. For a small sample of the scholarship on racial segregation and desegregation battles in the public education system in the US context, see Anderson, *Education of Blacks in the South*; Jelani Cobb, "The Failure of Desegregation," *New Yorker*, April 6, 2014; Fairclough, *Class of Their Own*; Carleton Mabee, *Black Education in New York State from Colonial to Modern Times* (Syracuse, NY: Syracuse University Press, 1979).
16 "Cuba y Puerto-Rico. 1844-octubre 27," Legislación Ultramarina, 4:46; Liras, *Resumen de la legislación de primera enseñanza*, viii–ix.
17 Lucia Provencio Garrigós, "Las maestras tituladas: Santiago de Cuba, 1842-1863," *Baluarte* 3 (2002): 49–50; "Cuba y Puerto-Rico. 1844-octubre 27," Legislación Ultramarina, 4:47.
18 Provencio Garrigós, "Las maestras tituladas," 60–62.
19 *Reglamento para la Escuela Normal Elemental bajo la dirección de los pp Escolapios* (Havana: Imprenta del Gobierno y Capitanía General, 1857), at https://archive.org/details/01ReglamentoEscuelaNormal1857/mode/2up
20 Provencio Garrigós, "Las maestras tituladas," 48–49.
21 Aline Helg, "Slave but Not Citizen: Free People of Color and Blood Purity in Colonial Spanish American Legislation" *Millars: Espai i Història* 42, no. 1 (2017): 75–99, http://dx.doi.org/10.6035/Millars.2017.42.4; Martinez-Alier, *Marriage, Class, and Color in Nineteenth-Century Cuba*, 15–18; Marcelo Martínez Alcubilla, *Diccionario de la administración española: Compilación de la novísima legislación de España, peninsular y ultramarina en todos los ramos de la administración pública* (Madrid: Administración, 1892): 890–891, http://books.google.com/books?id=_CIrAQAAMAAJ.
22 David Sartorius, "Colonial Transfusions: Cuban Bodies and Spanish Loyalty in the Nineteenth Century," in *The Cultural Politics of Blood, 1500-1900*, ed. Kimberly Anne Coles, Ralph Bauer, Zita Nunes, and Carla L. Peterson (New York: Palgrave Macmillan, 2015), 232.
23 Thanks to the University of Pittsburgh Press for permission to reproduce my article here. "Es de suponer que los maestros sean de la misma clase: What a Nineteenth-Century Teaching Application Reveals about Race, Power, and Education in Colonial Cuba," by Raquel Alicia Otheguy from *Cuban Studies* 49, ed. Alejandro de la Fuente, © 2020, reprinted by permission of the University of Pittsburgh Press.

24 Expediente sobre profesor de enseñanza al moreno libre José Moreno, 1856, leg. 114, no. 7311, Instrucción Pública, Archivo Nacional de Cuba (hereafter ANC).
25 Expediente sobre profesor de enseñanza al moreno libre José Moreno, ANC.
26 Expediente sobre profesor de enseñanza al moreno libre José Moreno, ANC.
27 Expediente sobre profesor de enseñanza al moreno libre José Moreno, ANC.
28 Expediente sobre profesor de enseñanza al moreno libre José Moreno, ANC.
29 Expediente sobre profesor de enseñanza al moreno libre José Moreno, ANC.
30 Expediente sobre profesor de enseñanza al moreno libre José Moreno, ANC.
31 Expediente sobre profesor de enseñanza al moreno libre José Moreno, ANC.
32 Expediente sobre profesor de enseñanza al moreno libre José Moreno, ANC.
33 Expediente sobre profesor de enseñanza al moreno libre José Moreno, ANC.
34 Vinat de la Mata, "Colores y dolores," 108.
35 Finch, *Rethinking Slave Rebellion in Cuba*, 121, 140, 221–229, conclusion.
36 Andrews, *Afro-Latin America*, 108; Paquette, *Sugar Is Made with Blood*, 106–108. Paquette notes that in 1861, free Blacks were still 15–20 percent of the total population and had doubled in number since 1817, despite the arrival of many enslaved Africans. This was the highest population of free people of color in the Americas, save for Brazil.
37 Finch, *Rethinking Slave Rebellion in Cuba*, 139, 221.
38 "Cartas de Miguel Gualba a Juan Gualberto Gomez," caja 24, exp. 1741, Adquisiciones, ANC.

Chapter 4. The 1878 Order to Build Schools for Children of Color, White Backlash, and the Effect on Black Teachers

1 Ferrer, *Insurgent Cuba*, 93–112; Lanier, *Directorio Central*, 6–7; Louis A. Pérez Jr., *Cuba between Empires, 1878–1902* (Pittsburgh, PA: University of Pittsburgh Press, 1983), chapter 1; Louis A. Pérez Jr., *Cuba between Reform and Revolution*, 96–117; Sartorius, *Ever Faithful*, 128–157.
2 Guía de forasteros, 1880–1884.
3 On Cuban Creoles of all political stripes in this era, see Ferrer, *Insurgent Cuba*; Lillian Guerra, "From Revolution to Involution in the Early Cuban Republic: Conflicts over Race, Class, and Nation, 1902–1906," in *Race and Nation in Modern Latin America*, ed. Nancy P. Appelbaum, Anne S. Macpherson, and Karin Alejandra Rosemblatt (Chapel Hill: University of North Carolina Press, 2003), 132–162; Bonnie Lucero, "Engendering Inequality: Masculinity and Racial Exclusion in Cuba, 1895–1902," PhD diss. (University of North Carolina, 2013); Louis A. Pérez Jr., *Cuba between Empires*.
4 Andrews, *Afro-Latin America*, 113; Ferrer, *Insurgent Cuba*, 49–80.
5 Scott, *Slave Empancipation in Cuba*, 45–126; McGillivray, *Blazing Cane*, chapter 1; Louis A. Pérez Jr., *Cuba between Reform and Revolution*, chapters 5 and 6; Corwin, *Spain and the Abolition of Slavery in Cuba*; Ferrer, *Insurgent Cuba*; Robert Whitney, "The Political Economy of Abolition: The Hispano-Cuban Elite and Cuban Slavery, 1868–1873," *Slavery and Abolition* 13, no. 2 (August 1992): 20–36.

6 Anselmo Alarcia, *Compilación legislativa de primera enseñanza vigente en la isla de Cuba* (Havana: Minerva, 1888), xi-x; José Esteban Liras, *La primera enseñanza en la isla de Cuba* (Havana: Elías Fernández Casona, 1893), xvi–xviii; *Real Decreto estableciendo un nuevo plan de estudios para la isla de Cuba* (Havana: Imprenta del Gobierno y Capitanía General por S.M., 1863), http://bdh-rd.bne.es/viewer.vm?id=0000110595&page=1.
7 For free children of color: "En cada población, según su importancia, se establecerán una o más escuelas para niños de color." For enslaved children: "sobre todo en lo relativo a la parte moral y religiosa."
8 Liras, *La primera enseñanza*, 5–6.
9 Expediente relativo a que se establescan escuelas para niños y niñas de color, 1878–1879, leg. 207, Instrucción Pública, Gobierno Municipal de Santiago de Cuba, Colonia, AHPSC. See also Lanier, *Directorio Central*; Helg, *Our Rightful Share*, 36; Liras, *Resumen de la legislación de primera enseñanza*, 15, 64.
10 Liras, *Resumen de la legislación de primera enseñanza*, 15–65.
11 Expediente relativo a que se establescan escuelas para niños y niñas de color, AHPSC. Lanier suggests that this happens differently; she says that in a November 20, 1878, circular the government also recognized the necessity of free primary education for children of color and recommended that municipal public schools be integrated. In those places where the public resisted such integration, separate free municipal schools should be created (Lanier, *Directorio Central*, 8). The version of the order I have seen is dated December 2, 1878. In his 1895 *Resumen de la legislación de primera enseñanza*, José Esteban Liras also says that in 1878 the central government ordered the admission of children of color into public schools of all kinds—secondary institutions, universities, and other centers of education (15)—but he later goes on to clarify that the November 26, 1878, order required the immediate creation of schools for children of color in each town, warning the city councils that if they couldn't do it quickly, they would have to admit Black children ("negros") in the municipal schools for Whites (64). Risquet appears to coincide with Lanier's interpretation. Risquet cites an 1878 circular by Governor General Martínez Campos recommending that city councils attend to the education of children of color and stating that the government was inclined to racially integrated education, but if that could not be accomplished, then separate schools should be built (Risquet, *Rectificaciones*, 104). I have not seen documentation to support this reading.
12 Expediente relativo a que se establescan escuelas para niños y niñas de color, AHPSC.
13 Ferrer, *Insurgent Cuba*, 99–111.
14 Liras, *Resumen de la legislación de primera enseñanza*, 64.
15 Expediente relativo a que se establescan escuelas para niños y niñas de color, AHPSC.
16 *Guía de forasteros*, 1883, 1884; Liras, *La primera enseñanza*.
17 *Guía de forasteros*, 1859, 1861.
18 *Guía de forasteros*, 1862, 1864, 1865.
19 *Guía de forasteros*, 1873.

20 Liras, *La primera enseñanza*, 12–14, 53–115.
21 Guía de forasteros, 1880–1884; Alfredo Dollero, *Cultura cubana: La provincia de Pinar del Río y su evolución* (Havana: Seoane y Fernández, 1921), 230–231.
22 Guía de forasteros, 1883, 267. For other examples of this kind of mirrored pairing, see the entries for the town of Cimarrones (257) and the town of Sabanilla del Encomendador (267).
23 Dollero, *Cultura cubana*, 230–231.
24 Guía de forasteros, 1880–1883.
25 Orlando García Martínez, *Esclavitud y colonización en Cienfuegos, 1819–1879* (Cienfuegos: Mecenas, 2012); Bonnie Lucero, *A Cuban City, Segregated: Race and Urbanization in the Nineteenth Century* (Tuscaloosa: University of Alabama Press, 2019).
26 Chira, *Patchwork Freedoms*, 17–23; Duharte Jimenez, *El negro en la sociedad colonial*; Knight, *Slave Society in Cuba*, 25–46; Lucero, "En*gendering* Inequality," 107.
27 Burkholder, *African American Dilemma*, 17.
28 Bacardí y Moreau, *Crónicas de Santiago de Cuba* 2:104.
29 Expediente relativo a que se establescan escuelas para niños y niñas de color, AHPSC.
30 Expediente relativo a que se establescan escuelas para niños y niñas de color, AHPSC.
31 Expediente relativo a que se establescan escuelas para niños y niñas de color, AHPSC.
32 Bacardí y Moreau, *Crónicas de Santiago de Cuba*, 2:391.
33 Expediente relativo a que se establescan escuelas para niños y niñas de color, leg. 207, AHPSC.
34 Expediente relativo a la estalación de la Academia de Artesanos, 1886, leg. 207, Instrucción Pública, Gobierno Municipal de Santiago de Cuba, Colonia, AHPSC.
35 Expediente relativo a que se eleve el número y categoría las escuelas Públicas de niños y niñas de color de esta ciudad, 1887, leg. 207, Instrucción Pública, Gobierno Municipal de Santiago de Cuba, Colonia, AHPSC.
36 "Las escuelas municipales y la raza de color," *La Fraternidad*, February 21, 1889.
37 Expediente relativo a la solicitud de Don Manuel Campo y D. Antonio Ferraro pidiendo se creen dos escuelas completas en esta ciudad para niños de color de ambos sexos, 1890, leg. 207, Instrucción Pública, Gobierno Municipal de Santiago de Cuba, Colonia, AHPSC.
38 Expediente relativo a la solicitud de Don Manuel Campo y D. Antonio Ferraro, AHPSC.
39 Actas Capitulares 1878, Fondo Ayuntamiento, Archivo Histórico Provincial de Cienfuegos (hereafter AHPC); Lucero, *Cuban City*, 127.
40 Enrique Edo, *Memoria histórica de Cienfuegos y su jurisdicción*, 3rd ed. (Havana: Úcar, García, 1943), 524–525; Lucero, *Cuban City*, 127.
41 Whitney, "Political Economy of Abolition."
42 García Martínez, *Esclavitud y colonización en Cienfuegos*, 69–74.
43 Actas Capitulares 1880, AHPC; Lucero, *Cuban City*, 127–128.
44 Actas Capitulares 1880, AHPC.

45 Actas Capitulares, 1882, AHPC.
46 Actas Capitulares, 1889, AHPC.
47 Actas Capitulares, 1892, AHPC.
48 Ferrer, *Insurgent Cuba*, 111.
49 Louis A. Pérez Jr., *Cuba between Empires*, 4–18.
50 Leg. 384, no. 22453, Instrucción Pública, ANC; leg. 582, no. 35822, Instrucción Pública, ANC.
51 Michael Zeuske, "Hidden Markers, Open Secrets: On Naming, Race-Marking, and Race-Making in Cuba," *New West Indian Guide* 76, no. 3/4 (2002): 224; Adriana Chira, "Uneasy Intimacies: Race, Family, and Property in Santiago de Cuba, 1803–1868," PhD diss., University of Michigan, 2016, 221–225, https://deepblue.lib.umich.edu/bitstream/handle/2027.42/120651/achira_1.pdf?sequence=1&isAllowed=y.
52 Leg. 680, no. 41358, Instrucción Pública, ANC.
53 Liras, *La primera enseñanza*, 84–115. All of the teachers of schools for children of color named in Cuban writer José Esteban Liras's 1893 compilation of municipal schools are also identified as "Don" or "Doña," but their race is left unmentioned, which suggests they are White. By the 1890s, free people of color had won the right to these honorifics. Liras mentions the racialized status of teachers of color such as Don Antonio Medina, suggesting that he would have done the same for the other teachers had they been people of color (74). In addition, some of the same teachers are listed in the 1884 Guía de forasteros (244), where they also appear with the honorifics, although other teachers, presumably Afro-descendants, are not listed with the honorifics.
54 Guía de forasteros, 1859, 1880–1881; *Boletín eclesiastico del Obispado de la Habana*, vol. 14 (Havana: A. Alvarez, 1893), 599; Heliodoro García Rojas, *San José de las Lajas: Evocaciones del pasado* (Havana: P. Fernández, 1944).
55 Liras, *La primera enseñanza*; Guía de forasteros, 1883.
56 *Directorio y guía para los maestros cubanos* (Cambridge, MA: E. W. Wheeler, 1900), at Harvard University Archives, Records of the Cuban Summer School, https://iiif.lib.harvard.edu/manifests/view/drs:493672069$5i; Guía de forasteros, 1881–1883.
57 Bacardí y Moreau, *Crónicas de Santiago de Cuba*, 6:391.
58 Guía de forasteros, 1883, 254; Guía de forasteros, 1884, 238. In the 1883 report, Gumersindo Franquis is identified as *pardo*, a free mulato, and Caridad Franquis is identified as *morena*, a free Black woman. In the 1884 report, they are both notably listed without an honorific, while teachers for children of White schools and teachers in schools for children of color in other towns are listed with the honorifics, suggesting their Whiteness. Caridad Gispert is also identified as a morena in the September 1878 issue of the *Gaceta de la Habana* in an article regarding her application for a property that had been abandoned by its owner, who had returned to the peninsula; the property on the corner of Calle Real and Calle Sol in Bejucal was in bad shape. It's possible this became the location of her school. Caridad Gispert outlived her husband, and in 1931 she owned a house at 28 Calle Cespedes that she was trying to sell. "Aviso," *Gaceta Oficial*, October 2, 1931.
59 Liras, *La primera enseñanza*, 53–54.

60 Guía de forasteros, 1865–1866, 222–234. They are all listed with the honorific *don*, which would not have been granted to Afro-descended men in the 1860s.
61 Burkholder, *African American Dilemma*, 19.
62 Jorge Castellanos and Isabel Castellanos, *Cultura afrocubana*, vol. 2 (Miami: Universal, 1990), 257–261; Ferrer, *Insurgent Cuba*, 129; Lucero, *Cuban City*, 85, 118–126; leg. 887, no. 53203, Instrucción Pública, ANC.
63 Leg. 887, no. 53203, Instrucción Pública, ANC.
64 *Estudios afrocubanos*: Revista Editada por la Sociedad de Estudios Afrocubanos 1 (1937): 146–147.

Chapter 5. Black Teachers, Sociedades de Color, and Separate Schools

1 Victoria María Sueiro Rodríguez, "Composición social y caracterización de las principales sociedades culturales y de instrucción y recreo en la región de Cienfuegos entre 1840 y 1899," *Espacio, Tiempo y Forma*, 5, no. 11 (1998): 329–330, https://doi.org/10.5944/etfv.11.1998.2950; Alfonso Quiroz, "La reforma educacional en Cuba, 1898–1909: Cambio y continuidad," in *Culturas encontradas: Cuba y los Estados Unidos*, ed. Rafael Hernandez and John H. Coatsworth (Cambridge, MA: Harvard University Press, 2001), 113–126.
2 Joan Casanovas, *Bread, or Bullets! Urban Labor and Spanish Colonialism in Cuba, 1850–1898* (Pittsburgh, PA: University of Pittsburgh Press, 1998), 69; Sueiro Rodríguez, "Composición social," 330.
3 Lanier, *Directorio Central*, 7; Sueiro Rodríguez, "Composición social," 337.
4 David T. Beito, *From Mutual Aid to the Welfare State: Fraternal Societies and Social Services, 1890–1967* (Chapel Hill: University of North Carolina Press, 2000); Sueiro Rodríguez, "Composición social," 329. For the labor movement and education, see Casanovas, *Bread, or Bullets!*, 83–85; Sueiro Rodríguez, "Composición social," 330; Araceli Tinajero, *El Lector: A History of the Cigar Factory Reader* (Austin: University of Texas Press, 2010), part 1.
5 Carleton Mabee, "Control by Blacks over Schools in New York State, 1830–1930," *Phylon* 40, no. 1 (1979): 29–40, https://doi.org/10.2307/274420; Burkholder, *An African American Dilemma*, 19.
6 Baumgartner, *In Pursuit of Knowledge*, 88. See also Burkholder, *An African American Dilemma*, 32; Prithi Kanakamedala, *Brooklynites: The Remarkable Story of the Free Black Communities That Shaped a Borough* (New York: NYU Press, 2024), 89–99.
7 Vinat de la Mata, "Colores y dolores," 115.
8 "Eulogia Pérez, viuda de Rosa," *El Album Cenfoguense: Revista Quincenal* 1, no. 5 (April 12, 1903): 1, Biblioteca Provincial de Cienfuegos Roberto García Valde, Cienfuegos, Cuba.
9 "Eulogia Pérez, viuda de Rosa," *El Album Cenfoguense*.
10 "Eulogia Pérez, viuda de Rosa," *El Album Cenfoguense*; *Directorio y guía para los maestros cubanos*, 42; "Notas quincenales," *Minerva: Revista Quincenal Dedicada a la Mujer de Color*, February 28, 1889; Guía de forasteros, 1883. The Cienfuegos

newspaper names her as Eulogia Pérez vda. [widow] de Rosa; the Guía de forasteros of 1883 has her as Eulogia Pérez and identifies her as parda; Minerva names her as Eduviges Pérez de Rosa, and the Harvard records have her as Sra. E. Pérez de Rosa.
11 Edo, *Memoria histórica de Cienfuegos*, 577–578.
12 "Vicente Silveira," *EcuRed*, https://www.ecured.cu/Vicente_Silveira. Her school only appears in the 1883 Guía de forasteros.
13 María Alejandra Aguilar Dornelles, "Heroísmo y conciencia racial en la obra de la poeta afrocubana Cristina Ayala," *Meridional: Revista Chilena de Estudios Latinoamericanos*, no. 7 (2016): 179+.
14 Guía de forasteros, 1862, 1863.
15 Guía de forasteros, 1884.
16 "Notas quincenales," *Minerva*, February 28, 1889.
17 Lucero, *Cuban City*, 127; Guía de forasteros, 1880–1881.
18 "Enseñanza primaria," *La Fraternidad*, August 31, 1888, Biblioteca Nacional José Martí, Havana.
19 Lanier, *Directorio Central*; Carmen V. Montejo Arrechea, *Sociedades de instrucción y recreo de pardos y morenos que existieron en Cuba colonial, período 1878–1898* (Veracruz, Mexico: Instituto Veracruzano de Cultura, 1993); Quiroz, "Free Association and Civil Society in Cuba"; Howard, *Changing History*; Rafael E. Tarragó, "Afro-Cuban Identity and the Black Press in Spanish Cuba, 1878–1898," in *Latin American Identities: Race, Ethnicity, Gender, and Sexuality*, Papers of the Forty-Sixth Annual Meeting of the Seminar on the Acquisition of Latin American Library Materials (SALALM) (Tempe, AZ: SALALM, 2001).
20 Elizabeth McHenry, "'Dreaded Eloquence': The Origins and Rise of African American Literary Societies and Libraries," *Harvard Library Bulletin* 6, no. 2 (Summer 1995): 32–56.
21 La Bella Unión, leg. 100, no. 4672, Gobierno General, ANC.
22 La Unión Fraternal, leg. 427, no. 13443, ANC.
23 Unión y Fraternidad, Registro de Asociaciones, ANC.
24 La Igualdad, leg. 99, no. 4663, Gobierno General, ANC; La Igualdad, leg. 100, no. 4663, Gobierno General, ANC.
25 La Igualdad, caja 1, exp. 13, Colonia, Registro de Asociaciones, AHPC; La Amistad, caja 1, exp. 15, Colonia, Registro de Asociaciones, AHPC.
26 Bacardí y Moreau, *Crónicas de Santiago de Cuba*, 7:200.
27 Bacardí y Moreau, *Crónicas de Santiago de Cuba*, 7:317, http://ufdc.ufl.edu/AA00062763/00006
28 Vinat de la Mata, "Colores y dolores," 115; "Notas Quincenales," *Minerva: Revista Quincenal Dedicada a la Mujer de Color*, January and July 1889.
29 "Notas Quincenales," *Minerva: Revista Quincenal Dedicada a la Mujer de Color*, January and July 1889.
30 Divina Caridad, leg. 435, no. 14640, Registro de Asociaciones, ANC.
31 El Buen Suceso, leg. 430, no. 13514, Asociaciones, ANC.
32 La Unión Fraternal, leg. 427, no. 13443, Registro de Asociaciones ANC.

33 Bella Unión Habanera, leg. 1336, no. 27343, Registro de Asociaciones, ANC.
34 *La Igualdad*, leg. 618, no. 17084, Registro de Asociaciones, ANC.
35 La Igualdad and El Progreso records, caja 1, exp. 13, AHPC; La Amistad, caja 1, exp. 15, AHPC.
36 Sartorius, *Ever Faithful*, 134.
37 Lucero, *Cuban City*, 126–127; La Igualdad, caja 1, exp. 13, AHPC; Sartorius, *Ever Faithful*, 147–148; Edo, *Memoria histórica de Cienfuegos*, 577–578.
38 Guía de forasteros, 1883, 275.
39 La Unión Fraternal, leg. 427, no. 13443, Asociaciones, Archivo Nacional de Cuba, Havana.
40 Bella Unión Habanera, ANC.
41 Divina Caridad, leg. 391, no. 11699, Registro de Asociaciones, ANC.
42 "Notas quincenales," *Minerva*, January 26, 1889.
43 Sartorius, *Ever Faithful*, 131.
44 Anderson, *Education of Blacks in the South*, 156, 170, 179, 181, 183–185.
45 Unión y Fraternidad, ANC.
46 La Unión Fraternal, leg. 427, no. 13443, Registro de Asociaciones, ANC.
47 *El Liceo*, leg. 416, no. 12158, Registro de Asociaciones, ANC.
48 Bella Unión Habanera, leg. 1336, no. 27343, Asociaciones, ANC.
49 Edo, *Memoria histórica de Cienfuegos*, 589.
50 *La Igualdad*, caja 1, exp. 13, AHPC; La Amistad, caja 1, exp. 15, AHPC.
51 Unión y Fraternidad, ANC.
52 Justo Legido, "Reformas que exige nuestra primera enseñanza," *La Fraternidad*, August 21, 1888.
53 Bella Unión Habanera, ANC.
54 Burkholder, *African American Dilemma*, 15.
55 Burkholder, *African American Dilemma*, 19.
56 Baumgartner, *In Pursuit of Knowledge*, 87, 109, 124.
57 Sueiro Rodríguez, "Composición social," 335.
58 Actas Capitulares, 1883, Fondo Ayuntamiento, AHPC; Sartorius, *Ever Faithful*, 145; Edo, *Memoria histórica de Cienfuegos*, 589.
59 Actas Capitulares, 1886, Fondo Ayuntamiento, AHPC; Sartorius, *Ever Faithful*, 146.
60 Actas Capitulares, 1884, Fondo Ayuntamiento, AHPC.
61 "Eulogia Perez, viuda de Rosa," *Album Cenfoguense: Revista Quincenal* 1, no. 5 (April 12, 1903).
62 Actas Capitulares, 1887, Fondo Ayuntamiento, AHPC.
63 Actas Capitulares, 1887–1891, Fondo Ayuntamiento, AHPC.
64 Lucero, *Cuban City*, 127.

Chapter 6. The Directorio Central de las Sociedades de la Raza de Color and the 1890s Campaign for Equal School Rights

1 "Cuestión Importante," *La Igualdad*, September 21, 1893.
2 Octavio R. Costa, *Juan Gualberto Gómez: Una vida sin sombra* (Miami: La Moderna

Poesía, 1950); Alejandro de la Fuente, *A Nation for All*; Ferrer, *Insurgent Cuba*; Helg, *Our Rightful Share*.
3. Lanier, *Directorio Central*, 24–27; Pappademos, *Black Political Activism in Cuba*, 125; Sartorius, *Ever Faithful*, 197–199.
4. Lanier, *Directorio Central*, 13–15.
5. "Aceptado," *La Igualdad*, August 1, 1893.
6. Ferrer, *Insurgent Cuba*, 129.
7. "Colegio de Señoritas," *La Igualdad*, February 24, 1894.
8. "Asamblea de las Sociedades de Color," *Patria*, no. 27, September 10, 1892.
9. Lanier, *Directorio Central*, 43; Memorias Presentadas a la Asamblea de Delegados de Sociedades de la raza de color, celebrada en la Habana en 1892, leg. 74, no. 4303–4305, Adquisiciones, ANC.
10. Leg. 74, no. 4304, Adquisiciones, ANC.
11. Leg. 74, no. 4303, Adquisiciones, ANC.
12. "Memoria de 'El Fénix de Trinidad,'" and "Memoria presentada a nombre de las sociedades Club de Oriente, Alcázar Antillano, de Santiago de Oriente," leg. 74, exp. 4303, Adquisiciones, ANC.
13. Leg. 74, no. 4303, Adquisiciones, ANC.
14. Leg. 74, no. 4304, Adquisiciones, ANC.
15. "Cuestión importante," *La Igualdad*, September 21, 1893.
16. "Dicatmen de la Comision del 1er Tema," leg. 74, no. 4304, Adquisiciones, ANC.
17. Frederick Douglass, March 1859, quoted in Zoë Burkholder, *African American Dilemma*, 9.
18. Leg. 74, no. 4303, Adquisiciones, ANC.
19. "Asamblea de las Sociedades de Color," *Patria*, no. 27, September 10, 1892.
20. Leg. 74, no. 4303, Adquisiciones, ANC.
21. Leg. 74, no. 4303, Adquisiciones, ANC.
22. "Memoria presentada a nombre de las sociedades 'Club de Oriente,' 'Alcázar Antillano,' de Santiago de Cuba," leg. 74, no. 4303, Adquisiciones, ANC.
23. "Memoria de 'El Fénix de Trinidad," leg. 74, no. 4303, Adquisiciones, ANC.
24. "Memoria de 'El Fénix de Trinidad,'" ANC.
25. Albert Gardner Robinson, *Cuba and the Intervention* (New York: Longmans, Green, 1905), 490.
26. "Memoria, 'El Casino de Artesanos de Holguín,'" leg. 74, exp. 4303, Adquisiciones, ANC.
27. "La instrucción como todos sabéis es la fuente donde el hombre bebe la sabia fructífera y vivicante de la libertad; ningún hombre instruido e ilustrado, fácilmente tolera las anomalías que el capricho a la suerte aciaga de un semejante, escudado con los cúmulos de circunstancia que lo favorezcan, establece como principio irrechazable la supeditación de *uno* sobre *otro*. Con la ilustración, desaparecerá el temor que decimos el temor desaparece la posibilidad de que, por muy poderoso, por muy protegido, de la suerte—siempre varía—que sea un hombre o un pueblo, intente dominar, negar el derecho a la libertad a aquel mismo hombre, su semejante,

a aquel mismo pueblo, su emulo." Enrique Cos and José L. Quesada, "Memoria, 'El Casino de Artesanos de Holguín,'" ANC.

28. Leg. 74, no. 4304, ANC.
29. "Cuestión Importante," *La Igualdad*, September 21, 1893.
30. "Cuestión Importante," *La Igualdad*, September 21, 1893.
31. "Parte Oficial," *Gaceta de la Habana*, leg. 887, no. 53203, Instrucción Pública, ANC.
32. "Parte Oficial," *Gaceta de la Habana*, ANC.
33. "Parte Oficial," *Gaceta de la Habana*, ANC.
34. "Parte Oficial," *Gaceta de la Habana*, ANC.
35. "Orden Público y Policia," *Gaceta de la Habana*, December 19, 1893, vol. 2, 1235–1236, leg. 887, no. 53203, Instrucción Pública, ANC.
36. "Reunión del Directorio," *La Igualdad*, December 16, 1893.
37. "Las resoluciones," *La Igualdad*, December 23, 1893.
38. Estinslao de Antonio, "Instrucción pública," *Gaceta de la Habana*, December 16, 1893, leg. 887, no. 53203, Instrucción Pública, ANC; *Estudios afrocubanos*, vol. 1 (1937): 146–147.
39. University of Havana rector to the three presidents of the Provincial Commissions of Public Education for Havana, Pinar del Río, Matanzas, Santa Clara, and Puerto Principe, leg. 887, no. 53203, Instrucción Pública, ANC.
40. "Notable circular," *La Igualdad*, January 4, 1894.
41. Roman Otero, Provincial Commission of Public Education of Santa Clara, to the Rector of the University of Havana, leg. 887, no. 53203, Instrucción Pública, ANC.
42. "Nuestro triunfo," *La Igualdad*, December 14, 1893 (originally misprinted as 1892).
43. "Nuestro triunfo," *La Igualdad*.
44. "Nuestro triunfo," *La Igualdad*.
45. "Carta del Sr. Labra," *La Igualdad*, December 26, 1893.
46. Ferrer, *Insurgent Cuba*, 130; Lanier, *Directorio Central*, 58–59.
47. Lanier, *Directorio Central*, 60.
48. "En El Regional," *La Igualdad*, December 26, 1893.
49. "La Consigna," *La Igualdad*, January 6, 1894.
50. "Así se hace," *La Igualdad*, January 18, 1894.
51. "Provocación," *La Igualdad*, January 2, 1894.
52. Gobierno General to king of Spain, December 8, 1894, leg. 887, no. 53203, ANC.
53. Rector to Captain General, leg. 887, no. 53203, Instrucción Pública, ANC.
54. "Nuestro triunfo," *La Igualdad*, December 14, 1893.
55. "Reunión del Directorio," *La Igualdad*, December 16, 1893.
56. "Reunión del Directorio," *La Igualdad*, December 16, 1893.
57. "Lo que procede," *La Igualdad*, January 2, 1894.
58. "El General Calleja," *La Igualdad*, January 2, 1894.
59. "La Consigna," *La Igualdad*, January 6, 1894; "Lo de Matanzas," *La Igualdad*, January 25, 1894.
60. "Cuestión importante," *La Igualdad*, September 21, 1893.
61. "Lo que procede," *La Igualdad*, April 26, 1894.
62. "Lo que procede," *La Igualdad*, April 26, 1894.

63 "Lo de Cienfuegos," *La Igualdad*, January 6, 1894.
64 "Escuelas municipales," *La Igualdad*, January 4, 1894.
65 *La Protesta* is cited in "Lo que dice la prensa," *La Igualdad*, December 26, 1893.
66 "Cuestión importante," *La Igualdad*, September 21, 1893.
67 "Opinión valiosa," *La Igualdad*, January 16, 1894.
68 "Lo que procede," *La Igualdad*, April 26, 1894.
69 Sartorius, *Ever Faithful*, 10.
70 "Escuelas municipales," *La Igualdad*, January 4, 1894.
71 "Escuelas municipales," *La Igualdad*.
72 "Escuelas municipales," *La Igualdad*.
73 "Cuestión importante," *La Igualdad*.
74 "Escuelas municipales," *La Igualdad*.
75 "Escuelas municipales," *La Igualdad*.

Chapter 7. "No Division by Color"

1 Ferrer, *Cuba: An American History*, 129–185; Louis A. Pérez Jr., *Cuba between Reform and Revolution*, 118–144.
2 Ferrer, *Insurgent Cuba*; Ferrer, *Cuba: An American History*; Philip S. Foner, *The Spanish-Cuban-American War and the Birth of American Imperialism, 1895–1902* (New York: Monthly Review Press, 1972), 2:672; Lucero, *Cuban City*; Lucero, *Revolutionary Masculinity*; Louis Pérez, *Cuba between Empires*; Emilio Roig de Leuchsenring, *La lucha cubana por la república, contra la anexión y la Enmienda Platt* (Havana: Oficina del Historiador de la Ciudad de La Habana, Colección Histórica Cubana Americana, 1952); Michael Zeuske, "'Los negros hicimos la independencia': Aspectos de la movilización afrocubana en un hinterland cubano; Cienfuegos entre colonia y república," in *Espacios, silencios y los sentidos de la libertad: Cuba entre 1878 y 1912*, ed. Fernando Martínez Heredia, Rebecca J. Scott, and Orlando F. García Martínez (Havana: Unión, 2001), 193–234.
3 Robert Lawrence Packard, Education in the Philippines, Cuba, Porto Rico, Hawaii, and Samoa, cited in US War Department, *Report on the Census of Cuba, 1899* (Washington, DC: Government Printing Office, 1900), 581.
4 Erwin Epstein, "The Peril of Paternalism: The Imposition of Education on Cuba by the United States," *American Journal of Education* 96, no. 1 (November 1987): 1–23; Foner, *Spanish-Cuban-American War*; Bonnie Lucero, "Civilization before Citizenship: Education, Racial Order, and the Material Culture of Female Domesticity in American-Occupied Cuba, 1899–1902," *Journal of Atlantic Studies* 12, no. 1 (2015): 26–49; Louis Pérez, "Imperial Design"; Louis Pérez, *Cuba between Empire*, 271.
5 Nancy P. Appelbaum, Anne S. Macpherson, and Karin Alejandra Rosemblatt, eds., *Race and Nation in Modern Latin America* (Chapel Hill: University of North Carolina Press, 2003); Alejandra Bronfman, *Measures of Equality: Social Science, Citizenship, and Race in Cuba, 1902–1940* (Chapel Hill: University of North Carolina Press, 2003); de la Fuente, *A Nation for All*, 40–42.
6 US War Department, *Report on the Census of Cuba, 1899*, 67, 100.
7 US War Department, *Report on the Census of Cuba, 1899*, 80–81, 96–97.

8 US War Department, *Report on the Census of Cuba, 1899*, 101.
9 US War Department, *Report on the Census of Cuba, 1899*, 148–150. Carlos Newland cites a higher literacy rate in Argentina (45.6 percent) in 1895 and a slightly lower rate in Chile (30.5 percent) in 1885, pointing out that together with Cuba, these countries had higher literacy rates because they saw a wave of European immigration at the end of the nineteenth century. Overall, the literacy rate in Latin America was 27 percent by 1900, so Cuba, Argentina, and Chile had above-average literacy rates for Latin America. Newland, "La educación elemental en Hispanoamérica," 357–361.
10 US War Department, *Report on the Census of Cuba, 1899*, 102, 152–153, 164.
11 Alejandro de la Fuente, *A Nation for All*; 56–60; Louis Pérez, *Cuba between Reform and Revolution*, 140–142.
12 US War Department, *Report on the Census of Cuba, 1899*, 585–615.
13 Mercedes García Tudurí, "La enseñanza en Cuba en los primeros cincuenta años de independencia," in *Historia de la nación cubana*, ed. Ramiro Guerra y Sánchez, José M. Pérez Cabrera, and Juan J. Remos (Havana: Historia de la Nación Cubana, 1952), 10–68; Enrique José Varona y Pera, *La instrucción pública en Cuba* (Havana: Rambla y Bouza, 1901), 19–22.
14 Epstein, "Peril of Paternalism," 4.
15 "3,313 Schools Open in Cuba," *New York Times*, September 22, 1900, 6. Despite the United States' actions and triumphant representation of its accomplishments in education, some scholars argue that the US empire's attempt at establishing educational structures abroad ultimately failed. See Sarah D. Manekin, "Spreading the Empire of Free Education, 1865–1905," PhD diss., University of Pennsylvania, 2009.
16 To Honorable Secretary of the Interior, June 2, 1899, entry 3, box 25, 1899: 4581–4798, record group (RG) 140, US National Archives and Records Administration (hereafter NARA).
17 C. M. Borrero, no. 339. "Carta a Borrero, subsecretario de Instrucción pública, pidiendole trabajo," 1899, Biblioteca Nacional; C. M. Borrero, no. 315, "Carta a Borrero felicitándolo por su nombramiento de SubSecretaría de Instrucción Pública," 1900, Biblioteca Nacional; C. M. Borrero, no. 250, "Cartas dirigidas a Esteban Borrero de diversas personas relacionadas con su cargo de Subsecretario de Instrucción Pública," 1900, Biblioteca Nacional; C. M. Borrero, "A mis compañeros y amigos los maestros de escuela de la Isla de Cuba. Habana, noviembre 10 de 1899," no. 354, *La Instrucción Pública*, Biblioteca Nacional; C. M. Borrero, "'Asuntos escolares.' Carta a María Teresa Arruebarrena con motivo de su matrimonio con Mr. Frye," no. 329, 1901, Biblioteca Nacional; C. M. Borrero, "Carta a. E. Frye sobre el Manual para Maestros de Instrucción Primaria," no. 273, Biblioteca Nacional.
18 Louis A. Pérez Jr., *Cuba between Empires*, 290.
19 Mario J. Minichino, "In Our Image: The Attempted Reshaping of the Cuban Educational System by the United States Government, 1898–1912" (PhD diss., University of South Florida, 2014), 152–155.
20 José Antonio González Lanuza to Major General John R. Brooke, October 20, 1899, entry 3, box 32, 1899, 5862–5983, RG 140, NARA.

21 María de los Ángeles Meriño Fuentes, *Gobierno municipal y partidos políticos en Santiago de Cuba, 1898–1912* (Santiago, Cuba: Santiago, 2001).
22 Marial Iglesias Utset, *A Cultural History of Cuba during the U.S. Occupation, 1898–1902*, trans. Russ Davidson (Chapel Hill: University of North Carolina Press, 2011); 10–13.
23 Report of Public Schools in City of Matanzas, Cuba, entry 3, box 9, 2303–2483, RG 140, NARA.
24 School Inspection Reports, entry 3, box 87, RG 140, NARA.
25 Inspection Reports for Santiago de Cuba Province, entry 3, box 62, RG 140, NARA.
26 Inspection Reports for Santiago de Cuba Province, NARA.
27 Reports on Schools, entry 102, box 2, RG 140, NARA.
28 Lucero, "Civilization before Citizenship," 9–13.
29 See, for example, *La Instrucción Primaria: Revista Quincenal*, no. 1 (August 10, 1902): 23.
30 Alfonso Quiroz, "Martí in Cuban Schools," in *The Cuban Republic and José Martí: Reception and Uses of a National Symbol*, ed. Mauricio Font and Alfonso Quiroz (New York: Lexington, 2006), 71–81.
31 Eduardo F. Pla, *Educación de la democracia* (Havana: P. Fernández, 1904).
32 Cuba, Convención constituyente, *Diario de Sesiones de la Convención Constituyente de la isla de Cuba* (Havana: La Convención, 1901), at University of Florida Digital Collections, https://ufdc.ufl.edu/UF00072606/00001/images.
33 *La Instrucción Primaria: Revista Quincenal*, vols. 1–6, 1902–1908; US War Department, *Report on the Census of Cuba, 1899*, 565–620; Cuba, Oficina Nacional del Censo, Victor H. Olmsted, and Henry Gannett, *Cuba: Population, History, and Resources, 1907* (Washington, DC: US Bureau of the Census, 1909), 246–249, at Library of Congress https://lccn.loc.gov/09035394.
34 *La Instrucción Primaria* 4, no. 1 (August 10, 1905): 9.
35 In September 1905, students of color attended at the same rates of matriculation (~75 percent of matriculated students attending) as White students as well as being matriculated proportionally to their share of the population. *La Instrucción Primaria* 4, no. 4 (September 1905): 456.
36 *La Instrucción Primaria* 1, no. 2 (August 25, 1902): 81.
37 The documents of the Secretaría de Instrucción Pública for the republican period are missing from Cuban archives.
38 *La Instrucción Primaria* 4, no. 16 (March 25, 1906): 545.
39 *Censo de la República de Cuba bajo la administración provisional de los estados unidos* (Washington, DC: Oficina del Censo de los Estados Unidos, 1908), 148–150, at Schomburg Center for Research in Black Culture, New York Public Library.
40 Oilda Martínez, Zoom interview with the author, June 7, 2022.
41 Martínez y Díaz, *Historia de la educación pública en Cuba*.
42 *La Instrucción Primaria* 1, no. 1 (August 10, 1902): 24.
43 Pappademos, *Black Political Activism in Cuba*, 64–91.
44 Castillo Bueno, *Reyita*, 55–56.

Epilogue

1 De la Fuente, *A Nation for All*, 141–147; Lisa Jarvinen, "The 'School Question' in an Imperial Context: Education and Religion during and Following the Occupations of Cuba and Puerto Rico," *History of Education Quarterly* 62 (2022): 84–106; Laurie Johnston, "Cuban Nationalism and Responses to Private Education in Cuba, 1902–1958," in *Ideologues and Ideologies in Latin America*, ed. Will Fowler (Westport, CT: Greenwood, 1997), 27–44; Quiroz, "La reforma educacional en Cuba"; Jason Yaremko, "The Path of Progress: Protestant Missions, Education, and U.S. Hegemony in the New Cuba, 1898–1940," in *American Post-Conflict Educational Reform: From the Spanish American War to Iraq*, ed. Noah W. Sobe (New York: Palgrave Macmillan, 2009), 53–74.

2 Danzie León et al., *Apuntes cronológicos*; Helg, *Our Rightful Share*, 146–226; Pappademos, *Black Political Activism*, 55–62.

3 Johnston, "Cuban Nationalism and Responses to Private Education in Cuba," 27–44.

4 Brunson, *Black Women, Citizenship, and the Making of Modern Cuba*, 98; Crumdy, "Teaching Revolution"; Oilda Martinez, Zoom interview with the author, June 7, 2022.

5 De la Fuente, *A Nation for All*, 260.

6 Benson, *Antiracism in Cuba*, 2–21; Danielle Pilar Clealand, *The Power of Race in Cuba: Racial Ideology and Black Consciousness during the Revolution* (New York: Oxford University Press, 2017); de la Fuente, *A Nation for All*, 275, 309; Esteban Morales Domínguez, *Race in Cuba* (New York: Monthly Review Press, 2013); Schultz, "Liberal Moment of the Revolution."

7 Benson, *Antiracism in Cuba*, 198–221.

8 Benson, *Antiracism in Cuba*, 96–101.

9 On race in contemporary Cuba, see Randal C. Archibold, "Inequality Becomes More Visible in Cuba as Economy Shifts," *New York Times*, February 24, 2015, https://www.nytimes.com/2015/02/25/world/americas/as-cuba-shifts-toward-capitalism-inequality-grows-more-visible.html; Benson, Rubiera Castillo, and Martiatu Terry, *Afrocubanas*; Clealand, *Power of Race in Cuba*; Alejandro de la Fuente, "Race and Income Inequality in Contemporary Cuba," *NACLA Report on the Americas* 44, no. 4 (July–August 2011), 30–33, 43, https://nacla.org/article/race-and-income-inequality-contemporary-cuba; Andy S. Gomez and Paul Webster Hare, "How Education Shaped Communist Cuba," *The Atlantic*, February 26, 2015, http://www.theatlantic.com/education/archive/2015/02/how-education-shaped-communist-cuba/386192/; Katrin Hansing, "Race and Inequality in the New Cuba: Reasons, Dynamics, and Manifestations," *Social Research: An International Quarterly* 84, no. 2 (2017): 331–349; Morales Domínguez, *Race in Cuba*; Roberto Zurbano, "For Blacks in Cuba, the Revolution Hasn't Begun," *New York Times*, March 23, 2013, https://www.nytimes.com/2013/03/24/opinion/sunday/for-blacks-in-cuba-the-revolution-hasnt-begun.html. For race and Cuban schools, see Blum, *Cuban Youth and Revolutionary Values*; Crumdy, "Teaching Revolution"; Erik Gleibermann, "Where Hip-

Hop Fits in Cuba's Anti-Racist Curriculum," *The Atlantic*, August 1, 2016, https://www.theatlantic.com/education/archive/2016/08/where-hip-hop-fits-in-cubas-anti-racist-curriculum/493682/; B. Denise Hawkins, "In Cuba, African Roots Run Deep, but it's a Lesson Students Aren't Learning in the Classroom," *NBC News*, September 1, 2017, https://www.nbcnews.com/news/nbcblk/cuba-african-roots-run-deep-it-s-lesson-students-aren-n767616.

10 Matthew F. Delmont, *Why Busing Failed: Race, Media, and the National Resistance to School Desegregation* (Oakland: University of California Press, 2016); Erickson, *Making the Unequal Metropolis*; Nicole Hannah Jones, "The Problem We All Live With," *This American Life*, episode 562, July 31, 2015, https://www.thisamericanlife.org/562/the-problem-we-all-live-with-part-one; Gary Orfield, Erica Frankenerg, Jongyeon Ee, and Jennifer B. Ayscue, "Harming Our Common Future: America's Segregated Schools 65 Years after Brown," Civil Rights Project—Proyecto Derecho Civiles at UCLA, May 10, 2019, University of California, Los Angeles, https://www.civilrightsproject.ucla.edu/research/k-12-education/integration-and-diversity/harming-our-common-future-americas-segregated-schools-65-years-after-brown/Brown-65-050919v4-final.pdf; Jeanne Theoharis, *A More Beautiful and Terrible History: The Uses and Misuses of Civil Rights History* (Boston: Beacon, 2018); Vanessa Siddle Walker, "Brown and Its Impact on Schools and American Life," *American Bar Association Focus on Law Studies* 19 (2004): 1–17; Vanessa Siddle Walker, "Second-Class Integration: A Historical Perspective for a Contemporary Agenda," *Harvard Educational Review* 79, no. 2 (2009): 269–284.

BIBLIOGRAPHY

Archival Collections and Libraries

Archivo Histórico Provincial Cienfuegos (AHPC), Cienfuegos, Cuba
  Actas Capitulares, Fondo Ayuntamiento
  Protocoles Notoriales
  Registro de Asociaciones
Archivo Histórico Provincial de Santiago de Cuba (AHPSC), Santiago, Cuba
  Gobierno Municipal, Colonia
Archivo Nacional de la República de Cuba (ANC), Havana
  Adquisiciones
  Audiencia de la Habana
  Donativos y Remisiones
  Especial
  Gobierno General
  Instrucción Pública
  Registro de Asociaciones
  Secretaría de la Presidencia
Biblioteca Nacional José Martí, Havana
  Manuscritos Borrero
  Manuscritos Escoto
  Manuscritos Sociedad Económica de Amigos del País
  Periodicals
Biblioteca Provincial de Cienfuegos Roberto García Valdés, Cienfuegos, Cuba
Centro de Información para la Educación, Havana
Escoto, José Augusto, Cuban History and Literature Collection, Houghton Library, Harvard University
Folks, Homer, Collection, Columbia University, New York
Fondos Raros y Valiosos, Biblioteca Provincial de Santiago de Cuba Elvira Cape, Santiago, Cuba
Instituto de Literatura y Lingüística José A. Portuondo, Havana
Latin American Pamphlet Collection, Houghton Library, Harvard University
Library of Congress Manuscripts Division, Washington, DC

Cuban Educational Association Papers
Rodríguez, José Ignacio, Papers
Wilson, James Harrison, Papers
Wood, Leonard, Papers
Massachusetts Historical Society, Boston
New-York Historical Society, New York
Schomburg Center for Research in Black Culture, New York Public Library
US National Archives and Records Administration (NARA)
Record groups 48, 60, 140, 199, 350, College Park, MD
Record group 395, Washington, DC

Secondary Sources

Adelman, Jeremy. *Sovereignty and Revolution in the Iberian Atlantic*. Princeton, NJ: Princeton University Press, 2006.
Agüero, Pedro de. *La instrucción pública en la isla de Cuba*. Havana: El Iris, 1867.
Aguilar Dornelles, María Alejandra. "Heroísmo y conciencia racial en la obra de la poeta afrocubana Cristina Ayala." *Meridional: Revista Chilena de Estudios Latinoamericanos*, no. 7 (2016): 179+.
Aguilera-Manzano, José María. "The Role of Higher Education Reform in the Construction of Cuban Identity." *Latin Americanist* 54, no. 2 (2010): 95–111.
Alarcia, Anselmo. *Compilación legislativa de primera enseñanza vigente en la isla de Cuba*. Havana: Minerva, 1888.
Alberto, Paulina L. *Terms of Inclusion: Black Intellectuals in Twentieth-Century Brazil*. Chapel Hill: University of North Carolina Press, 2011.
Alberto, Paulina Laura, George Reid Andrews, and Jesse Hoffnung-Garskof, eds. *Voices of the Race: Black Newspapers in Latin America, 1870–1960*. New York: Cambridge University Press, 2022.
Anderson, James D. *The Education of Blacks in the South, 1860–1935*. Chapel Hill: University of North Carolina Press, 1988.
Andrews, George Reid. *Afro-Argentines, 1800–2000*. New York: Oxford University Press, 2004.
Andrews, George Reid. *Afro-Latin America, 1800–2000*. New York: Oxford University Press, 2004.
Appelbaum, Nancy P., Anne S. Macpherson, and Karin Alejandra Rosemblatt, eds. *Race and Nation in Modern Latin America*. Chapel Hill: University of North Carolina Press, 2003.
Archibold, Randal C. "Inequality Becomes More Visible in Cuba as Economy Shifts," *New York Times*, February 24, 2015. https://www.nytimes.com/2015/02/25/world/americas/as-cuba-shifts-toward-capitalism-inequality-grows-more-visible.html.
Ayala, Cesar J. "Social and Economic Aspects of Sugar Production in Cuba, 1880–1930." *Latin American Research Review* 30, no. 1 (1995): 95–124.

Bacardí y Moreau, Emilio. *Crónicas de Santiago de Cuba*. 10 volumes. Santiago, Cuba: Arroyo Hermanos, 1923. At http://ufdc.ufl.edu/AA00062763/00006.

Bachiller y Morales, Antonio. *Apuntes para la historia de las letras, y de la instrucción pública de la isla de Cuba*. 3 volumes. Havana: P. Massana, 1859–1861. At University of Florida Digital Collections, https://ufdc.ufl.edu/en/AA00081487/00001/images.

Bachiller y Morales, Antonio. "Apuntes para la historia de las letras en la isla de Cuba." *Revista de la Habana*, March 1–September 1, 1854.

Baker, Lee D. *Anthropology and the Racial Politics of Culture*. Durham, NC: Duke University Press, 2010.

Baldwin, Davarian L. Foreword to *Ideas in Unexpected Places: Reimagining Black Intellectual History*, edited by Brandon R. Byrd, Leslie M. Alexander, and Russell Rickford, xi–xvii. Evanston, IL: Northwestern University Press, 2022.

Barcia, Manuel. *The Great African Slave Revolt of 1825: Cuba and the Fight for Freedom in Matanzas*. Baton Rouge: Louisiana State University Press, 2012.

Barcia, Manuel. *Seeds of Insurrection: Domination and Resistance on Western Plantations, 1808–1848*. Baton Rouge: Louisiana State University Press, 2008.

Barcia, Manuel. *West African Warfare in Bahia and Cuba: Soldier Slaves in the Atlantic World, 1807–1844*. New York: Oxford University Press, 2014.

Barcia, María del Carmen. *Los ilustres apellidos: Negros en la Habana colonial*. Havana: Boloña, 2009.

Barcia, María del Carmen. "Poder étnico y subversión social: Los batallones de pardos y morenos de Cuba." *Islas* 1, no. 1 (2005): 6–9.

Barrachina, María Agustina. "Entre la igualdad y la segregación: Las disputas por la educación de los afrodescendientes en el Buenos Aires postrosista." *Claves: Revista de Historia* 5, no. 9 (2019): 115–143.

Barragán Goetz, Philis M. *Reading, Writing and Revolution: Escuelitas and the Emergence of a Mexican American Identity in Texas*. Austin: University of Texas Press, 2020.

Barreto, Amilcar Antonio, "Enlightened Tolerance or Cultural Capitulation? Contesting Notions of American Identity." In *Colonial Crucible, Empire in the Making of the Modern American State*, edited by Alfred W. McCoy and Francisco A. Scarano, 145–150. Madison: University of Wisconsin Press, 2009.

Baumgartner, Kabria. *In Pursuit of Knowledge: Black Women and Educational Activism in Antebellum America*. New York: New York University Press, 2019.

Beito, David T. *From Mutual Aid to the Welfare State: Fraternal Societies and Social Services, 1890–1967*. Chapel Hill: University of North Carolina Press, 2000.

Bennett, Herman L. *Colonial Blackness: A History of Afro-Mexico*. Bloomington: Indiana University Press, 2009.

Bennett, Herman L. "The Subject in the Plot: National Boundaries and the 'History' of the Black Atlantic." *African Studies Review* 43, no. 1, special issue on the diaspora (April 2000): 101–124.

Benson, Devyn Spence. *Antiracism in Cuba: The Unfinished Revolution*. Chapel Hill: University of North Carolina Press, 2016.

Benson, Devyn Spence. "Redefining Mestizaje: How Trans-Caribbean Exchanges Solidified Black Consciousness in Cuba." *Small Axe: A Caribbean Journal of Criticism* 25, no. 2 (2021): 91–108.

Benson, Devyn Spence, Daisy Rubiera Castillo, and Inés María Martiatu Terry, eds. *Afrocubanas: History, Thought, and Cultural Practices*. New York: Rowman and Littlefield International, 2020.

Bergad, Laird W. "Slavery in Cuba and Puerto Rico, 1804 to Abolition." In *The Cambridge World History of Slavery*, volume 4, edited by David Eltis, Stanley L. Engerman, Seymour Drescher, and David Richardson, 98–128. Cambridge, England: Cambridge University Press, 2017.

Berlin, Ira. *Many Thousands Gone: The First Two Centuries of Slavery in North America*. Cambridge, MA: Harvard University Press, 1998.

Best, Stephen, and Saidiya Hartman. "Fugitive Justice." *Representations* 92, no. 1 (2005): 1–15. https://doi.org/10.1525/rep.2005.92.1.1.

Bevis, Teresa Brawner, and Christopher J. Lucas. *International Students in American Colleges and Universities: A History*. New York: Palgrave Macmillan, 2007.

Blackburn, Robin. *The Overthrow of Colonial Slavery, 1776–1848*. Verso, 1989.

Blinkhorn, Martin. "Spain: 'The Spanish Problem' and the Imperial Myth." *Journal of Contemporary History* 15, no. 1 (January 1980): 5–25.

Blum, Denise F. *Cuban Youth and Revolutionary Values: Educating the New Socialist Citizen*. Austin: University of Texas Press, 2011.

Boyd, Carolyn P. *Historia Patria: Politics, History, and National Identity in Spain, 1875–1975*. Princeton, NJ: Princeton University Press, 1997.

Briggs, Laura. *Reproducing Empire: Race, Sex, Science, and US Imperialism in Puerto Rico*. Berkeley: University of California Press, 2003.

Britton, John A., ed. *Molding the Hearts and Minds: Education, Communications, and Social Change in Latin America*. Wilmington, DE: Scholarly Resources, 1994.

Brock, Lisa. "Questioning the Diaspora: Hegemony, Black Intellectuals, and Doing International History from Below." *Issue: A Journal of Opinion* 24, no. 2 (1996): 9–12.

Brock, Lisa, and Digna Castañeda Fuertes, eds. *Between Race and Empire: African-Americans and Cubans before the Cuban Revolution*. Philadelphia, PA: Temple University Press, 1998.

Bronfman, Alejandra. *Measures of Equality: Social Science, Citizenship, and Race in Cuba, 1902–1940*. Chapel Hill: University of North Carolina Press, 2003.

Brown, Jacqueline Nassy. *Dropping Anchor, Setting Sail: Geographies of Race in Black Liverpool*. Princeton, NJ: Princeton University Press, 2005.

Brown, Vincent. *The Reaper's Garden: Death and Power in the World of Atlantic Slavery*. Cambridge, MA: Belknap Harvard University Press, 2008.

Brunson, Takkara. *Black Women, Citizenship, and the Making of Modern Cuba*. Gainesville: University of Florida Press, 2021.

Buck-Morss, Susan. *Hegel, Haiti, and Universal History*. Pittsburgh, PA: University of Pittsburgh Press, 2009.

Burkholder, Zoë. *An African American Dilemma: A History of School Integration and Civil Rights in the North.* New York: Oxford University Press, 2021.
Butler, Kim. D. "Defining Diaspora, Refining a Discourse." *Diaspora* 10, no. 2 (2001): 189–219.
Byrd, Brandon R. "The Rise of African American Intellectual History." *Modern Intellectual History* 18, no. 3 (2021): 833–864. doi:10.1017/S1479244320000219.
Byrd, Brandon R., Leslie M. Alexander, and Russell Rickford. Introduction to *Ideas in Unexpected Places: Reimagining Black Intellectual History*, edited by Byrd, Alexander, and Rickford, 3–11. Evanston, IL: Northwestern University Press, 2022.
Callahan, Megan. "'The Dangers' of Literacy: How Literacy Laws in Early America Ensured the Continuation of Slavery and the Oppression of Enslaved Peoples." PhD diss., State University of New York at Stony Brook, 2020.
Cañizares Márquez, José Antonio. "La política de instrucción pública en Cuba (1863–1898): El problema de la segunda enseñanza." PhD diss., Universidad Nacional de Educación a Distancia, 2019.
Cárdenas, Diana Sosa. *Los pardos: Caracas en las postrimerías de la colonia.* Caracas: Universidad Católica Andrés Bello, 2010.
Carnoy, Martin. *Education as Cultural Imperialism.* New York: David McKay, 1974.
Carr, Barry. "Identity, Class, and Nation: Black Immigrant Workers, Cuban Communism, and the Sugar Insurgency, 1925–1934." *Hispanic American Historical Review*, 78 no. 1 (February 1998): 83–116.
Carreras, Julio Angel. *Esclavitud, abolición y racismo.* Havana: Editorial de Ciencias Sociales, 1985.
Caruso, Marcelo. "Latin American Independence: Education and the Invention of New Polities." *Paedagogica Historica* 46, no. 4 (August 2010): 409–417.
Caruso, Marcelo. "Literacy and Suffrage: The Politicisation of Schooling in Postcolonial Hispanic America (1810–1850)." *Paedagogica Historica* 46, no. 4 (August 2010): 463–478.
Casanovas, Joan. *Bread, or Bullets! Urban Labor and Spanish Colonialism in Cuba, 1850–1898.* Pittsburgh, PA: University of Pittsburgh Press, 1998.
Castañeda Delgado, Paulino, and Juan Marchena Fernández. "Notas sobre la educación pública en Cuba, 1816–1863." *Jahrbuch für Geschichte von Staat Lateinamerikas* 21 (1984): 264–282.
Castellanos, Jorge, and Isabel Castellanos. *Cultura afrocubana.* Volume 2. Miami: Universal, 1990.
Castillo Bueno, María de los Reyes. *Reyita: The Life of a Black Cuban Woman in the Twentieth Century.* Durham, NC: Duke University Press, 2000.
Castro Monterrey, Pedro, Sandra Estévez Rivero, and Olga Portuondo Zúñiga, eds. *Por la Identidad del negro cubano.* Santiago, Cuba: Caserón, 2011.
Chase, Michelle. *Revolution within the Revolution: Women and Gender Politics in Cuba, 1952–1962.* Chapel Hill: University of North Carolina Press, 2015.
Chávez Rodríguez, Justo A. *Bosquejo histórico de las ideas educativas en Cuba.* Havana: Pueblo y Educación, 1996.

Childs, Matt D. *The 1812 Aponte Rebellion in Cuba and the Struggle against Atlantic Slavery*. Chapel Hill: University of North Carolina Press, 2006.
Childs, Matt D. "Gendering the African Diaspora in the Iberian Atlantic," In *Women of the Iberian Atlantic*, edited by Sarah E. Owens and Jane E. Mangan, 232, 242–244. Baton Rouge: Louisiana State University Press, 2012.
Childs, Matt D. "'Sewing' Civilization: Cuban Female Education in the Context of Africanization, 1800–1860." *The Americas* 54, no. 1 (July 1997): 83–107.
Chinea, Jorge. *Race and Labor in the Hispanic Caribbean: The West Indian Worker Experience in Puerto Rico, 1800–1850*. Gainesville: University Press of Florida, 2005.
Chinea, Jorge. "Race, Colonial Exploitation, and West Indian Immigration in Nineteenth-Century Puerto Rico, 1800–1850." *The Americas* 52, no. 4, (1996): 495–515.
Chira, Adriana. *Patchwork Freedoms: Law, Slavery, and Race beyond Cuba's Plantations*. Cambridge, England: Cambridge University Press, 2022.
Chomsky, Aviva. "'Barbados or Canada?': Race, Immigration, and Nation in Early Twentieth-Century Cuba." *Hispanic American Historical Review* 80, no. 3 (2000): 415–462.
Clealand, Danielle Pilar. *The Power of Race in Cuba: Racial Ideology and Black Consciousness during the Revolution*. New York: Oxford University Press, 2017.
Cobb, Jelani. "The Failure of Desegregation." *New Yorker*, April 6, 2014. https://www.newyorker.com/news/news-desk/the-failure-of-desegregation.
Conde Rodríguez, Alicia. "Cultura y educación en los años iniciales de la República de Cuba." *Cubaliteraria: Portal de literatura cubana*, April 8, 2014.
Connolly, Brian, and Marisa Fuentes. "Introduction: From Archives of Slavery to Liberated Futures?" *History of the Present* 6, no. 2 (Fall 2016): 105–116.
Cooper, Frederick, Thomas C. Holt, and Rebecca J. Scott. *Beyond Slavery: Explorations of Race, Labor, and Citizenship in Postemancipation Societies*. Chapel Hill: University of North Carolina Press, 2000.
Cordoví Nuñez, Yoel. *Magisterio y nacionalismo en las escuelas públicas de Cuba, 1899–1920*. Havana: Editorial de Ciencias Sociales, 2012.
Corwin, Arthur F. *Spain and the Abolition of Slavery in Cuba, 1817–1886*. Austin: University of Texas Press, 1967.
Costa, Octavio R. *Juan Gualberto Gomez: Una vida sin sombra*. 2nd edition. Miami: La Moderna Poesía, 1984 [1950].
Cowling, Camila. *Conceiving Freedom: Women of Colour, Gender, and the Abolition of Slavery in Havana and Rio de Janeiro*. Chapel Hill: University of North Carolina Press, 2013.
Cowling, Camila. "Gendered Geographies: Motherhood, Slavery, Law, and Space in Mid-Nineteenth-Century Cuba." *Women's History Review* 27, no. 6 (June 2017): 939–953.
Cropper, Tubyez. *What Could Have Been*. Video. New Haven, CT: Beinecke Library, Yale University, 2022. At YouTube, https://www.youtube.com/watch?v=gmXF3N62Olo.

Crumdy, Angela. "Teaching Revolution: Women Primary School Teachers, Race, and Social Reproduction in Cuba." PhD diss., City University of New York, 2022. https://academicworks.cuny.edu/gc_etds/4927.
Crumdy, Angela. "'This Isn't to Get Rich': Double Morality and Black Women Private Tutors in Cuba." In *Black Women in Latin America and the Caribbean: Critical Research and Perspectives*, edited by Melanie A. Medeiros and Keisha-Khan Y. Perry, 95–112. New Brunswick, NJ: Rutgers University Press, 2023.
Cruz-Taura, Graciella. "Revolution and Continuity in the History of Education in Cuba." *Cuba in Transition* 18 (2008): 168–180. https://ascecuba.org//c/wp-content/uploads/2014/09/v18-cruztaura.pdf.
Cuba. Ley y Reglamento de la Abolición de la Esclavitud de 13 de febrero de 1880. Havana: Imprenta del Gobierno y Capitanía General por S. M., 1880. At University of Florida Digital Collections, https://ufdc.ufl.edu/UF00103332/00001/images.
Cuba. *Plan y reglamento para las escuelas gratuitas de enseñanza mutua de esta ciudad, Pueblo-Nuevo y Ceiba-Mocha*. Matanzas, Cuba: Imprenta de la Real Marina, 1835.
Cuba. *Reglamento para la Escuela Normal Elemental bajo la dirección de los pp Escolapios*. Havana: Imprenta del Gobierno y Capitanía General, 1857. At https://archive.org/details/01ReglamentoEscuelaNormal1857/mode/2up.
Cuba, Comisión Militar de Matanzas. *Colección de los fallos pronunciados por una sección de la Comisión militar establecida en la ciudad de Matanzas para convocer de la causa de conspiración de la gente de color, etc*. Matanzas, Cuba: Imprenta de Gobierno, 1844.
Cuba, Convención Constituyente. *Diario de sesiones de la Convención Constituyente de la isla de Cuba*. Havana, La Convención, 1901. At University of Florida Digital Collections, https://ufdc.ufl.edu/UF00072606/00001/images.
Cuba, Ministerio de Educación. *La educación en los cien años de lucha*. Havana: Pueblo y Educación, 1968.
Cuba, Oficina Nacional del Censo, Victor H. Olmsted, and Henry Gannett, *Cuba: Population, History, and Resources, 1907*. Washington, DC: US Bureau of the Census, 1909. At Library of Congress, https://lccn.loc.gov/09035394.
Cunningham, Candace. "*I Hope They Fire Me*": Black Teachers in the Fight for Equal Education. Athens: University of Georgia Press, forthcoming.
Dagbovie, Pero Gaglo. "Exploring a Century of Historical Scholarship on Booker T. Washington." *Journal of African American History* 92, no. 2 (Spring 2007): 239–264.
Danzie León, Bárbara, Loreto Raúl Ramos Cárdenas, Doreya Gómez Véliz, and Iván Dalai Vázquez Maya. *Apuntes cronológicos sobre el Partido Independiente de Color*. Santiago, Cuba: Santiago, 2010.
Deere, Carmen Diana. "Here Come the Yankees! The Rise and Decline of United States Colonies in Cuba, 1898–1930." *Hispanic American Historical Review* 78, no. 4 (November 1998): 729–765.
de la Fuente, Alejandro. *Havana and the Atlantic in the Sixteenth Century*. Chapel Hill: University of North Carolina Press, 2008.

de la Fuente, Alejandro. *A Nation for All: Race, Inequality, and Politics in Twentieth-Century Cuba*. Chapel Hill: University of North Carolina Press, 2001.

de la Fuente, Alejandro. "Race and Income Inequality in Contemporary Cuba." *NACLA Report on the Americas* 44, no. 4 (July–August 2011), 30–33, 43. https://nacla.org/article/race-and-income-inequality-contemporary-cuba.

de la Fuente, Alejandro, and Ariela J. Gross. *Becoming Free, Becoming Black: Race, Freedom, and Law in Cuba, Virginia, and Louisiana*. New York: Cambridge University Press, 2020.

Delmont, Matthew F. *Why Busing Failed: Race, Media, and the National Resistance to School Desegregation*. Oakland: University of California Press, 2016.

Del Monte, Domingo. *Escritos*. Volume 1. Havana: Cultural, 1929. At University of Florida Digital Collections, https://ufdc.ufl.edu/UF00075391/00001.

del Moral, Solsiree. *Negotiating Empire: The Cultural Politics of Schools in Puerto Rico, 1898–1952*. Madison: University of Wisconsin Press, 2013.

del Moral, Solsiree. "'Una niña humilde y de color': Sources for the History of an Afro-Puerto Rican Childhood." *Journal of Caribbean History* 53, no. 2 (2019): 192–222.

Deschamps Chapeaux, Pedro. *Los batallones de pardos y morenos libres*. Havana: Arte y Literatura, 1976.

Deschamps Chapeaux, Pedro. *El negro en el periodismo cubano en el siglo XIX*. Havana: Revolución, 1963.

Deschamps Chapeaux, Pedro. *El negro en la economía habanera del siglo XIX*. Havana: Unión de Escritores y Artistas de Cuba, 1971.

Deschamps Chapeaux, Pedro. *Rafael Serra y Montalvo, obrero incansable de nuestra independencia*. Havana: Unión de Escritores y Artistas de Cuba, 1975.

Deschamps Chapeaux, Pedro, and Juan Pérez de la Riva. *Contribución a la historia de la gente sin historia*. Havana: Editorial de Ciencias Sociales, 1974.

Directorio y guía para los maestros cubanos. Cambridge, MA: E. W. Wheeler, 1900. At Harvard University Archives, Records of the Cuban Summer School, https://iiif.lib.harvard.edu/manifests/view/drs:493672069$5i.

Dollero, Alfredo. *Cultura cubana: La provincia de Pinar del Río y su evolución*. Havana: Seoane y Fernández, 1921.

Du Bois, W. E. B. *The Souls of Black Folk*. New York: Dover, 1994.

Dubois, Laurent. *Avengers of the New World: The Story of the Haitian Revolution*. Cambridge, MA: Harvard University Press, 2004.

Duharte Jimenez, Rafael. *El negro en la sociedad colonial*. Santiago, Cuba: Oriente, 1988.

Duke, Cathy. "The Idea of Race: The Cultural Impact of American Intervention in Cuba, 1898–1912." In *Politics, Society, and Culture in the Caribbean: Selected Papers of the XIV Conference of Caribbean Historians*, edited by Blanca G. Silvestrini, 87–108. San Juan: Universidad de Puerto Rico, 1983.

Edo, Enrique. *Memoria histórica de Cienfuegos y su jurisdicción*. 3rd edition. Havana: Úcar, García, 1943.

Edwards, Brent Hayes. *The Practice of Diaspora: Literature, Translation, and the Rise of Black Internationalism*. Cambridge, MA: Harvard University Press, 2003.

Edwards, Erika Denise. *Hiding in Plain Sight: Black Women, the Law, and the Making of a White Argentine Republic*. Tuscaloosa: University of Alabama Press, 2020.

Epstein, Erwin. "The Peril of Paternalism: The Imposition of Education on Cuba by the United States." *American Journal of Education* 96, no. 1 (November 1987): 1–23.

Erickson, Ansley T. *Making the Unequal Metropolis: School Desegregation and Its Limits*. Chicago: University of Chicago Press, 2016.

Esdaile, Charles. *Spain in the Liberal Age: From Constitution to Civil War, 1808–1939*. Oxford, England: Blackwell, 2000.

Espinoza, G. Antonio. "National Education Systems: Latin America." In *The Oxford Handbook of the History of Education*, edited by John L. Rury and Eileen H. Tamura, 199–212. New York: Oxford University Press, 2019.

Estévez Rivero, Sandra. "La instrucción pública: Forjada de la conciencia política entre negros y mulatos libres en la ciudad de Santiago de Cuba (1526–1868)." In *Por la identidad del negro cubano*, edited by Pedro Castro Monterrey, Sandra Estévez Rivero, and Olga Portuondo Zúñiga, 41–64. Santiago, Cuba: Caserón, 2011.

Fairclough, Adam. *A Class of Their Own: Black Teachers in the Segregated South*. Cambridge, MA: Belknap, 2007.

Fairclough, Adam. *Teaching Equality: Black Schools in the Age of Jim Crow*. Athens: University of Georgia Press, 2001.

Fear-Segal, Jacqueline. *White Man's Club: Schools, Race, and the Struggle of Indian Acculturation*. Lincoln: University of Nebraska Press, 2007.

Fernández Robaina, Tomás. *El negro en Cuba, 1902–1958: Apuntes para la historia de la lucha contra la discriminación racial*. Havana: Editorial de Ciencias Sociales, 1990.

Ferrer, Ada. *Cuba: An American History*. New York: Scribner, 2021.

Ferrer, Ada. *Freedom's Mirror: Cuba and Haiti in the Age of Revolution*. New York: Cambridge University Press, 2014.

Ferrer, Ada. "Haiti, Free Soil, and Antislavery in the Revolutionary Atlantic." *American Historical Review* 117, no. 1 (February 2012): 40–66.

Ferrer, Ada. *Insurgent Cuba: Race, Nation, and Revolution, 1868–1898*. Chapel Hill: University of North Carolina Press, 1999.

Ferrer, Ada. "Introduction to Part II." In *Breaking the Chains: The Afro-Cuban Fight for Freedom and Equality, 1812–1912*, edited by Aisha Finch and Fannie Rushing, 131–137. Baton Rouge: Louisiana State University Press, 2019.

Figueroa, Luis A. *Sugar, Slavery, and Freedom in Nineteenth Century Puerto Rico*. Chapel Hill: University of North Carolina Press, 2005.

Finch, Aisha K. "The Repeating Rebellion: Slave Resistance and Political Consciousness in Nineteenth-Century Cuba, 1812–1844." In *Breaking the Chains: The Afro-Cuban Fight for Freedom and Equality, 1812–1912*, edited by Aisha Finch and Fannie Rushing, 138–157. Baton Rouge: Louisiana State University Press, 2019.

Finch, Aisha K. *Rethinking Slave Rebellion in Cuba: La Escalera and the Insurgencies of 1841–1844*. Chapel Hill: University of North Carolina Press, 2015.

Finch, Aisha. "'What Looks Like a Revolution': Enslaved Women and the Gendered Terrain of Slave Insurgencies in Cuba, 1843–1844." *Journal of Women's History* 26, no. 1 (2014): 112–134. doi:10.1353/jowh.2014.0007.

Finch, Aisha K., and Fannie Rushing, eds. *Breaking the Chains, Forging the Nation: The Afro-Cuban Fight for Freedom and Equality, 1812–1912*. Baton Rouge: University of Louisiana Press, 2019.

Findlay, Eileen. *Imposing Decency: The Politics of Sexuality and Race in Puerto Rico, 1870–1920*. Durham, NC: Duke University Press, 1999.

Fitchen, Edward D. "Primary Education in Colonial Cuba: Spanish Tool for Retaining 'La Isla Siempre Leal?'" *Caribbean Studies* 14, no. 1 (April 1974): 105–120.

Foner, Philip S. *The Spanish-Cuban-American War and the Birth of American Imperialism, 1895–1902*. 2 vols. New York: Monthly Review Press, 1972.

Forment, Carlos E., and Emilio Bacardí Moreau. *Crónicas de Santiago de Cuba: Continuación de la obra de Emilio Bacardí*. Santiago, Cuba: Arroyo, 1953.

Fradera, Josep M. "Quiebra imperial y reorganización política en las antillas españolas, 1810–1868." *Boletín del Centro de Investigaciones Históricas* 9 (1997): 289–323.

Franklin, Sarah L. *Women and Slavery in Nineteenth-Century Colonial Cuba*. Rochester, NY: University of Rochester Press, 2012.

Fuentes, Marisa. *Dispossessed Lives: Enslaved Women, Violence, and the Archive*. Philadelphia: University of Pennsylvania Press, 2016.

Gaddis, John Lewis. *The Landscape of History: How Historians Map the Past*. New York: Oxford University Press, 2002.

Gaines, Kevin. *Uplifting the Race: Black Leadership, Politics, and Culture in the Twentieth Century*. Chapel Hill: University of North Carolina Press, 1996.

García, Gloria. *Conspiraciones y revueltas: La actividad política de los negros en Cuba, 1790–1845*. Santiago, Cuba: Oriente, 2003.

García, Guadalupe. *Beyond the Walled City: Colonial Exclusion in Havana*. Oakland: University of California Press, 2016.

García Aguero, Salvador. "Lorenzo Menéndez (o Meléndez), el negro en la Educación cubana." *Revista Bimestre Cubana* 39. no. 3 (May–June 1937): 351–358.

García Martínez, Orlando. *Esclavitud y colonización en Cienfuegos, 1819–1879*. Cienfuegos, Cuba: Mecenas, 2012.

García Rojas, Heliodoro. *San José de las Lajas: evocaciones del pasado*. Havana: P. Fernández, 1944.

García Tudurí, Mercedes. "La enseñanza en Cuba en los primeros cincuenta años de independencia." In *Historia de la nación cubana*, edited by Ramiro Guerra y Sánchez, José M. Pérez Cabrera, and Juan J. Remos, 10–68. Havana: Historia de la Nación Cubana, 1952.

García Yero, Cary Aileen. "Sights and Sounds of Cubanidad: Race, Nation, and the Arts in Cuba, 1938–1958." PhD diss., Harvard University, 2020.

Gatewood, Willard B. *Aristocrats of Color: The Black Elite, 1880–1920*. Bloomington: Indiana University Press, 1990.

Gatewood, Willard B. *Black Americans and the White Man's Burden, 1898–1903*. Chicago: University of Illinois Press, 1975.

Generals, Donald. "Booker T. Washington and Progressive Education: An Experimentalist Approach to Curriculum Development and Reform." *Journal of Negro Education* 69, no. 3 (Summer 2000): 215–234.
Gilmore, Glenda Elizabeth. *Gender and Jim Crow: Women and the Politics of White Supremacy in North Carolina, 1896–1920.* Chapel Hill: University of North Carolina Press, 1996.
Giroux, Henry A. "Theories of Reproduction and Resistance in the New Sociology of Education: A Critical Analysis." *Harvard Educational Review* 53, no. 3 (August 1983): 257–293.
Givens, Jarvis R. *Fugitive Pedagogy: Carter G. Woodson and the Art of Black Teaching.* Cambridge, MA: Harvard University Press, 2021.
Gleibermann, Erik. "Where Hip-Hop Fits in Cuba's Anti-Racist Curriculum." *The Atlantic*, August 1, 2016. https://www.theatlantic.com/education/archive/2016/08/where-hip-hop-fits-in-cubas-anti-racist-curriculum/493682/.
Gómez, Andy S., and Paul Webster Hare. "How Education Shaped Communist Cuba." *The Atlantic*, February 26, 2015. http://www.theatlantic.com/education/archive/2015/02/how-education-shaped-communist-cuba/386192/.
González, José Luis. *Puerto Rico, The Four-Storyed Country: The Question of An Afro-Mestizo Culture.* Princeton, NJ: M. Weiner, 1993.
González de los Ríos, Pelayo. "Ensayo histórico-estadístico de la instrucción pública de la isla de Cuba, libro Segundo, de la instrucción intelectual: Primera parte de la instrucción primaria, capítulo III." In *Memorias de la Sociedad Económica de la Habana*, Anales de Fomento, series 5, volume 9. Havana: Imprenta de Tiempo, 1864.
Goode, Joshua. *Impurity of Blood: Defining Race in Spain, 1870–1930.* Baton Rouge: Louisiana State University Press, 2009.
Gordon, Peter. "Dame Schools." In *The Oxford Companion to British History*. Oxford, England: Oxford University Press, 2015.
Greenbaum, Susan. *More Than Black: Afro-Cubans in Tampa.* Gainesville: University Press of Florida, 2002.
Grillo, Evelio. *Black Cuban, Black American: A Memoir.* Houston: Arte Público, 2000.
Guerra, Lillian. "From Revolution to Involution in the Early Cuban Republic: Conflicts over Race, Class, and Nation, 1902–1906." In *Race and Nation in Modern Latin America*, edited by Nancy P. Appelbaum, Anne S. Macpherson, and Karin Alejandra Rosemblatt, 132–162. Chapel Hill: University of North Carolina Press, 2003.
Guerra, Lillian. *The Myth of José Martí: Conflicting Nationalisms in Early Twentieth-Century Cuba.* Chapel Hill: University of North Carolina Press, 2005.
Guillard Limonta, Norma R. "To Be a Black Woman, a Lesbian, and an Afro-Feminist in Cuba Today." *Black Diaspora Review* 5, no. 2 (Spring 2016): 81–97.
Guridy, Frank Andre. *Forging Diaspora: Afro-Cubans and African Americans in a World of Empire and Jim Crow.* Chapel Hill: University of North Carolina Press, 2010.
Guridy, Frank A. "From Solidarity to Cross-Fertilization: Afro-Cubans/African-

American Interaction during the 1930s and 1940s." *Radical History Review* 87 (2003): 19–48.

Hahn, Steven. *A Nation under Our Feet: Black Political Struggles in the Rural South from Slavery to the Great Migration.* Cambridge, MA: Belknap, 2005.

Hansing, Katrin. "Race and Inequality in the New Cuba: Reasons, Dynamics, and Manifestations." *Social Research: An International Quarterly* 84, no. 2 (2017): 331–349.

Harper, Elizabeth P. "Dame Schools." In *Encyclopedia of Educational Reform and Dissent,* edited by Thomas C. Hunt, James C. Carper, Thomas J. Lasley, and C. D. Raisch, 258–260. Thousand Oaks, CA: Sage, 2010.

Harroun, Gilbert K. "The Cuban Educational Association of the United States." *American Monthly Review of Reviews* 20 (1899): 334–335.

Hartman, Saidiya. *Lose Your Mother: A Journey along the Atlantic Slave Route.* New York: Farrar, Straus, and Giroux, 2007.

Hartman, Saidiya. "Venus in Two Acts." *Small Axe* 26 (June 2008): 1–14.

Hawkins, B. Denise. "In Cuba, African Roots Run Deep, but It's a Lesson Students Aren't Learning in the Classroom." *NBC News,* September 1, 2017. https://www.nbcnews.com/news/nbcblk/cuba-african-roots-run-deep-it-s-lesson-students-aren-n767616.

Helg, Aline. *Our Rightful Share: The Afro-Cuban Struggle for Equality, 1886–1912.* Chapel Hill: University of North Carolina Press, 1995.

Helg, Aline. "Slave but Not Citizen: Free People of Color and Blood Purity in Colonial Spanish American Legislation." *Millars: Espai i Història* 42, no. 1 (2017): 75–99. http://dx.doi.org/10.6035/Millars.2017.42.4.

Hellwig, David J. "The African-American Press and United States Involvement in Cuba, 1902–1912." In *Between Race and Empire: African-Americans and Cubans before the Cuban Revolution,* edited by Lisa Brock and Digna Castañeda Fuertes. Philadelphia, PA: Temple University Press, 1998.

Hernández Rodríguez, Rafael, and Dick Cluster. *The History of Havana.* New York: Palgrave Macmillan, 2006.

Hicks, Anasa. "Dubious Victimhood: Labor, Race, Age and Honor in Republican Cuban Courts." In *The Global History of Black Girlhood,* edited by Corinne T. Field and LaKisha Michelle Simmons, 68–81. Chicago: University of Illinois Press, 2022.

Hicks, Anasa. *Hierarchies at Home: Domestic Service in Cuba from Abolition to Revolution.* New York: Cambridge University Press, 2022.

Hierrezuelo, María Cristina. "Women 'of Color' in Santiaguera Colonial Society: A Commentary." In *Afrocubanas: History, Thought, and Cultural Practices,* edited by Devyn Spence Benson, Daisy Rubiera Castillo, and Inés María Martiatu Terry, 39–56. New York: Rowman and Littlefield International, 2020.

Higginbotham, Evelyn Brooks. *Righteous Discontent: The Women's Movement in the Black Baptist Church, 1880–1920.* Cambridge: Harvard University Press, 1993.

Higginson, J. H. "Dame Schools." *British Journal of Educational Studies* 22, no. 2 (1974): 166–181. https://doi.org/10.2307/3119841.

Hines, Michael. *A Worthy Piece of Work: The Untold Story of Madeline Morgan and the Fight for Black History in Schools.* Boston: Beacon, 2022.

Hitchman, James H. "Unfinished Business: Public Works in Cuba, 1898–1902." *The Americas* 31, no. 3 (January 1975): 335–359.
Hoernel, Robert B. "Sugar and Social Change in Oriente, Cuba, 1886–1946." *Journal of Latin American Studies* 8, no. 2 (November 1976): 215–249.
Hoffnung-Garskof, Jesse. *Racial Migrations: New York City and the Revolutionary Politics of the Spanish Caribbean*. Princeton, NJ: Princeton University Press, 2019.
Howard, Phillip A. *Changing History: Afro-Cuban Cabildos and Societies of Color in the Nineteenth Century*. Baton Rouge: Louisiana State University Press, 1998.
Huerta Martínez, Ángel. *La enseñanza primaria en Cuba en el siglo XIX, 1812–1868*. Seville: Excma. Diputación Provincial de Sevilla, 1992.
Iglesias Utset, Marial. *A Cultural History of Cuba during the U.S. Occupation, 1898–1902*. Translated by Russ Davidson. Chapel Hill: University of North Carolina Press, 2011.
Jackson, David H. *Booker T. Washington and the Struggle against White Supremacy*. New York: Palgrave Macmillan, 2008.
Jacobson, Stephen. "'The Head and Heart of Spain': New Perspectives on Nationalism and Nationhood." *Social History* 29, no. 3 (August 2004): 393–407.
Jacoby, Karl. *The Strange Career of William Ellis: The Texas Slave Who Became a Mexican Millionaire*. New York: W. W. Norton, 2016.
James, C. L. R. *The Black Jacobins: Toussaint L'Ouverture and the San Domingo Revolution*. New York: Random House, 1963.
James, Winston. *Holding Aloft the Banner of Ethiopia: Caribbean Radicalism in Early Twentieth-Century America*. New York: Verso, 1998.
Jarvinen, Lisa. "The 'School Question' in an Imperial Context: Education and Religion during and Following the Occupations of Cuba and Puerto Rico." *History of Education Quarterly* 62 (2022): 84–106.
Jensen, Larry R. *Children of Colonial Despotism: Press, Politics, and Culture in Cuba, 1790–1840*. Tampa: University of South Florida Press, 1988.
Jiménez Román, Miriam. "Un Hombre (Negro) del Pueblo: José Celso Barbosa and the Puerto Rican 'Race' Toward Whiteness." *Centro* 8, nos. 1–2 (1996): 8–29.
Jiménez Román, Miriam, and Juan Flores, eds. *The Afro-Latin@ Reader: History and Culture in the United States*. Durham, NC: Duke University Press, 2010.
Johnson, Sherry. *The Social Transformation of Eighteenth-Century Cuba*. Gainesville: University Press of Florida, 2001.
Johnston, Laurie. "Cuban Nationalism and Responses to Private Education in Cuba, 1902–1958." In *Ideologues and Ideologies in Latin America*, edited by Will Fowler, 27–44. Westport, CT: Greenwood, 1997.
Jones, Brian P. *The Tuskegee Student Uprising*. New York: New York University Press, 2022.
Jones, Nicole Hannah. "The Problem We All Live With." *This American Life*, episode 562, July 31, 2015. https://www.thisamericanlife.org/562/the-problem-we-all-live-with-part-one.
Kaestle, Carl. *Pillars of the Republic: Common Schools and American Society, 1780–1860*. New York: Hill and Wang, 1983.

Kanakamedala, Prithi. *Brooklynites: The Remarkable Story of the Free Black Communities That Shaped a Borough*. New York: NYU Press, 2024.

Kelley, Robin D. G. *Freedom Dreams: The Black Radical Imagination*. Boston: Beacon, 2002.

Kelley, Robin D. G. "Why Black Marxism? Why Now?." Foreword to *Black Marxism: The Making of the Black Radical Tradition*, by Cedric J. Robinson, xi–xxvi. 3rd edition. Chapel Hill: University of North Carolina Press, 2000.

Kimball, Richard B. *Cuba and the Cubans: Comprising a History of the Island of Cuba, Its Present Social Political and Domestic Condition; Also, Its Relation to England and the United States*. New York: Samuel Hueston, 1850.

King, James F. "The Colored Castes and American Representation in the Cortes of Cádiz." *Hispanic American Historical Review* 33, no. 1 (February 1953): 33–64.

Kinsbruner, Jay. *Not of Pure Blood: The Free People of Color and Racial Prejudice in Nineteenth Century Puerto Rico*. Durham, NC: Duke University Press, 1996.

Kiple, Kenneth F. *Blacks in Colonial Cuba, 1774–1899*. Gainesville: University Presses of Florida, 1976.

Klein, Herbert S. "The Colored Militia of Cuba: 1568–1868." *Caribbean Studies* 6, no. 2 (July 1966): 17–27.

Knight, Franklin. *Slave Society in Cuba during the Nineteenth Century*. Madison: University of Wisconsin Press, 1974.

Landers, Jane G. *Atlantic Creoles in the Age of Revolutions*. Cambridge, MA: Harvard University Press, 2010.

Lanier, Oilda Hevia. *El Directorio Central de las Sociedades Negras de Cuba, 1886–1894*. Havana: Editorial de Ciencias Sociales, 1996.

Larson, Brooke. *The Lettered Indian: Race, Nation, and Indigenous Education in Twentieth-Century Bolivia*. Durham, NC: Duke University Press, 2024.

Latham, Henry. *Black and White: A Journal of a Three Months' Tour in the United States*. London: Macmillan, 1867.

Lewis, Earl. *In Their Own Interests: Race, Class, and Power in Twentieth-Century Norfolk, Virginia*. Berkley: University of California Press, 1993.

Liras, José Esteban. *La primera enseñanza en la isla de Cuba*. Havana: Elías Fernández Casona, 1893.

Liras, José Esteban. *Resumen de la legislación de primera enseñanza vigente en la isla de Cuba, 1895*. Havana: La Propagandista, 1895.

Litwack, Leon F. *Trouble in Mind: Black Southerners in the Age of Jim Crow*. New York: Alfred A. Knopf, 1998.

López, Oresta. "Las maestras en la historia de la educación en Mexico: Contribuciones para hacerlas visibles." *Sinéctica* 3 (2006): 4–16.

Lovejoy, Henry B. *Prieto: Yorùbá Kingship in Colonial Cuba during the Age of Revolution*. Chapel Hill: University of North Carolina Press, 2019.

Lowe, Lisa. *The Intimacies of Four Continents*. Durham, NC: Duke University Press, 2015.

Lucero, Bonnie. "Civilization before Citizenship: Education, Racial Order, and the Material Culture of Female Domesticity in American-Occupied Cuba, 1899–1902." *Journal of Atlantic Studies* 12, no. 1 (2015): 26–49.

Lucero, Bonnie. *A Cuban City, Segregated: Race and Urbanization in the Nineteenth Century.* Tuscaloosa: University of Alabama Press, 2019.
Lucero, Bonnie "En*gendering* Inequality: Masculinity and Racial Exclusion in Cuba, 1895–1902." PhD diss., University of North Carolina, 2013.
Lucero, Bonnie. "Racial Geographies, Imperial Transitions: Property Ownership and Race Relations in Cienfuegos, Cuba, 1894–1899." *Journal of Transnational American Studies* 3, no. 2 (2011).
Lucero, Bonnie. *Revolutionary Masculinity and Racial Inequality: Gendering War and Politics in Cuba.* Albuquerque: University of New Mexico Press, 2018.
Lynch, John. *Latin American Revolutions, 1808–1826: Old and New World Origins.* Norman: University of Oklahoma Press, 1994.
Mabee, Carleton. *Black Education in New York State from Colonial to Modern Times.* Syracuse, NY: Syracuse University Press, 1979.
Mabee, Carleton. "Control by Blacks over Schools in New York State, 1830–1930." *Phylon* 40, no. 1 (1979): 29–40. https://doi.org/10.2307/274420
MacDonald, Victoria-María. *Latino Education in the United States: A Narrated History from 1513–2000.* New York: Palgrave Macmillan, 2004.
Manekin, Sarah D. "Spreading the Empire of Free Education, 1865–1905." PhD diss., University of Pennsylvania, 2009.
Mann, Kristin. "Shifting Paradigms in the History of the African Diaspora and of Atlantic History and Culture." *Slavery and Abolition: A Journal of Slave and Post Slave Studies* 22, no. 1 (2001): 1–2.
Marable, Manning. *Malcolm X: A Life of Reinvention.* New York: Viking, 2011.
Marks, George P., ed. *The Black Press Views American Imperialism, 1898–1900.* New York: Arno, 1971.
Martin, Leona S. "Nation Building, International Travel, and the Construction of the Nineteenth-Century Pan-Hispanic Woman's Network." *Hispania* 87, no. 3 (September 2004): 439–446.
Martínez Alcubilla, Marcelo. *Diccionario de la administración española: Compilación de la novísima legislación de España, peninsular y ultramarina en todos los ramos de la administración pública.* Madrid: Administración, 1892. https://bvpb.mcu.es/es/consulta/registro.do?id=440732.
Martínez-Alier, Verena. *Marriage, Class, and Color in Nineteenth-Century Cuba: A Study of Racial Attitudes and Sexual Values in a Slave Society.* Ann Arbor: University of Michigan Press, 1974.
Martínez y Díaz, José F. *Historia de la educación pública en Cuba desde el descubrimiento hasta nuestros días y causas de su fracaso.* Pinar del Río, Cuba: Casa Villalba, 1943.
Matos Rodríguez, Félix. "*Libertas Citadinas*: Free Women of Color in San Juan, Puerto Rico." In *Beyond Bondage: Free Women of Color in the Americas*, edited by David Barry Gaspar and Darlene Clark Hine, 202–218. Chicago: University of Illinois Press, 2004.
Matos Rodríguez, Félix. "'¿Quién Trabajará?': Domestic Workers, Urban Slaves, and the Abolition of Slavery in Puerto Rico." In *Puerto Rican Women's History: New Per-*

spectives, edited by Félix V. Matos Rodríguez and Linda D. Delgado, 62–82. Armonk, NY: M. E. Sharpe, 1998.

Maynes, Mary Jo. *Schooling in Western Europe: A Social History.* Albany: State University of New York Press, 1985.

McCadden, Joseph J. "The New York to Cuba Axis of Father Varela." *The Americas* 20, no. 4 (April 1964): 376–392.

McGillivray, Gillian. *Blazing Cane: Sugar Communities, Class, and State Formation in Cuba, 1868-1959.* Durham, NC: Duke University Press, 2009.

McHenry, Elizabeth. "'Dreaded Eloquence': The Origins and Rise of African American Literary Societies and Libraries." *Harvard Library Bulletin* 6, no. 2 (Summer 1995): 32–56.

McLeod, Marc C. "Undesirable Aliens: Race, Ethnicity, and Nationalism in the Comparison of Haitian and British West Indians." *Journal of Social History* 31, no. 3 (Spring 1998): 599–623.

Mena, Luz. "Stretching the Limits of Gendered Spaces: Black and Mulatto Women in 1830s Havana." *Cuban Studies* 36 (2005): 87–104.

Meriño Fuentes, María de los Ángeles. *Gobierno municipal y partidos políticos en Santiago de Cuba (1898-1912).* Santiago, Cuba: Santiago, 2001.

Meyer, John W., David Tyack, Joane Nagel, and Audri Gordon. "Public Education as Nation-Building in America: Enrollments and Bureaucratization in the American States, 1870–1930." *American Journal of Sociology* 85, no. 3 (November 1979): 591–613.

Minichino, Mario J. "In Our Image: The Attempted Reshaping of the Cuban Educational System by the United States Government, 1898-1912." PhD diss., University of South Florida, 2014.

Mintz, Sidney, and Richard Price. *The Birth of African-American Culture: An Anthropological Perspective.* Boston: Beacon, 1992.

Mirabal, Nancy Raquel. *Suspect Freedoms: The Racial and Sexual Politics of Cubanidad in New York, 1823-1957.* New York: New York University Press, 2017.

Mitchell, Mary Niall. *Raising Freedom's Child: Black Children and Visions of the Future After Slavery.* New York: NYU Press, 2008.

Montejo Arrechea, Carmen Victoria. *Sociedades de iInstrucción y recreo de pardos y morenos que existieron en Cuba colonial, período 1878-1898.* Veracruz, Mexico: Instituto Veracruzano de Cultura, 1993.

Montgomery, Rebecca S. *The Politics of Education in the New South: Women and Reform in Georgia, 1890-1930.* Baton Rouge: Louisiana State University Press, 2006.

Moore, Robin. *Nationalizing Blackness: Afrocubanismo and Artistic Revolution in Havana, 1920-1940.* Pittsburgh, PA: University of Pittsburgh Press, 1997.

Morales Domínguez, Esteban. *Race in Cuba.* New York: Monthly Review Press, 2013.

Moreno Fraginals, Manuel. *El ingenio: Complejo económico-social cubano de azúcar.* Havana: Editorial de Ciencias Sociales, 1978.

Morgan, Jennifer L. *Laboring Women: Reproduction and Gender in New World Slavery.* Philadelphia: University of Pennsylvania Press, 2004.

Morgan, Jennifer. "Partus Sequitur Ventrum: Law, Race, and Reproduction in Colonial Slavery." *Small Axe* 22, no. 1 (2018): 1–17.
Morris, Robert C. *Reading, 'Riting, and Reconstruction: The Education of Freedmen in the South, 1861–1870.* Chicago: University of Chicago Press, 1976.
Morrison, Karen Y. "Civilization and Citizenship through the Eyes of Afro-Cuban Intellectuals during the First Constitutional Era, 1902–1940." *Cuban Studies* 30 (2000): 76–99.
Morrison, Karen Y. *Cuba's Racial Crucible: The Sexual Economy of Social Identities, 1750–2000.* Bloomington: Indiana University Press, 2015.
Morúa Delgado, Martín. *Integración cubana y otros ensayos.* Havana: Comisión Nacional del Centenario de don Martín Morúa Delgado, 1957.
Moses, Wilson Jeremiah. *Creative Conflict in African American Thought: Frederick Douglass, Alexander Crummell, Booker T. Washington, W.E.B. Du Bois, and Marcus Garvey.* Cambridge, England: Cambridge University Press, 2004.
Moss, Hilary J. *Schooling Citizens: The Struggle for African American Education in Antebellum America.* Chicago: University of Chicago Press, 2009.
Muñoz, Laura K. *Desert Dreams: Mexican Arizona and the Politics of Educational Equity.* Philadelphia: University of Pennsylvania Press, 2023.
Neem, Johann. *Democracy's Schools: The Rise of Public Education in America.* Baltimore, MD: Johns Hopkins University Press, 2017.
Negrín Fajardo, Olegario. "Maestros y educadores españoles en el siglo XVIII," *Cuadernos de estudios del siglo XVIII* 15 (2017): 117–157. doi:10.17811/cesxviii.15.2005.117–157.
Neverdon-Morton, Cynthia. "Self-Help Programs as Educative Activities of Black Women in the South, 1895–1925: Focus on Four Key Areas." *Journal of Negro Education* 51, no. 3 (Summer 1982): 207–221.
Newland, Carlos. "La educación elemental en Hispanoamerica: Desde la independencia hasta la centralización de los sistemas educativos nacionales." *Hispanic American Historical Review* 71, no. 2 (May 1991): 335–364.
Norman, Matthew, and Fiona McAuslan. *The Rough Guide to Havana.* London: Rough Guides, 2010.
Norrell, Robert J. *Up from History: The Life of Booker T. Washington.* Cambridge, MA: Harvard University Press, 2009.
Nwankwo, Ifeoma Kiddoe. *Black Cosmopolitanism: Racial Consciousness and Transnational Identity in the Nineteenth-Century Americas.* Philadelphia: University of Pennsylvania Press, 2005.
O'Brien, Kenneth B. "The Cuban Educational Association: An Early Experiment in International Education." *Journal of Negro Education* 32, no. 1 (Winter 1963): 6–15.
Opatrny, Josef. "José Antonio Saco's Path toward the Idea of Cubanidad." *Cuban Studies* 24 (1994): 39–56.
Orfield, Gary, Erica Frankenerg, Jongyeon Ee, and Jennifer B. Ayscue. "Harming Our Common Future: America's Segregated Schools 65 Years after Brown." Civil Rights Project—Proyecto Derecho Civiles at UCLA, May 10, 2019, University of California, Los Angeles. https://www.civilrightsproject.ucla.edu/research/k-12

-education/integration-and-diversity/harming-our-common-future-americas-segregated-schools-65-years-after-brown/Brown-65-050919v4-final.pdf.

Ossenbach, Gabriela. "Research into the History of Education in Latin America: Balance of the Current Situation." *Paedagogica Historica* 36, no. 3 (2000): 841–867.

Ossenbach Sauter, Gabriela. "Política educativa española para la isla de Cuba en el siglo XIX (1837–1868)." *Historia de la Educación* 2 (1983): 263–274.

Otheguy, Raquel Alicia. "Education in Empire, Nation, and Diaspora: Black Cubans' Struggle for Schooling, 1850–1910." PhD diss., Stony Brook University, 2016.

Packard, Robert Lawrence, and US Bureau of Education. *Education in the Philippines, Cuba, Porto Rico, Hawaii, and Samoa.* Washington, DC: Government Printing Office, 1901. At Library of Congress, https://www.loc.gov/item/06015968/.

Palmié, Stephan. *Wizards and Scientists: Explorations in Afro-Cuban Modernity and Tradition.* Durham, NC: Duke University Press, 2002.

Pando, Dalen. "Juan Gualberto Gomez, A Cuban Portrait." *Caribbean Quarterly* 5 (1958): 78–84.

Pappademos, Melina. *Black Political Activism and the Cuban Republic.* Chapel Hill: University of North Carolina Press, 2011.

Paquette, Robert L. *Sugar Is Made with Blood: The Conspiracy of La Escalera and the Conflict between Empires over Slavery in Cuba.* Middletown, CT: Wesleyan University Press, 1988.

Patterson, Orlando. *Slavery and Social Death: A Comparative Study.* Cambridge, MA: Harvard University Press, 1982.

Payne, Stanley G. *A History of Spain and Portugal.* Madison: University of Wisconsin Press, 1973.

Payne, Stanley G. *Spain: A Unique History.* Madison: University of Wisconsin Press, 2011.

Perera Díaz, Aisnara. *Para librarse de lazos, antes buena familia que buenos brazos: Apuntes sobre la manumisión en Cuba.* Santiago, Cuba: Oriente, 2009.

Pérez, Emma. *Historia de la pedagogía en Cuba desde los orígenes hasta la guerra de independencia.* Havana: Cultural, 1945.

Pérez, Lisandro. *Sugar, Cigars, and Revolution: The Making of Cuban New York.* New York: NYU Press, 2018.

Pérez, Louis A. Jr. *Cuba between Empires, 1878–1902.* Pittsburgh, PA: University of Pittsburgh Press, 1983.

Pérez, Louis A. Jr. *Cuba between Reform and Revolution.* 3rd edition. New York: Oxford University Press, 2006.

Pérez, Louis A. Jr. "The Imperial Design: Politics and Pedagogy in Occupied Cuba, 1899–1902." *Cuban Studies/Estudios Cubanos* 12 (July 1982): 1–19.

Perkinson, Henry J. *The Imperfect Panacea: American Faith in Education.* 4th edition. New York: McGraw-Hill, 1995.

Pimenta, João Paulo G. "Education and the Historiography of Ibero-American Independence: Elusive Presences, Many Absences." *Paedagogica Historica* 46, no. 4 (August 2010): 419–434.

Pla, Eduardo F. *Educación de la democracia*. Havana: P. Fernández, 1904.

Pla, José. *La raza de color: Necesidad de instruir y moralizar a los individuos de color y de fomentar el matrimonio entre los patrocinados*. Matanzas, Cuba: El Ferro-Carril, 1881.

Portuondo Zúñiga, Olga. *Entre esclavos y libres de Cuba colonial*. Santiago, Cuba: Oriente, 2003.

Provencio Garrigós, Lucía. "Construyendo identidades desde la excepcionalidad: Mujer, divorciada, y maestra en Santiago de Cuba, siglo XIX." *Revista de Indias* 68, no. 243 (2008): 177–206.

Provencio Garrigós, Lucía. "Las maestras tituladas: Santiago de Cuba, 1842–1863." *Baluarte* 3 (2002): 47–70.

Provencio Garrigós, Lucía. "¡Mujeres a la escuela! Lo que quería ser público y resultó privado. Santiago de Cuba a principios del siglo XIX." In *Historia de las mujeres en América Latina*, edited by Sara Beatriz Guardia, 209–244. Lima: Centro de Estudios la Mujer en la Historia de América Latina, 2012.

Provencio Garrigós, Lucía. "La *Trampa* discursiva del elogio a la maternidad cubana del siglo XIX." *Americanía*, no. 1 (2011): 42–73.

Quiroz, Alfonso W. "Free Association and Civil Society in Cuba, 1787–1895." *Journal of Latin American Studies* 48, no. 1 (February 2011): 33–64.

Quiroz, Alfonso. "Martí in Cuban Schools." In *The Cuban Republic and José Martí: Reception and Uses of a National Symbol*, edited by Mauricio Font and Alfonso Quiroz, 71–81. New York: Lexington, 2006.

Quiroz, Alfonso. "La reforma educacional en Cuba, 1898–1909: Cambio y continuidad." In *Culturas encontradas: Cuba y los Estados Unidos*, edited by Rafael Hernandez and John H. Coatsworth, 113–126. Cambridge, MA: Harvard University Press, 2001.

Rael, Patrick. *Black Identity and Black Protest in the Antebellum North*. Chapel Hill: University of North Carolina Press, 2002.

Rasmussen, Birgit Brander. "'Attended with Great Inconveniences': Slave Literacy and the 1740 South Carolina Negro Act." *PMLA* 125, no. 1 (2010): 201–203. http://www.jstor.org/stable/25614450.

Reese, William J. "The Origins of Progressive Education." *History of Education Quarterly* 41, no. 1, (Spring 2001): 1–24.

Reid, Michele. "Protesting Service: Free Black Reponses to Cuba's Reestablished Militia of Color, 1854–1865." *Journal of Colonialism and Colonial History* 5, no. 2 (2004): 1–22.

Reid-Vazquez, Michele. "Tensions of Race, Gender, and Midwifery in Colonial Cuba." In *Africans to Colonial Spanish America: Expanding the Diaspora*, edited by Rachel O'Toole, Sherwin Bryant, and Ben Vinson III, 186–205. Chicago: University of Illinois Press, 2012.

Reid-Vazquez, Michele. *The Year of the Lash: Free People of Color in Cuba and the Nineteenth-Century Atlantic World*. Athens: University of Georgia Press, 2011.

Reimers, Fernando. "Education and Social Progress." In *The Cambridge Economic History of Latin America*, volume 2, edited by Victor Bulmer-Thomas, John Coatsworth, and Roberto Cortes-Conde, 427–480. Cambridge, England: Cambridge University Press, 2006.

Reyes, Juan Justo. *Memoria sobre los progresos que ha hecho la instrucción pública bajo la protección de la Real Sociedad Patriótica de la Habana desde que se puso en activo ejercicio su clase de educación*. Havana: Imprenta del Gobierno y Capitanía General, 1830.

Ris, Ethan. *Other People's Colleges: The Origins of American Higher Education Reform*. Chicago: University of Chicago Press, 2022.

Risquet, Juan Felipe. *Rectificaciones: La cuestión político-social en la isla de Cuba*. Havana: Patria, 1900.

Roberts, Neil. *Freedom as Marronage*. Chicago: University of Chicago Press, 2015.

Robinson, Albert Gardner. *Cuba and the Intervention*. New York: Longmans, Green, 1905.

Robinson, Cedric J. *Black Marxism: The Making of the Black Radical Tradition*. 3rd edition. Chapel Hill: University of North Carolina Press, 2000.

Rodríguez, Daniel A. *The Right to Live in Health: Medical Politics in Postindependence Havana*. Chapel Hill: University of North Carolina Press, 2020.

Roig de Leuchsenring, Emilio. *La lucha cubana por la república, contra la anexión y la Enmienda Platt*. Havana: Oficina del Historiador de la Ciudad de La Habana, Colección Histórica Cubana Americana, 1952.

Roldán de Montaud, Inés. "La carrera de un alto funcionario moderado en Cuba: Vicente Vázquez Queipo (1804–1893)." In *L'État dans ses colonies: Les administrateurs de l'empire espagnol au XIXe siècle*, edited by Jean-Phillipe Luis, 137–156. Madrid: Casa de Velázquez, 2015. https://books.openedition.org/cvz/1196?lang=en.

Rousseau, Pablo L., and Pablo Díaz de Villegas. *Memoria descriptiva, histórica y biográfica de Cienfuegos, 1819–1919*. Havana: El Siglo XX, 1920.

Rury, John L., and Eileen H. Tamura, eds. *The Oxford Handbook of the History of Education*. New York: Oxford University Press, 2019.

Saco, José Antonio. *Memorias sobre caminos en la isla de Cuba*. New York: G. F. Bunce, 1830.

Safford, Frank. *The Ideal of the Practical: Colombia's Struggle to Form a Technical Elite*. Austin: University of Texas Press, 1976.

Salvatore, Ricardo D. "Imperial Revisionism: U.S. Historians of Latin America and the Spanish Colonial Empire (ca. 1915–1945)." *Journal of Transnational American Studies* 5, no. 1 (2013): 1–54.

Sartorius, David. "Colonial Transfusions: Cuban Bodies and Spanish Loyalty in the Nineteenth Century." In *The Cultural Politics of Blood, 1500–1900*, edited by Kimberly Anne Coles, Ralph Bauer, Zita Nunes, and Carla L. Peterson, 229–250. New York: Palgrave Macmillan, 2015.

Sartorius, David. *Ever Faithful: Race, Loyalty, and the Ends of Empire in Spanish Cuba*. Durham, NC: Duke University Press, 2013.

Sartorius, David. "My Vassals: Free-Colored Militias in Cuba and the Ends of the Spanish Empire." *Journal of Colonialism and Colonial History* 5, no. 2 (2004).
Scarano, Francisco. "Liberal Pacts and Hierarchies of Rule: Approaching the Imperial Transition in Cuba and Puerto Rico." *Hispanic American Historical Review* 78, no. 4 (November 1998): 583–601.
Schaffer, Kirwin R. "Freedom Teaching: Anarchism and Education in Early Republican Cuba, 1898–1925." *The Americas* 80, no. 2 (October 2003): 151–183.
Schmidt-Nowara, Christopher. *The Conquest of History: Spanish Colonialism and National Histories in the Nineteenth Century*. Pittsburgh, PA: University of Pittsburgh Press, 2006.
Schmidt-Nowara, Christopher. *Empire and Anti-Slavery: Spain, Cuba, and Puerto Rico, 1833–1874*. Pittsburgh, PA: University of Pittsburgh Press, 1999.
Schmidt-Nowara, Christopher. "The Specter of Las Casas: José Antonio Saco and the Persistence of Spanish Colonialism in Cuba." *Itinerario* 25, no. 2 (2001): 93–109. doi:10.1017/S0165115300008846.
Schneider, Elena. "African Slavery and Spanish Empire: Imperial Imaginings and Bourbon Reform in Eighteenth-Century Cuba and Beyond." *Journal of Early American History* 5 (2015): 3–29.
Schultz, Rainer. "The Liberal Moment of the Revolution: Cuba's Early Educational Reforms, 1959–1961." *Cuban Studies*, no. 49 (2020): 215–236. https://www.jstor.org/stable/26983800.
Scott, Julius. *The Common Wind: Afro-American Currents in the Age of the Haitian Revolution*. New York: Verso, 2018.
Scott, Rebecca J. *Slave Emancipation in Cuba: The Transition to Free Labor, 1860–1899*. Pittsburgh, PA: University of Pittsburgh Press, 1985.
Sensbach, Jon F. *Rebecca's Revival: Creating Black Christianity in the Atlantic World*. Cambridge, MA: Harvard University Press, 2005.
Serra, Rafael. *Ensayos políticos*. 1st series. New York: El Porvenir, 1892.
Serra, Rafael. *Ensayos políticos*. 2nd series. New York: P. J. Díaz, 1896.
Serra, Rafael. *Ensayos políticos*. 3rd series. New York: A. W. Howes, 1899.
Serra, Rafael. *Para blancos y negros: Ensayos políticos, sociales y económicos*. 4th series. Havana: El Score, 1907.
Shaffer, Kirwin. *Anarchism and Countercultural Politics in Early Twentieth-Century Cuba*. Gainesville: University Press of Florida, 2005.
Shaw, Stephanie J. *What a Woman Ought to Be and Do: Black Professional Women Workers during the Jim Crow Era*. Chicago: University of Chicago Press, 1996.
Smallwood, Stephanie E. "The Politics of the Archive and History's Accountability to the Enslaved." *History of the Present* 6, no. 2 (2016): 117–132. https://doi.org/10.5406/historypresent.6.2.0117.
Smallwood, Stephanie. *Saltwater Slavery: A Middle Passage from Africa to American Diaspora*. Cambridge, MA: Belknap, 2008.
Smithsonian American Art Museum. "Literacy as Freedom." Washington, DC, September 2014. https://americanexperience.si.edu/wp-content/uploads/2014/09/Literacy-as-Freedom.pdf.

Sobe, Noah W. *American Post-Conflict Educational Reform: From the Spanish-American War to Iraq.* New York: Palgrave Macmillan, 2009.
Sosa Rodríguez, Enrique, and Alejandrina Penabad Félix. *Historia de la educación en Cuba.* 10 volumes. Havana: Pueblo y Educación, 2005.
Spain. Guía de forasteros de la siempre fiel isla de Cuba. Volumes 1837–1884. Havana: Imprenta del Gobierno y Capitanía General por S. M. At Library of Congress, https://www.loc.gov/item/44027902/.
Spain. Resumen del Censo de Población de la Isla de Cuba a fin del año de 1841. Havana: Imprenta del Gobierno por S. M., 1842.
Spain, Ministerio de Ultramar. Legislación Ultramarina. 16 volumes. Madrid, 1865–1869. At University of Florida Digital Collections, https://ufdc.ufl.edu/AA00080854/00001.
Spain, Ministerio de Ultramar. *Real Decreto estableciendo un nuevo plan de estudios para la isla de Cuba.* Havana: Imprenta del Gobierno y Capitanía General por S. M., 1863. At Biblioteca Digital Hispánica, http://bdh-rd.bne.es/viewer.vm?id=0000110595&page=1.
Span, Christopher M., and Brenda N. Sanya. "Education and the African Diaspora." In *The Oxford Handbook of the History of Education,* edited by John L. Rury and Eileen H. Tamura, 399–412. New York: Oxford University Press, 2019.
Spencer, Samuel R. Jr. *Booker T. Washington and the Negro's Place in American Life.* Boston: Little, Brown, 1955.
Spivey, Donald. *Schooling for the New Slavery: Black Industrial Education, 1868–1915.* London: Greenwood, 1978.
Spring, Joel. *Deculturalization and the Struggle for Equality: A Brief History of the Education of Dominated Cultures in the United States.* New York: McGraw Hill, 2001.
Stepan, Nancy. *The Hour of Eugenics: Race, Gender, and Nation in Latin America.* Ithaca, NY: Cornell University Press, 1991.
Stoner, K. Lynn. *From the House to the Streets: The Cuban Woman's Movement for Legal Reform, 1898–1940.* Durham, NC: Duke University Press, 1991.
Studnicki-Gizbert, Daviken. *A Nation upon the Ocean Sea: Portugal's Atlantic Diaspora and the Crisis of the Spanish Empire, 1492–1640.* New York: Oxford University Press, 2007.
Suárez y Romero, A. "Educación: Enseñanza privada." *Revista de la Habana,* 1854, 209.
Sueiro Rodríguez, Victoria María. "Composición social y caracterización de las principales sociedades culturales y de instrucción y recreo en la región de Cienfuegos entre 1840 y 1899." *Espacio, Tiempo y Forma* 5, no. 11 (1998): 327–342.
Sweet, James H. *Recreating Africa: Culture, Kinship, and Religion in the African-Portuguese World, 1441–1770.* Chapel Hill: University of North Carolina Press, 2003.
Tanck, Dorothy. "Escuelas, colegios y conventos para niñas y mujeres indígenas en el siglo XVIII." In *Obedecer, servir y resistir: La educación de las mujeres en la historia de México,* edited by Adelina Arredondo. Mexico City: Universidad Pedagógica Nacional, 2003.
Tannenbaum, Frank. *Slave and Citizen.* Boston: Beacon, 1946.

Tarragó, Rafael E. "Afro-Cuban Identity and the Black Press in Spanish Cuba, 1878–1898." In *Latin American Identities: Race, Ethnicity, Gender, and Sexuality*, Papers of the Forty-Sixth Annual Meeting of the Seminar on the Acquisition of Latin American Library Materials (SALALM) (Tempe, AZ: SALALM, 2001).
Tejera, Diego Vicente. *Blancos y negros: Conferencia dada en Cayo Hueso en 7 de noviembre de 1897*. Havana: Patria, 1900.
Theoharis, Jeanne. *A More Beautiful and Terrible History: The Uses and Misuses of Civil Rights History*. Boston: Beacon, 2018.
Thompson, Owen. "School Desegregation and Black Teacher Employment." *Review of Economics and Statistics* 104, no. 5 (2022): 962–980.
Tinajero, Araceli. *El Lector: A History of the Cigar Factory Reader*. Austin: University of Texas Press, 2010.
Trelles, Carlos Manuel. *Matanzas en la independencia de Cuba*. Havana: Avisador Comercial, 1928.
Trouillot, Michel-Rolph. *Silencing the Past: Power and the Production of History*. Boston: Beacon, 1995.
US War Department. *Report on the Census of Cuba, 1899*. Washington, DC: Government Printing Office, 1900.
Valdés Guada, Alberto. *La Educación en Cienfuegos durante la República, 1902–1958*. Cienfuegos: Editorial Universidad de Cienfuegos, 1997.
Varella, Claudia, and Manuel Barcia. *Wage-Earning Slaves: Coartación in Nineteenth-Century Cuba*. Gainesville: University of Florida Press, 2020.
Varona y Pera, Enrique José. *La instrucción pública en Cuba*. Havana: Rambla y Bouza, 1901.
Vaughan, Mary Kay. *Cultural Politics in Revolution: Teachers, Peasants, and Schools in Mexico, 1930–1940*. Tucson: University of Arizona Press, 1997.
Vaughan, Mary Kay. *The State, Education, and Social Class in Mexico, 1880–1928*. DeKalb: Northern Illinois University Press, 1982.
Villoldo, Julio. *Necesidad de colegios cubanos: El genio de los pueblos, la escuela laíca*. Havana: El Siglo XX, 1914.
Vinat de la Mata, Raquel. "Colores y dolores de la educación femenina en Cuba (siglo XIX)." In *Emergiendo del silencio: Mujeres negras en la historia de Cuba*, edited by Oilda Hevia Lanier and Daisy Rubiera Castillo, 89–130. Havana: Editorial de Ciencias Sociales, 2016.
Vinat de la Mata, Raquel. *Luces en el silencio: Educación femenina en Cuba 1648–1898*. Havana: Política, 2005.
Vinson, Ben III. *Bearing Arms for His Majesty: The Free-Colored Militia in Colonial Mexico*. Stanford, CA: Stanford University Press, 2002.
Vogel, Sara, and Ofelia García. "Translanguaging." In *Oxford Research Encyclopedia of Education*. New York: Oxford University Press, 2017. doi:10.1093/acrefore/9780190264093.013.181.
Walker, Vanessa Siddle. "Brown and Its Impact on Schools and American Life." *American Bar Association Focus on Law Studies* 19 (2004): 1–17.

Walker, Vanessa Siddle. "Second-Class Integration: A Historical Perspective for a Contemporary Agenda." *Harvard Educational Review* 79, no. 2 (2009): 269–284.

Walker, Vanessa Siddle. *Their Highest Potential: An African American School Community in the Segregated South*. Chapel Hill: University of North Carolina Press, 2000.

Weinberg, Gregorio. *Modelos educativos en la historia de América Latina*. Buenos Aires: A-Z, 1995.

Whitney, Robert. "The Political Economy of Abolition: The Hispano-Cuban Elite and Cuban Slavery, 1868–1873." *Slavery and Abolition* 13, no. 2 (August 1992): 20–36.

Whitney, Robert. *State and Revolution in Cuba: Mass Mobilization and Political Change, 1920–1940*. Chapel Hill: University of North Carolina Press, 2001.

Williams, Danielle Terrazas. *A Capital of Free Women: Race, Legitimacy, and Liberty in Colonial Mexico*. New Haven, CT: Yale University Press, 2022.

Williams, Eric. *Capitalism and Slavery*. 3rd edition. Chapel Hill: University of North Carolina Press, 2021.

Williams, Heather Andrea. *Self-Taught: African American Education in Slavery and Freedom*. Chapel Hill: University of North Carolina Press, 2005.

Woodward, C. Van. *The Strange Career of Jim Crow*. New York: Oxford University Press, 2002.

Yacou, Alain. *Essor des plantations et subversión antiesclavagiste à Cuba, 1791–1845*. Paris: Karthala, 2010.

Yaremko, Jason. "The Path of Progress: Protestant Missions, Education, and U.S. Hegemony in the New Cuba, 1898–1940." In *American Post-Conflict Educational Reform: From the Spanish American War to Iraq*, edited by Noah W. Sobe, 53–74. New York: Palgrave Macmillan, 2009.

Zambrana Valdés, Ramón. "Los niños." *Revista de la Habana* 2 (1853–1854): 53–54.

Zeleza, Paul Tiyambe. "Rewriting the African Diaspora: Beyond the Black Atlantic." *African Affairs* 104, no. 414 (2005): 35–68.

Zeuske, Michael. "Hidden Markers, Open Secrets: On Naming, Race-Marking, and Race-Making in Cuba." *New West Indian Guide* 76, no. 3/4 (2002): 211–241.

Zeuske, Michael. "'Los negros hicimos la independencia': Aspectos de movilización afrocubana en un hinterland cubano; Cienfuegos entre colonia y república." In *Espacios, silencios y los sentidos de la libertad: Cuba entre 1878 y 1912*, edited by Fernando Martínez Heredia, Rebecca J. Scott, and Orlando F. García Martínez. 193–234. Havana: Unión, 2001.

Zeuske, Michael. "Two Stories of Gender and Slave Emancipation in Cienfuegos and Santa Clara, Central Cuba: Microhistorical Approaches to the Atlantic World." In *Gender and Slave Emancipation in the Atlantic World*, edited by Pamela Scully and Diana Paton, 181–198. Durham, NC: Duke University Press, 2005.

Zimmerman, Andrew. *Alabama in Africa: Booker T. Washington, the German Empire, and the Globalization of the New South*. Princeton, NJ: Princeton University Press, 2010.

Zurbano, Roberto. "For Blacks in Cuba, the Revolution Hasn't Begun." *New York Times*, March 23, 2013. https://www.nytimes.com/2013/03/24/opinion/sunday/for-blacks-in-cuba-the-revolution-hasnt-begun.html.

INDEX

Page numbers in *italics* indicate illustrations.

Abakuá religious society, 11, 64, 65
Academia Nocturna Gratuita, 172n10
African Americans: compared to Afro-descended Cubans, 153; disenfranchisement of, 152; and education, 22, 97, 120, 123, 125, 186n2; marginalization of, 152–53; and mutual aid societies, 117; violence against, 152; and White supremacy, 152
African diaspora, 60
African ethnic organizations. *See* Cabildos de nación
Africans: and armed rebellions, 28, 51, 55, 58, 65; and Black Cuban Creoles, 65; and education, 5, 30, 92, 172n9; enslaved, 3, 5, 13, 28, 92, 94, 188n36; and gender, 3; increased numbers of, 27, 28, 45; and miscegenation, 152; missionaries and, 172n9; and mulato/mulata persons, 65; and sugar economy, 5, 6, 28
Afro-descended Caribbean persons, 172n9
Afro-descended Cubans: and activism, 1, 3, 10; and armed rebellions, 4, 8, 12, 18, 19, 20, 27, 47, 48, 49, 51, 52, 54, 55, 58, 59, 63, 65, 149, 151, 153; and assimilation, 140; and Black newspapers, 16; and bourgeois norms, 11; censuring of, 128; and civil rights, 143, 150; and class, 56, 65, 137–38, 143; and colonialism, 11, 18, 128; community among, 10; compared to African Americans, 153; and concerns for wider Cuban society, 142; and Cuban independence movement, 132, 134, 140, 148; and Cuban nationhood and identity, 9, 10, 128; cultural differences among, 65; and culture, 143; and employment, 165; and equality, 3, 9; exiled, 128, 130, 133; and Fidel Castro government, 169; in government records, 17; on harmony within Cuban society, 148–49; and health, 165; impact of, on Cuban society, 9; increased numbers of, 27, 32, 35, 44, 45, 76, 153; and integration of public spaces, 107–8, 129, 136–37, 141; as intellectuals, 1, 16, 86–87, 128, 133, 142; intellectual history of, 14; and liberation, 2, 3, 58; and loyal subjectivity, 128; and militia service, 52; and mutual aid societies, 2, 3; occupations of, 56; organizational traditions of, 9, 110, 169; as parents, 1; and participation in Cuban society, 76, 81, 104, 136; and patriarchy, 11; and patronage, 11; as political office holders, 11; and political parties, 128–29, 168, 169; and political rights, 9; population figures for, 159, 199n35; and post-independence myth of racial equality, 11; as property owners, 120; and racial discrimination, 5, 18, 170; racialization of, 23–24; and racial justice, 140; and racial solidarity, 66, 67, 119; and racial uplift, 143; and resistance to racial oppression, 11; and response to segregation, 11–12; scholarship on, 11; and separatist political organization, 149; settlement patterns of, 96, 153; and slavery and abolition, 3, 9, 11, 13; social networks of, 56; and social status, 18, 65; and Spanish colonial government, 7, 27, 65, 73, 76, 78, 81–82, 88, 90, 91, 103, 107–8, 128, 134, 137, 140, 142, 145, 148, 150; and Spanish constitution, 134, 144, 145; as taxpayers, 101, 120; terms for, 23, 116; during US occupation of Cuba, 151, 152–54, 157; and violence, 11, 13, 168; and voting rights, 11, 145, 153, 154,

228 · Index

163, 164; and White Cuban Creoles, 27, 76, 91; and White resistance to integration, 142, 143. See also Free people of color; Women of color, Cuban
Afro-descended Cubans, and education: in 18th century, 33; and 1893 civil rights orders, 127, 139–40, 141–42, 145; and access to education, 9, 15, 35, 47, 76, 83, 84, 85, 94, 96, 125, 158; and Afro-descendants' place in Cuban society, 91, 109; and broader campaign for equality and rights, 134, 136, 171n1; and class, 128, 136; and drop-outs, 165; and education as political and social tool, 85, 112, 122, 128, 133, 134, 148, 167; and education for all Cubans, 1, 126, 133; and education for newly freed enslaved persons, 99; and equal school rights, 97, 108, 111, 126, 128, 150, 168, 170; and Fidel Castro government, 22–23, 49, 169, 170; and freedom and liberation, 22, 67, 69; and free education, 167, 168; historical records on, 52; impact of slavery on, 132, 136, 145–46; importance of, 67, 110, 119, 145, 146, 147, 167; and literacy, 153–54; and loyal subjectivity, 100; and militias, 54; and municipal schools, 16, 17, 21, 108–9, 112, 120; and national public school system, 171n1; and oppositional politics, 52; petitions by, 89, 101, 108; and political consciousness, 72; and political parties, 168; and race of teachers of students of color, 112; and racial justice, 147, 148, 168; and racially integrated schools, 1, 21, 110, 158, 164; and racial solidarity, 59, 66, 67, 69–70, 112; and racial uplift, 170; and school funding, 109, 110, 111; and school registration and attendance, 154, 164–65, 199n35; schools established by, 21–22, 110, 111; and separate schooling projects, 140; and sociedades de color / mutual aid society schools, 21, 109; and Spanish colonial government, 85, 93, 108; and valorization of Black teachers and students, 22; and vocational education, 99; and White Cuban Creoles, 100, 148; and White Cubans, 133; and White resistance to school desegregation, 142; and White supremacy, 133–34, 167. See also Black Cuban educational tradition; Directorio Central de las Sociedades de la Raza de Color; Escuelitas de amigas / home schools; Maestras amigas; Militiamen-teachers, Afro-descended Cuban; Municipal schools; Private schools for students of color; Sociedades de color / mutual aid societies, schools of; Teachers, Afro-descended Cuban

Afro-descended Latin Americans, 12–13, 23, 177n41
Aguacate, Cuba, 117
Alcázar Antillano sociedad de color / mutual aid society, 133
Alexander, Leslie M., 17
Alfonso XII, Cuba, 89, 95, 96, 106
Almedia de Soriano, Dorotea, 116
Alonso Rojas, Cuba, 96
Alto Songo, Cuba, 161
Anglican Church, 172n9
Antilles, 140
Aponte, José, 49, 64, 186n34
Aponte rebellion, 54, 58, 64, 186n34
Apuntes para la historia de las letras y de la instrucción pública de la isla de Cuba (Bachiller), 42
Argentina, 14, 198n9
Arjona, Beatriz, 114–16
Arjona, Vicente Silveira, 114, 116
Aultman, Dwight, 162

Bachiller y Morales, Antonio: on Afro-descended militiamen turned teachers, 40; on Black Cubans teaching White children, 44, 45; on education for boys, 42; on education for girls, 42–43, 46; on escuelitas de amigas, 40, 42, 43, 45, 46; on free schools, 31, 42; on maestras amigas, 40, 41, 42, 43; on number of schools and students, 181n31; on schools in Havana, 41; and Sociedad Económica, 31; works by, 42, 181n31
Bahía Honda, Cuba, 96
Baja, Cuba, 96
Baracoa, Cuba, 89, 95
Barba, Gabriel Doroteo, 55–56, 57, 66
Barcia, Manuel, 4, 58
Basilia Rodríguez, Elena, 113, 118
Bataller, Felipe, 118

Baumgartner, Kabria, 112, 171n1
Bayamo, Cuba, 95, 106
Bejucal, Cuba, 89, 95, 106, 191n58
Belén school, 34, 80
Bella Unión Habanera sociedad de color / mutual aid society, 120, 122
Bello, Andrés, 8
Benites, Juan José, 61, *62*
Benson, Devyn Spence, 169
Berrayarza, Filmena, 116
Black Cuban Creoles, 33, 65, 110, 153, 154. *See also* White Cuban Creoles
Black Cuban educational tradition: and 1893 civil rights orders, 167; and 1895–98 war of independence, 151, 167; and access to education, 1, 111, 121, 150; and activism, 1, 7, 10, 17, 18; and agency, 12; and armed rebellion, 2, 3, 12; and Black-run schools, 1–2, 10, 14, 17, 122, 167; and Black thought, 10; and class, 18, 170; and co-ed education, 2, 150; as counter to racist assumptions of US occupiers, 151; and Cuban nationalism, 12; and Cuban public education system, 2, 19; and curricula, 2; and desire to solve social ills, 19; and Directorio Central de las Sociedades de la Raza de Color, 131–32; and education as political and social tool, 148, 167; and education for adults, 121, 122; and education for all Cubans, 3, 150, 169; and education for girls, 2, 6, 10, 17, 121, 122, 167; and equality, 3, 23; and equal school rights, 2, 17, 97; and freedom and liberation, 1, 19, 20, 21, 23, 73, 110, 170; and free education, 2, 10, 17, 120, 121–22, 127, 150, 167, 168; free persons and, 6; and gender, 18, 170; goals of, 55, 150; historical resources on, 15, 17; and history of Cuban education, 14; and identity, 10, 69; importance of, 170; and importance of education, 167; and initiative, 12; late 19th-century/early 20th-century legacy of, 22; and liberation for all Cubans, 3; and literacy, 10, 73; maestras amigas and, 68, 108; militiamen-teachers and, 68, 108; and municipal schools, 3, 12, 109; and mutual aid societies / sociedades de color, 3, 12, 17, 18; and newspaper pieces on education, 16; and official censorship of Black schools, 17; and oppositional politics, 3, 20, 51, 52; and opposition to race science and White supremacy, 10, 19; and organizations of people of color, 129; origins of, 108; overlooking of, 169; and participation in wider Cuban society, 12, 109; and political consciousness, 51, 69; and political protest, 122; and public schools, 12, 18; and race-based organizing, 12, 127; and racial integration in Cuban society, 51; and racial justice, 148; and racially integrated classrooms, 2, 3, 10, 17, 122, 150, 164, 167, 169; and racial segregation, 11; and racial separation, 109; and racial solidarity, 55, 73; and racial uplift, 18–19, 73; and rejection of mainstream vision for education, 51–52; and school creation, 10, 12, 18; and school desegregation, 3, 10, 12, 14, 18, 128, 150; and school funding, 122; and separate race-based schools, 51, 167; and sociedades de color / mutual aid societies, 120, 170; strategies of, 18; and teachers of color, 70, 121; and theories of power, 13; and US occupation of Cuba, 151, 167; and White Cuban Creoles, 6–7, 9; and White Cubans, 73; and White students, 3, 5, 10, 12, 119, 121, 167; and White supremacy, 19, 23, 167; and women's history, 13. *See also* 1893 civil rights order; Afro-descended Cubans, and education; Cuba, education in; Directorio Central de las Sociedades de la Raza de Color; Escuelitas de amigas / home schools; Maestras amigas; Militiamen-teachers, Afro-descended Cuban; Municipal schools; Private schools for students of color; Sociedades de color / mutual aid societies, schools of; Teachers, Afro-descended Cuban
Black Cubans. *See* Afro-descended Cubans
Black diaspora, 14
Black history, 13, 16
Black intellectual history, 12, 13, 14
Black Marxism (Robinson), 13
Blum, Denise, 49
Bonilla, Juan, 130, 133
Borrego, Pilar, 55, 64, 65–67, 68
Borrero Echavarría, Esteban, 156
Boston, MA, 106, 123

230 · Index

Bravo y Joven, Governor, 138
Brazil, 188n36
Brooke, George M., 160, 161, 162
Brooke, John, 157
Brooklyn, NY, 112, 123
Brown v. Board of Education of Topeka, 1, 170
Burkholder, Zoë, 22, 171n1
Byrd, Brandon R., 17

Cabezas, Cuba, 89, 95, 96
Cabildos de nación: Afro-descended Cuban rebels and, 65; definition of, 11; free people of color and, 66; historical records of, 53; importance of, 66; leadership in, 53; militiamen of color and, 53, 64; Nuestra Señora de Belén, 64; organization of, 119; as part of Afro-descendant Cuban organizational tradition, 110; and rebellion conspiracies, 64; San Benito de Palermo, 64; schools associated with, 53; and sociedades de color / mutual aid societies, 111, 140
Calleja, Emilio, 139
Calzada, José, 55
Camajuani, Cuba, 89, 95
Campo, Manuel, 100, 125
Cardenas, Cuba, 89, 95
Caribbean, 12-13, 69, 172n9
Caridad (maestra de amiga), 49-50
Carvajal, Juan Manuel, 31
Casino de Artesanos sociedad de color / mutual aid society, 132
Casino Popular La Bella Unión sociedad de color / mutual aid society, 119
Castillo Bueno, María de los Reyes (Reyita), 25, 26, 49, 50, 167
Castro, Fidel, 22
Catholics and Catholicism: Bethlemites, 6; conservative nature of, 175n23; convents and monasteries of, 6, 31, 41; and education, 6, 31, 41, 168, 173n17; Jesuits, 6, 80; lay confraternities *(cofradías)* of, 11; nuns, 6; Oblate Sisters of Charity, 169; and plantation slavery, 172n9; priests, 6, 67, 114; San Francisco de Sales, 6; and social legitimacy, 4; in Spain, 172n9, 175n23; Ursulines, 6
Centro de Cocineros La Bella Unión sociedad de color / mutual aid society, 119

Childs, Matt, 35, 46, 180n6
Chile, 198n9
Chinese, 153
Chira, Adriana, 4
Cienfuegos, Cuba: and 1878 education order, 97, 101-4, 124; Afro-descended population in, 96, 97, 101; free education in, 120; location of, 96; schools in, 101, 102-4, 114, 116, 119, 123, 124, 125-26; sociedades de color / mutual aid societies in, 114, 117-18, 119, 120, 123; sugar economy in, 96, 102; teachers of color in, 114, 115, 116, 119, 123; White sociedades / mutual aid societies in, 110
Cienfuegos province, Cuba, 101, 140-41
Cimarrones, Cuba, 89, 95
Coaffar de Marquez, Felicia, 114
Cofradías, 110
Coimbra de Valverde, Ursula, 116
Colegio de Santiago, 48
Colored School in Brooklyn, 123
Consolación del Sur, Cuba, 96
Corral Falso de Macuriges, Cuba, 89, 95
Creoles (term), 2. *See also* Black Cuban Creoles; Cuban Creoles; White Cuban Creoles
Cuartero, Angela, 116
Cuba: and 1876 Spanish constitution, 88, 134; 1901 constitution of, 154; abolition of slavery in, 1, 2, 3, 14, 90-91, 94, 96, 98, 99, 102, 107, 108, 112, 124, 125, 132, 140, 159; administrative reorganization of provinces and towns in, 88; Africans in, 27; anticolonialism in, 11, 104; Black consciousness in, 48, 49; blood purity in, 78; British occupation of, 53; Chinese in, 153; demographic shifts in, 94; and European immigration, 198n9; founding of, as Spanish colony, 3; freedom of assembly in, 88, 111; freedom of the press in, 7, 16, 111; free people of color in, 3, 6; gender in, 43; militias in, 52; national identity in, 27; population figures for, 153, 154-55; post-independence myth of racial equality in, 11; private and public spheres in, 43; publishing in, 16, 110; and race, 6, 9, 52, 78, 83, 140, 169; rebellions in, 20; scholarship on Black childhood in, 178n51; scholarship on Black history in, 13; slaveholding elites in, 15; slavery in, 1, 3, 4, 7, 11, 20, 27,

60, 73; as Spanish colony, 1; US occupation of, 17, 22, 105, 114, 116, 150–51, 152–64, 167; voting in, 153, 154; women's history in, 13

Cuba, armed rebellions in: 1795–99 annual slave rebellions, 58; 1812 Aponte slave rebellion, 54, 58, 64, 186n34; in 1820s-1840s, 58, 63, 64; 1837–44 annual slave rebellions, 58, 64; 1843–44 Escalera rebellion, 48, 49, 63, 67, 72, 73, 79, 86, 110; 1953–59 Cuban Revolution, 49, 50, 169; Afro-descended Cubans and, 4, 12, 18, 19, 20, 27, 47, 48, 51, 52, 54, 55, 58, 59, 65, 149; and Black political consciousness, 59; against colonialism, 12, 51, 63, 64, 67, 71, 108; and desire for new political order, 69; and education, 68–70; enslaved persons and, 4, 18, 20, 27, 47, 48, 51, 55; free people of color and, 4, 12, 20, 27, 47, 51, 58; and literacy, 54, 64–65, 69; maestras amigas and, 49; male teachers and, 51; militiamen of color and, 12, 19, 20, 51, 52, 54; militiamen-teachers and, 108, 149; mulato persons and, 20, 54; official responses to, 58, 72, 73, 79, 86; as political acts, 51; scholarship on, 58–59; against slavery, 20, 51, 58, 63, 64, 67, 71, 108; Spaniards' participation in, 63; and suspicion of involvement by British abolitionists, 58; teachers of color and, 3, 12, 16, 18, 20, 64; White Cubans and, 63; women of color and, 13. *See also* 1868–78 war of independence; 1895–98 war of independence

Cuba, economy of: 1990 reforms of, 169; and enslaved persons and slavery, 5, 23, 28, 32, 58; expansion of, 27, 28, 51, 58, 96, 102; and sugar, 1, 2, 5–6, 23, 27, 28, 32, 44, 45, 51, 58, 96, 102, 168; White Cuban Creoles and, 29, 30, 44, 45, 71, 102

Cuba, education in: and 1857 Spanish education law, 91; and 1863 education law, 75, 78, 91, 92; and 1868–78 war of independence, 95, 151; and 1880 education law, 75, 93–94, 101, 104, 124; and 1895–98 war of independence, 150, 151–52, 156; 1900 reorganization of, 154; and 1960s literacy campaign, 49, 170; abroad, 6; access to, 26, 33, 76, 94, 96, 125, 165; administration of, 26, 29, 48, 61, 72, 74, 75, 80; and armed rebellions, 68–70; and Black schools and organizations, 22–23; and blood purity, 81; and Catholic schools, 168; and Christianity, 31; and class, 26; and co-ed education, 92; in convents and monasteries, 6, 31; curricula for, 75, 92, 94; and debates about race and colonialism, 92; and drop-outs, 165; efforts to extend to all Cubans, 121; enslaved people and, 92; and equal school rights movement, 108, 170; establishment of, 26; Fidel Castro government and, 22–23, 49, 169, 170; former Cuban exiles and, 156; former enslaved persons and, 99; free, 2, 26, 30–31, 41, 75, 77, 87; funding of, 8, 29, 30–32, 74, 75, 77, 91, 101–2, 103, 109; and gender, 6, 31; government reports on, 105, 106, 181n30, 191n53, 191n58; and hiring of teachers, 154; historical resources on, 15, 158, 165; as ideological battleground, 27; legislation related to, 4, 8, 11, 12, 20, 26, 44; and literacy, 8, 31, 169, 198n9; and local school boards, 166; mandatory, 75, 91; and marginalization of free people of color, 32; and municipal schools, 3, 8, 16, 20, 21, 31–32, 88–89, 91–92, 97–104; and neglect of public school system, 169; and number of schools, 30, 31, 154–55; and patronage, 168; as political and social tool, 163; and possible US annexation of Cuba, 152; as prerequisite for modern Cuba, 31, 164; and present-day racial disparities, 23, 170; and primary schools, 2, 6, 8, 26, 31; principles of, 26; and private schools, 168; as privilege, 85; and public education system, 2, 4, 6, 20, 22, 27, 31, 41, 49, 72, 75–76; quality of, 133; and race of teachers of students of color, 80–82, 83, 112; and racial desegregation, 1–2, 21, 22–23, 127, 143; and racial hierarchy, 9; racially integrated, 21, 93, 94, 163; and racial segregation, 7, 11, 12, 16, 20, 21, 44, 46, 72, 73, 74–75, 76, 79, 80–81, 82, 83, 86, 87, 91, 94; during republican period, 168; in rural areas, 49; scholarship on, 13, 26; and school attendance, 199n35; and secondary education, 143; and segregation by gender, 44, 75, 92, 96, 103; and social control, 80, 84, 99, 104; and sociedades de color / mutual aid society schools, 109;

232 · Index

Spanish colonial government and, 3, 7, 17–18, 20–21, 27, 29, 30, 31, 32, 49, 72, 80, 84, 85, 87, 181n30; students of color and, 88–89, 91–92, 94, 163; in sugar-company towns, 168; and teacher-training schools, 78, 91; and teaching licenses, 78; and text books, 154; and transition from slavery to freedom, 97; during US occupation, 22, 151, 152, 154–58, 164; vocational, 99; and wealth, 6, 75, 77; White Cuban Creoles and, 87; and White private schools, 22, 165; and White supremacy, 21, 75, 82, 83, 108, 111. *See also* 1844 education law; 1878 education order; Afro-descended Cubans, and education; Black Cuban educational tradition; Escuelitas de amigas / home schools; Maestras amigas; Militiamen-teachers, Afro-descended Cuban; Municipal schools; Plan General de Instrucción Pública para las Islas de Cuba y Puerto-Rico; Private schools for students of color; Private schools, White; Sociedad Económica de Amigos del País / Real Sociedad Económica de la Habana / Real Sociedad Patrótica de la Habana; Sociedades de color / mutual aid societies, schools of; Teachers, Afro-descended Cuban; White Cuban Creoles, and education

Cuba, Republic of: and anti-racism, 170; and education, 22–23, 49, 165–66, 169, 170; patronage in, 166; and racial inequality, 166

Cuba, Spanish colonial government in: and 1839 rebellion, 65; and 1863 education law, 94; and 1868–78 war of independence, 90; and 1878 education order, 94, 98, 99, 108, 137; and 1880 education law, 93–94; and 1885 and 1887 decrees on rights of Afro-descended Cubans, 137; and 1893 civil rights orders, 127, 138, 139, 140, 148; and abolition of slavery, 102, 108; and administration of education, 75; and admission of students of color to municipal schools, 138; and Afro-descended Cubans, 7, 73, 76, 78, 81–82, 103, 128, 134, 137–38, 142, 145, 148; captain general as highest-ranking member of, 61; and civil rights, 143, 148, 150; and class, 137–38; conspiracies against, 64; and constitutional rule, 76; Cuban Creoles and, 7; and Directorio Central de las Sociedades de la Raza de Color, 12, 130, 136–38, 142, 143, 144, 147; and doubts about Cubans' loyalty to Spain, 54, 58, 63; and education, 3, 7, 17–18, 20–21, 27, 29, 30, 31, 32, 48, 49, 72, 73–74, 75–76, 85, 87, 93, 94, 181n30; education reports published by, 95, 105, 106, 181n30, 191n53, 191n58; and efforts to gain loyalty of people of color, 73, 88, 90, 91, 104, 107; and efforts to prevent people of color from uniting, 65; and efforts to retain Cuba as Spanish colony, 90, 93; and enslaved persons, 6, 30, 78; exodus of, from Cuba, 15; and free education, 32; and free people of color, 6, 53–54, 72–73, 74, 84, 85, 100; and increase in Afro-descended Cuban population, 76; and individual rights, 72, 90; and integration of public spaces, 107–8, 129, 136–37; lawsuits against, 141; and liberal reforms, 7, 90; and local governments, 72, 90; and loyal subjectivity, 84; and maestras amigas, 54; and midwives, 49; and military rule, 76, 110; and militiamen, 18, 53, 54, 61; and militiamen-teachers, 40, 51, 54, 57, 66, 68, 71–73, 80, 87; and municipal schools, 88–89, 91, 104, 124, 127; and press censorship, 7, 52, 76, 110; and Puerto Rico, 90; and race of teachers in Black schools, 81–82; and racial divisions, 67; and racial equality, 134; and racial hierarchy, 72, 79, 85; and racially integrated schools, 93, 94; and racially segregated schools, 104; and racial oppression, 84; rebellions against, 12, 51; and responses to armed rebellions, 58, 72, 73; and restrictions on assembly, 110; and restrictions on publishing, 110; and rural Cubans, 74; and school administration, 18; and school desegregation, 21, 127; and school segregation, 12, 20, 76, 79, 85; and schools for students of color, 88–89, 97, 98, 99, 100, 101–2, 103, 104; and slavery, 66; and social control, 80, 84, 86; and social hierarchies, 137; and Sociedad Económica, 72; and teachers of color, 4, 73, 78, 85, 86; and

teaching licenses, 79, 80; and trade policies, 72, 90; and White Cuban Creoles, 21, 27, 29, 30, 31, 71, 74, 75–76, 78, 91, 92, 93, 94, 100, 101–2, 104, 107, 124; and White Cubans, 88, 137; and White supremacy, 9, 48, 74, 93
Cuba Libra movement, 151, 163
Cuban Creoles, 6–7, 12, 90. *See also* Black Cuban Creoles; White Cuban Creoles; White Cuban Creoles, and education
Cubanidad / Cuban national identity: Afro-descended Cubans and, 9, 10, 128; and Black Cuban educational tradition, 10; conflicting views of, 9; scholarship on, 9; teachers of color and, 27, 28; White Cuban Creoles and, 9, 10, 30; women and, 9; workers and, 9
Cuban independence movement: during 1868–1878 war of independence, 104; and abolition of slavery, 104; Afro-descended Cubans and, 107, 128, 132, 134, 140, 142, 148; Cuban Creoles and, 107; Cuban exiles and, 104, 156; and racial equality, 104, 105, 108, 132; White Cuban Creoles and, 104
Cuban National Archive, 15
Cuban Partido Independiente de Color, 129

De Antonio, Estanislao, 139
Del Monte, Domingo, 29, 43
Del Moral, Solsiree, 178n51
Del Toro, Ana, 37, 45, 48
Department of Havana, 162
Department of Justice and Public Education, 157
Department of Matanzas, 159
Department of Public Education, 156, 164, 165, 166
Deschamps Chapeaux, Pedro, 55, 64
Desegregation. *See under* 1893 civil rights orders; Afro-descended Cubans, and education; Black Cuban educational tradition; Cuba, education in; Directorio Central de las Sociedades de la Raza de Color
Diario de la Habana, 32, 57
Díaz, María de Jesus, 113
Directorio Central de las Sociedades de la Raza de Color: and 1876 Spanish constitution, 134, 142, 144; and 1878 education order, 131, 137; and 1885 and 1887 civil rights decrees, 136–37; 1892 meeting of, 130–31, 133–34, 135, 161; and 1893 civil rights orders, 127, 138, 139, 140, 145; and access to education, 131, 132; on benefits of school desegregation, 132, 135; and civil rights, 127, 129, 130, 136–37; and concerns about caste system, 132, 137; as continuation of Black Cuban educational tradition, 131; creation of, 12, 127, 129; and Cuban independence movement, 132–33, 142; education as first priority of, 127–28, 130–31, 145; and education as tool of liberation, 134–35, 195n27; and education for all Cubans, 135; and education for girls, 130; and education of formerly enslaved persons, 132; effectiveness of, 129, 151; and equal school rights, 128, 129, 135, 148, 168, 170; and harmony within Cuban society, 142–43, 146, 149; and *La Igualdad* newspaper, 142, 144, 147; leaders of, 128, 129; non-Cuban support for, 144; and political parties, 128–29, 130; purpose of, 12, 129, 130; and racially integrated schools, 21, 127, 130, 131, 132, 137, 161; and racial solidarity, 149; and racial uplift, 170; and school desegregation, 132, 135, 149, 151, 163; schools created by, 130; and Spanish colonial government, 12, 127, 130, 134, 136–38, 142, 143, 144, 147; strategies of, 142, 145, 147, 148; and traditions of race-based organizing, 149; as umbrella organization, 21, 127, 129; and Western customs, 128; and White resistance to integration, 143–44, 148
Douglass, Frederick, 132
DuBois, W. E. B., 10
Dumas, Claudio, 159
D'Wolf, Dionisia, 116

Economy. *See* Cuba, economy of
Education. *See* 1893 civil rights orders; Afro-descended Cubans, and education; Black Cuban educational tradition; Cuba, education in; Directorio Central de las Sociedades de la Raza de Color; Escuelitas de amigas / home schools; Maestras amigas; Militiamen-teachers, Afro-descended Cu-

234 · Index

ban; Municipal schools; Private schools for students of color; Private schools, White; Sociedades de color / mutual aid societies, schools of; Teachers, Afro-descended Cuban; White Creole Cubans, and education

1844 education law: and curricula, 75, 77; and education administration, 48, 72, 74, 75–77; and enslaved persons, 187n14; expansion of provisions of, 92; as first law for public education in Cuba and Puerto Rico, 72, 74, 75, 77, 91; importance of, 84; passage and finalization of, 48, 72, 74; and private and public education, 75; and race of teachers in Black schools, 80–81; and racially segregated schools, 72, 74–75, 76–77, 79, 80, 81, 82, 86, 88, 104; and racial segregation in Cuban society, 73; and requirement for schools based on population, 74, 75, 76, 98; and school funding, 74, 75; Spanish precursor of, 76; and students of color, 83, 92; and teacher salaries, 77; teachers of color and, 72, 73, 77–78, 82–83, 86; and teacher training, 78; and teaching licenses, 72, 75, 77–78, 82; and textbooks, 76; and tuition, 75, 77; White Cuban Creoles and, 75–76; White teachers and, 78. *See also* Cuba, education in

1868–78 war of independence: and anticolonialism, 87; and antislavery ideology, 8, 87, 104; and Cuban national ideology, 28; as demarcation point, 52, 92, 104; failure of, 20, 21, 104; and impact on education, 88, 114, 151; and Pact of Zanjón, 16, 21, 88, 92, 93, 94, 102, 104, 110, 144; slavery during, 8, 90, 159; Spanish authorities and, 90; White Cuban Creoles and, 90, 104

1878 education order: Afro-descended Cubans and, 89, 108, 125–26; Directorio Central de las Sociedades de la Raza de Color and, 131; historical interpretation of, 189n11; motives for issuing, 93; and municipal schools for students of color, 88–89, 91, 92–93, 94, 95, 97–100, 101–3, 105, 106, 107, 108, 112, 124, 125–26, 131, 137; newspapers and, 98, 136, 144; and postsecondary education, 94, 189n11; and racial integration of municipal schools, 89, 91, 93, 94–95, 96, 97, 99, 100, 101, 102–3, 104, 108, 124, 125–26, 131, 189n11; and racially segregated municipal schools, 89, 94, 96, 101, 103, 104, 107, 129–30, 137, 189n11; and secondary education, 94, 189n11; significance of, 94; Spanish colonial government and, 88–89, 93, 97, 98, 99, 100, 101, 102, 103, 104, 107, 108, 137, 189n11; teachers of color and, 89, 105, 106, 112; White Cubans and, 89, 93, 94–95, 97–104, 105, 107, 112, 120, 124; White teachers and, 89, 105–6, 112

1893 civil rights orders: and 1876 Spanish constitution, 144–45; Directorio Central de las Sociedades de la Raza de Color and, 127, 138, 139, 140, 143, 145, 147, 148; and equal school rights, 146; impact of, on Cuban republic, 148; and integration of public spaces, 141, 142, 148; lawsuits related to, 141; newspapers and, 139–40, 141, 142–47; and school desegregation, 127, 138–39, 141, 142, 143–44, 145, 146–47, 148; Spanish colonial government and, 127, 138–39, 140, 146, 147, 148; White Cubans and, 140–41, 142–43, 146–47, 148

1895–98 war of independence: Afro-descended Cubans and, 22, 107, 148, 153; and anti-racist rhetoric, 8; and Cuban nationhood, 128; as demarcation point, 113; and education, 22; impact of, 150, 151, 154–55, 156; organization of, outside Cuba, 128; places fought, 150; start of, 150

El Album Cenfoguense: Revista Quincenal, 115

El Buen Suceso sociedad de color / mutual aid society, 118

El Club de Oriente sociedad de color / mutual aid society, 133

El Fénix de Trinidad sociedad de color / mutual aid society, 133

El Liceo sociedad de color / mutual aid society, 120

El negro en la economía habanera del siglo XIX (Deschamps Chapeaux), 64

El País, 116, 121

El Progreso sociedad de color / mutual aid society (Cienguegos), 118, 119, 123

El Progreso sociedad de color / mutual aid society (Havana), 118, 120

El Progreso sociedad de color / mutual aid society (Santiago de Cuba), 100, 118
El Regional, 141
El Teatro Tacón, 141
Enslaved persons: and 1868-78 war of independence, 8, 90; Africans as, 3, 5, 13, 28, 92, 94, 188n36; and armed rebellions, 4, 18, 20, 27, 47, 48, 51, 55, 57, 58, 59, 72, 73; and cabildos de nación, 53, 110; and Christian doctrine, 172n9; in cities, 171n6; and class, 65; and coartación/self-purchase, 3, 4; and education, 4, 5, 19, 30, 35, 47, 57, 66, 71, 92, 94, 172n10, 187n14; and emancipation, 67, 90-91, 94, 98; escaped (maroons), 60; female, 13; and free people of color, 3-4, 37, 56, 57, 171n6; and Haitian Revolution, 5; import of, 5; increased numbers of, 6, 30, 58; and literacy, 49, 59-60, 69, 172n9; and manumission, 3, 4, 8, 96-97; occupations and activities of, 5, 38, 181n23; and organizational tradition, 110; and racial solidarity, 66; and rebellion conspiracies, 64, 65; and resistance, 12, 13, 47, 71, 86; scholarship on, 12, 13; and slave codes, 4, 172n9; and social status, 51; and Spaniards, 171n6; and Spanish colonial government, 6, 78; and sugar economy, 1, 5, 102; White Creole Cubans and, 6, 30
Equal school rights: and 1893 civil rights orders, 146; Afro-descended Cubans and, 97, 108, 111, 126, 128, 150, 168, 170; Black Cuban educational tradition and, 2, 17, 97; Directorio Central de las Sociedades de la Raza de Color and, 128, 129, 135, 148, 168, 170; *La Igualdad* newspaper on, 146; maestras amigas and, 97; teachers of color and, 17, 117
Escalera, Julian, 119
Escalera rebellion. *See under* Cuba, armed rebellions in
Escuelitas de amigas / home schools: and class, 38, 42, 45; and co-ed classrooms, 19, 42, 44, 45; continued operation of, 48, 49, 114, 166, 169; curricula in, 38, 41, 42-43, 47, 48; definition of, 2, 19; and education for girls, 45, 46, 48; and free education, 41; funding of, 111; historical records on, 41, 42, 166; importance of, 42; in Latin America, 182n42; numbers of, 48; official censure of, 17; as part of Black Cuban organizational tradition, 110; as predecessors of national public education system, 19; and private and public spheres, 43; and racial integration, 19, 25, 33, 44, 54, 77; in Spain, 182n42; and students of color, 38; and tuition, 19, 25, 41; unofficial nature of, 25, 46, 54; White Cuban Creoles and, 40, 42, 46; and White students, 19, 38. *See also* Maestras amigas
Esperanza, Cuba, 89, 95

Ferraro, Antonio, 100, 125
Ferrer, Ada, 8, 15
Filomeno, Francisco, 31
Finch, Aisha, 13, 20, 59
Florencia, Roberto, 55, 57
Florida, 56, 60, 67, 128, 156
Franquis, Caridad Gispert de, 106, 191n58
Franquis Arango, Gumersindo, 106, 191n58
Fraternidad, 118
Free people of color: and 1844 public education law, 76; and 1878 education order, 97; and adaptation, 85; and armed rebellions, 4, 12, 20, 27, 47, 51, 57, 58, 65, 72, 73; and cabildos de nación, 53, 66, 110; in cities, 171n6; and class, 65; and discrimination, 28; and economic mobility, 4, 36; economic rebuilding by, 86; and education, 4, 12, 28, 30, 32, 33, 35, 36, 37, 57, 61, 88, 94, 97, 167; and enslaved persons, 3-4, 57, 65, 171n6; formerly enslaved persons as, 3, 14, 19, 37, 67, 90, 94, 99, 100, 122, 128, 132; and gender, 3, 4, 18; and honorifics, 191n53; importance of teaching to, 37; increased numbers of, 35, 86, 188n36; and loyal subjectivity, 53-54, 58, 61, 66, 76, 100; and magisterio, 36, 37, 66; marginalization of, 32; as militiamenteachers, 51; and militia service, 11, 37, 40, 52, 66; mulato/mulata persons as, 3, 6, 41, 159; and municipal schools, 100; and mutual aid societies, 88; occupations of, 37, 56, 61, 86, 99; and organizational tradition, 110; and participation in Cuban society, 86; petitions by, 100; politicization of, 86; population figures for, 3, 159; and private schools, 116; and property ownership, 4; and

resistance to racial oppression, 11, 37, 47, 58, 71; restrictions on, 6, 73, 90; rights of, 4, 87; settlement patterns of, 3, 96; as slaveholders, 4, 37, 56; and social legitimacy, 4, 51; and social recognition, 4; and social status, 65, 66; and socioeconomic mobility, 4; and Spanish colonial government, 6, 68, 71, 72–73, 74, 84, 85, 100; and strategies of liberation, 85; as taxpayers, 101; as teachers, 6, 36, 88, 106; and teaching licenses, 37, 79, 84; terms for, 23, 191n58; in urban settings, 86; and violence, 86; and wealth, 36, 37, 56, 66; and White Cuban Creoles, 6, 71. *See also* Afro-descended Cubans; Mulato/mulata persons

Gaceta de la Habana, 138, 191n58
Galindo, Manuela, 106
García, Gloria, 59
García, José Isaac, 116
Givens, Jarvis, 69
Gómez, José Policeto, 61, *62*, 63, 67, 68
Gómez, Juan Gualberto: and 1878 education order, 135; and 1885 and 1887 rulings on access to public spaces, 136–37; and 1893 civil rights orders, 139, 140; background of, 129; as Black intellectual, 86, 128; and Cuban independence, 129; and Directorio Central de las Sociedades de la Raza de Color, 128–29, 136, 139; education of, 86, 116, 129; exile of, 128; as journalist, 129; and political parties, 128–29; and racial democracy, 129; and Spanish colonial government, 136–37, 138, 140, 144
González, Félix, 38, 39
González, Natividad G., 116
González Lanuza, José Antonio, 156, 157
Great Britain, 30, 53, 58, 182n42
Gualba, Miguel, 86, 116, 118
Guanabacoa, Cuba, 78, 91, 106, 116, 165
Guanajay, Cuba, 89, 95, 114
Guantánamo, Cuba, 64
Guerra, Lillian, 9
Guía de forasteros, 95, 105, 106, 181n30, 191n53, 191n58
Guines, Cuba, 89, 95
Gutiérrez, Carmita, 172n10

Gutiérrez de la Concha, José, 80, 91

Haiti and Haitian Revolution, 5, 12, 58, 84, 130
Harper's Weekly, 60
Harvard University, 106, 114–16
Havana, Cuba: and 1895–98 war of independence, 158; Afro-descended Cubans in, 96; female students in, 6, 33, 35, 41; free people of color in, 3, 84; location of, 96; maestras amigas in, 6, 41; male students in, 33, 35, 41; militiamen and militiamen-teachers in, 67, 79; as national capital, 158; neighborhoods and townships in, 31, 67, 78, 105, 141; population of, 3, 158; primary education in, 41; private schools for people of color in, 116; publishing in, 16; residential segregation in, 171n6; and school funding, 31; schools in, 6, 31, 33, 34–35, 38, 41, 56, 67, 80, 89, 95, 106, 119, 130; secondary schooling in, 164; and Sociedad Económica, 31; sociedades de color / mutual aid societies in, 117, 118, 119; streets in, 67, 186n34; students of color in, 33, 34, 56, 95, 106, 119, 130; teacher examining commission in, 77, 79; teachers of color in, 37, 47–48, 67, 113, 116, 119; theaters and cafés in, 141; walls of, 181n23; White resistance to integration in, 141; White students in, 33, 34–35, 56; White teachers in, 105, 121
Havana province, Cuba, 140–41, 153, 158–59, 162–63
Hernández, Juan, 116
Herrera, Desiderio, 31
Hicks, Anasa, 178n51
Hijas del Progreso, 119
Holguín, Cuba, 132, 134
Home schools. *See* Escuelitas de amigas / home schools

Iglesias Utset, Marial, 158
Independentistas / independence fighters, 8
Indians, 152
Inspección General de Estudios / Junta Superior de Instrucción Pública, 75–76
Integration. *See under* 1878 education order; 1893 civil rights orders; Afro-descended Cubans; Black Cuban educational tradition; Cuba, Spanish colonial government in;

Directorio Central de las Sociedades de la Raza de Color; Escuelitas de amigas / home schools; La Igualdad (newspaper); Militiamen of color, as teachers; Municipal schools; White Cubans

James, C. L. R., 12
Jiménez Zúñiga, José, 116
Junta Superior de Instrucción Pública / Inspección General de Estudios, 75–76

La Amistad sociedad de color / mutual aid society, 118, 123, 125
Labalette, Petrona, 113
La Bella Unión Habanera sociedad de color / mutual aid society, 117, 120
Labra, Rafael María, 139–40
La Coruña, Spain, 66
La Divina Caridad sociedad de color / mutual aid society, 118, 120
La Fraternidad, 116, 121
La Igualdad (newspaper): on 1893 civil rights orders, 139–40, 144–45, 146; and Directorio Central de las Sociedades de la Raza de Color, 142, 144, 147; on education for people of color, 1–2, 127, 135–36, 143, 144, 145–47; on equal school rights, 146; on harmony in Cuban society, 142–43, 147; on harmony in integrated schools, 132, 146–47; on integration of public spaces, 145; Juan Gualberto Gómez and, 144; on racial solidarity, 142; and White resistance to integration, 143–44, 146–47
La Igualdad sociedad de color / mutual aid society (Cienfuegos), 117–18, 119, 123
La Igualdad sociedad de color / mutual aid society (Havana), 117, 118
La Instrucción Primaria, 164, 165, 166
Lanier, Oilda Hevia, 189n11
La Nueva Era, 141
Lapatier, Juan Tranquilino, 131, 133
La Protesta, 144
Latin America: Afro-Latin American studies in, 11; Catholic Church in, 175n23; education in, 6, 8, 14, 23, 147, 175n23, 182n42; empirical inquiry in, 175n23; and European immigration, 198n9; former Spanish colonies in, 8; freedom and equality in, 23; independence movements in, 76; intellectual currents in, 175n23; liberal reforms in, 90; literacy in, 8, 60, 154, 198n9; racial oppression in, 133; scientific racism in, 152; self-government in, 152; teachers of students of color in, 112; White supremacy in, 14, 23
La Unión Fraternal sociedad de color / mutual aid society, 117, 118, 120
La Unión sociedad de color / mutual aid society, 118
La Unión y Fraternidad sociedad de color / mutual aid society, 117, 120, 121
Legislation and decrees: 1740 Negro Act (SC, US), 60; 1857 education law (Spain), 91; 1863 education law (Cuba), 75, 78, 91, 94; 1870 Moret Law (Spain), 90; 1880 education law (Cuba), 75, 93–94, 101, 104; 1885 decree on rights of Afro-descended Cubans (Cuba), 107–8, 136–37; 1887 decree on rights of Afro-descended Cubans (Cuba), 107, 108, 136–37; 1888 assembly right law (Cuba), 111; Civil Rights Act of 1964 (US), 170; on municipal school signs, 141; slave codes (Cuba), 73; slave codes (US), 60, 172n9. *See also* 1844 education law; 1878 education order; 1893 civil rights orders
Le Louvre café, 141
Lersundi, Francisco, 74
Liras, José Esteban, 189n11, 191n53
Llorente, Leocadia, 105
L'Ouverture School, 155
Loyal subjectivity: Afro-descended Cubans and, 100, 128; free people of color and, 53–54, 58, 61, 66, 76, 100; maestras amigas and, 53; magisterio and, 68, 76, 80; militiamen of color and, 53, 58, 66, 68; militiamen-teachers of color and, 61, 63, 68, 80; Spanish colonial government and, 84; women of color and, 53
Lucero, Bonnie, 163
Lujarzo, Martín, 45

Macagua, Cuba, 89, 95, 96
Macuriges / Corral Falso de Macuriges, Cuba, 89, 95, 96

Madrigal, Félix, 119
Maestras amigas: 19th-century terms for, 180n6; Afro-descended Cuban women as, 2, 5, 19, 25, 26, 27, 28, 36, 37, 38, 40, 41, 42, 43, 44, 45, 48, 49, 71, 180n6; ages of, 25; and armed rebellions, 49; and Black Cuban educational tradition, 108; and Black political consciousness, 72; and class, 18, 28, 39, 43, 47, 129; and co-ed education, 19, 26, 36, 44, 46, 47, 48, 57, 68; and consciousness-raising, 48; continued operation of, 48, 49, 71, 169; curricula of, 38, 39, 41, 42–43, 47, 48, 49, 50, 67; definition of, 5; and education for girls, 26, 27, 37, 68, 124; education of, 25, 28, 49; and equal school rights, 97; and feminization of teaching, 38; formerly enslaved persons as, 28; former occupations of, 40; and free education, 19, 25, 26, 28, 36, 39, 40–41, 46, 56, 57, 68, 87, 120; free people of color as, 28; and gender roles, 43; historical records on, 17, 19, 26, 39, 41, 42, 48, 49, 167, 180n6; importance of, 2, 26, 27, 39, 42, 46, 48, 49, 169–70; and income, 68; in Latin America, 182n42; and literacy, 54, 60, 67; and loyal subjectivity, 53; memoirs of, 25; motives of, 114; mulata women as, 17, 19, 26, 37, 43, 49; and national identity and ideology, 28; number of, 41; and opposition, 19; as precursors of licensed female teachers of color, 114; and private and public spheres, 47; and public schools, 167; and racial hierarchy, 47; and racially integrated education, 19, 25, 26, 27, 28, 33, 45, 46, 47, 48, 49, 57, 68, 87; and racial solidarity, 68; and resistance to racial oppression, 28, 29, 36, 44, 47, 50, 71, 72; and resistance to social norms, 43; scholarship on, 180n6; and schools in homes (escuelitas de amigas), 2, 4–5, 19, 25, 27, 36, 38, 40, 41, 43, 48, 49, 71, 87, 180n6; and segregation, 47; and separation from official school system, 68; and social status, 54; in Spain, 38, 182n42; and Spanish colonial government, 46, 49; and teaching licenses, 5, 25, 27, 37, 38, 39, 40, 49, 52, 71, 72, 82, 86; throughout the Americas, 38; and wealth, 38–39, 46; and White Cuban Creoles, 5, 28–29, 39–40, 44, 46, 47–48, 49, 57, 68, 71, 169; and White Cubans, 5, 20, 68; and White students, 9, 19, 39, 40, 45, 47, 60, 87, 120; widespread impact of, 49. *See also* Teachers, Afro-descended Cuban

Magisterio: and 1878 education order, 89; Afro-descended Cubans and, 12, 40, 65, 71, 106, 108, 113; attempts to expel free people of color from, 9; definition of, 4, 36, 51; free people of color and, 4, 36, 37, 58, 66, 76; and gender, 4, 39, 113; and loyal subjectivity, 68, 76, 80; mulato/mulata persons and, 71; and private schools for students of color, 89, 112; and racial solidarity, 51; and racial uplift, 73; and recognition, 4, 58, 66; and social change, 70; and social legitimacy, 4; and social status, 56, 58, 62; in Spain, 66; and wealth, 56; White Cubans and, 9, 37, 39, 40. *See also* Escuelitas de amigas / home schools; Maestras amigas; Militiamen of color, as teachers; Teachers, Afro-descended Cuban

Marianao, Cuba, 89, 95
Mariel, Cuba, 96
Maroons, 60
Martí, José, 108, 169
Martínez Acosta, Elvira, 98, 106
Martínez Campos, Arsenio, 136, 144, 189n11
Martínez y Díaz, José F., 181n31
Matanzas, Cuba: and 1893 civil rights orders, 138; cafés in, 141; education for girls in, *160;* emancipation in, 159; militiamen of color in, 61, 63; rebellion conspiracy in, 63; schools in, 34, 89, 95, 96, 159; Sociedad Económica in, 34; and US occupation of Cuba, 159; wage workers in, 159
Matanzas province, Cuba: 1893 civil rights orders in, 140; education in, 34, 157, 158, 159–60, *161;* landholders in, 159; location of, 140–41; people of color in, 140–41, 153, 158–59; population of, 160; provincial authorities in, 61, 138, 139, 157; Sociedad Económica in, 34; and sugar economy, 140–41, 158; and US occupation of Cuba, 155, 156, 158; White resistance to racial integration in, 140–41
Medina, Antonio, 86–87, 116, 129, 191n53
Meléndez, Lorenzo, 55, 56, 57

Militiamen of color: and 1812 Aponte rebellion, 64; and 1843–44 Escalera rebellion, 63; assertion of rights by, 54; and benefits of militia service, 52–53, 55, 66; and Black community life, 53; and cabildos de nación, 53; and community leadership, 53; disbanding of, 79; free men as, 37, 40, 52, 53; and legal equality, 53; and literacy, 54, 64–65; and loyal subjectivity, 53, 58, 66, 68; mulato men as, 52, 53, 54, 55, 67; numbers of, 52; and political resistance, 11; as property owners, 53; and recognition, 58; as slaveholders, 53; and social status, 18, 40, 52, 57, 58; and Spanish colonial government, 18, 51, 53–54, 55, 61; and travel, 54; and wealth, 53, 66; and well-being of others, 55; and White Cubans, 40, 51

Militiamen of color, as teachers: and 1812 Aponte rebellion, 54, 64; and 1839 rebellion, 67; and 1843–44 Escalera rebellion, 63, 67; and Afro-descended Cubans' place in Cuban society, 23, 55; and anticolonialism, 87; and armed rebellions of unspecified date, 12, 18, 19, 20, 51, 52, 55, 59, 68, 71–72, 80, 85, 108, 149; assertion of rights by, 54; and benefits of militia service, 54, 87; and Black Cuban educational tradition, 108; and Black political consciousness, 72; and cabildos de nación, 64; and class, 129; and co-ed education, 57; and collaboration with enslaved persons, 67; and community among Afro-descended Cubans, 51, 58; as community leaders, 55, 85; and curricula, 40, 57, 61, 67, 68; and education as vehicle for rights and recognition, 62; and education for girls, 56, 68; and enslaved students, 57, 66; and freedom and liberation, 27–28, 72; free men as, 51; importance of, 2; and income, 54, 68; and literacy, 60, 67, 68, 69; and loyal subjectivity, 61, 63, 68, 80; mulato men as, 71; and opposition to slavery, 87; and patriarchy, 68; and political activism, 12, 59; and political opposition, 52, 59; privileges of, 57–58; and racial integration in Cuban society, 51; and racially integrated classrooms, 55, 56, 67, 87; and racial solidarity, 51, 54–55, 66, 67, 68, 69–70; and recognition, 87; and resistance to racial oppression, 18, 51; schools established by, 56, 61, 64, 67; and separate race-based schools, 51; and social status, 18, 51, 54, 56, 57, 67, 68, 85, 87; and Spanish colonial government, 18, 20, 46, 51, 54, 57, 61, 66, 68, 71–73, 80, 87; and teaching licenses, 18, 20, 51, 54, 55, 59, 61, 62, 63, 68, 85, 87, 111; and tuition, 56, 57, 68; and wealth, 18, 56, 57; and well-being of others, 55, 58; and White Cuban Creoles, 55, 57; and White Cubans, 18, 40, 51, 56, 68; and White students, 56, 60, 66, 87, 120

Militias: Afro-descended Cuban rebels and, 65; Black corps of, 52, 54, 55, 56, 61, 63, 64, 71, 79, 110; and Black Cuban organizational tradition, 110; during British occupation of Cuba, 53; draft for, 79; establishment of, 52; free people of color and, 11, 18, 52, 64, 66, 79; mulato corps of, 52, 54, 55, 61, 67, 79, 110; official recognition of, 18; prevalence of service in, 52; reinstatement of, 79, 110; and rights, 62; and social status, 18, 40, 62; White corps of, 52

Minerva, 116, 118
Missionaries, 129, 168, 172n9
Monte, José, 157
Monzón, León, 55, 64, 65–67, 68
Moreno, Isabel, 105
Moreno, José, 79–82, 83, 85, 89, 106
Morenos. *See* Free people of color
Morgan, Jennifer, 13
Moro González, Antonio, 134
Morúa Delgado, Martín, 141
Moss, Hilary, 14
Moya, Mariano, 55
Mulato/mulata persons: and armed rebellions, 20, 54, 65, 71–72; and Black Cuban Creoles, 65; and Black Cuban educational tradition, 70; and civil rights, 143; and class, 56, 143; and concept of freedom, 13; definition of, 3, 23, 79; and education, 6, 9, 15, 4, 491, 167; as free persons, 3, 6; in government records, 17; and literacy, 54; as maestras amigas, 17, 19, 26, 41; and militia service, 52, 53, 54, 55, 67, 71; and municipal schools, 95; occupations of, 56; and private schools for students of color, 112, 114, 116; racialization

of, 23–24; and racial oppression, 69; and racial solidarity, 66; and school creation, 12; and segregated municipal schools, 17; social networks of, 56; and sociedades de color / mutual aid societies, 119; and sociedades de color / mutual aid society schools, 12, 122; as students, 3, 33; as teachers, 3, 6, 18, 37, 41, 42, 45, 73, 82, 86, 89, 106, 116, 121, 122, 151, 166, 168; terms for, 114, 191n58; and voting rights, 154

Municipal schools: and 1844 education law, 92; and 1863 education law, 91–92, 94; and 1878 education order, 21, 88–89, 91, 92–93, 94–95, 96, 97–99, 100, 101–6, 107, 108, 112, 120, 131, 136, 189n11; and 1880 education law, 93–94, 101; and 1893 civil rights orders, 138, 139, 141; and class, 159; curricula in, 92, 112; and education for girls, 95, 96, 97, 98, 160; enrollment numbers for, 133; funding of, 31–32, 91, 95, 101–3; and law on signs displayed at, 141; numbers of, 92, 96, 112, 139, 145; photo of, 155; and racial integration, 21, 89, 91, 93, 94, 95, 96, 97, 99, 100, 101, 102, 103, 108, 124, 127, 131, 132, 133, 135, 136, 137, 138, 150, 189n11; and segregation by gender, 95, 96, 97, 103; sociedades de color / mutual aid societies and, 100; Spanish colonial government and, 31, 88–89, 91, 97, 98, 99, 100, 101, 102, 103–4, 108, 124, 127; and students of color, 16, 17, 88–89, 91–93, 94, 95, 97–100, 101–3, 108–9, 110, 112, 129–30, 131, 132, 133; teachers at, 21, 89, 106, 112, 133, 191n58; White Cuban Creoles and, 31–32, 91, 92, 93, 94–95, 97–104, 112, 120; and White students, 94, 95, 96, 98–99, 101, 102, 103, 105, 106, 107, 133, 189n11

Mutual aid societies. *See* Sociedades de color / mutual aid societies

Nantucket, MA, 123
National Academy of Education/Spencer annual meeting, 177n41
National Association for Colored Women, 186n2
Nat Turner rebellion, 60
Nazaria, Victoria, 45
Negociado de Instrucción, 80, 81, 83, 84
Negros (term), 23
Newland, Carlos, 198n9
New York, NY, 16, 113, 128, 130, 133
Nuestra Senora de la Caridad school, 95
Nuestra Señora de los Desamaprados school, 87, 116
Nuestra Señora de Lourdes school, 114, 123
Nueva Paz, Cuba, 95, 105

Oriente, Cuba, 150, 161

Packard, Robert Lawrence, 151
Pact of Zanjón. *See under* 1868–78 Cuban war of independence
Palma Soriano, Cuba, 161
Palmira, Cuba, 89, 95, 96
Paquette, Robert, 171n6, 188n36
Pardos. *See* Mulato/mulata persons
Partido Independiente de Color (PIC), 11, 149, 168, 169
Paso Real San Diego, Cuba, 95
Pastor, Juana, 37, 113, 114
Patria, 133
Patrocinados. *See* Free people of color: formerly enslaved persons as
Peñalver, María Faustina, 37, 39
Pérez, Emma, 172n10
Pérez, Eulogia/Eduviges, 114, 115, 116, 123, 124, 125
Pérez de Castro, Teresa, 118
Perico, Cuba, 89, 95, 96
Philippines, 151
Pimentel, María de Jesus, 113
Piñeiro, Eloisa, 113
Pla, Eduardo, 164
Placetas, Cuba, 116
Plan General de Instrucción Pública para las Islas de Cuba y Puerto-Rico. *See* 1844 education law
Private schools, for students of color: access to, 169; administration of, 111, 113; adult students and, 111; criticisms and defenses of, 116; curricula of, 113; and education for girls, 114, 123, 124; establishment of, 111–12, 116, 117; funding of, 111, 112, 123, 124, 125; increased numbers of, 111, 112; motives for establishing, 111; as part of Black Cuban

educational tradition, 132; precursors of, 111, 112; racially integrated, 111, 114; and racial solidarity, 112–13; segregated by gender, 114, 116; Sociedad Económica and, 34; and sociedades de color / mutual aid societies, 113; teachers of color and, 89, 111, 112, 113, 114, 123, 124; tuition-free, 114, 123, 124; White students and, 111, 114, 117. *See also* Escuelitas de amigas / home schools

Private schools, White, 22, 165, 168, 169, 170

Protestants, 168, 172n9

Provincial Commission of Primary Education of Havana, 80, 81, 82, 84, 85

Puerto Principe, Cuba, 31, 139, 153

Puerto Rico: civil rights supporters in, 144; Cuban prisoners in, 64; education in, 72, 74, 75, 91, 151; scholarship on Black childhood in, 178n51; as Spanish colony, 90; teacher examining commission in, 77

Punta Brava, Cuba, 113

Punta y Colón neighborhood, Havana, Cuba, 141

Ramos, Luis A., 114

Ranchuelo, Cuba, 89, 95

Real Audiencia de La Habana, 80

Real Audiencia Pretorial, 81, 84

Real Colegio de Belén, 34, 80

Real Sociedad Económica de la Habana / Real Sociedad Patrótica de la Habana. *See* Sociedad Económica de Amigos del País

Recreo, Matanzas province, Cuba, *161*

Regla, Cuba, 15, 105, 162

Reid-Vazquez, Michele, 49, 73

Reol, Josefa, 105–6

Resumen de la legislación de primera enseñanza (Liras), 189n11

Revista de la Habana (Zambrana Valdes), 38

Reyes, Juan Justo, 30, 31, 34, 41, 42, 45

Reyita: The Life of a Black Cuban Woman in the Twentieth Century (Castillo Bueno), 25

Rickford, Russell, 13, 17, 177n41

Risquet, Juan, 66, 189n11

Robinson, Cedric, 13, 58

Rochester, NY, 15

Rodríguez, Alicia Conde, 10

Rodríguez de Tío, Lola, 144

Sabanilla del Encomendador, Cuba, 89, 95

Saco, José Antonio, 32, 41

Sagua la Grande, Cuba, 89, 95, 140

Saint Domingue, 5, 28, 159

San Antonio de Pádua school, 95

Sancti Spíritus, Cuba, 95, 106, 113

San Diego de los Baños, Cuba, 95

San Diego de Núñez, Cuba, 96

San Fernando school, 116

San José de las Lajas, Cuba, 89, 95, 96, 105

San Luis, Santiago de Cuba province, Cuba, 96, 161, *162, 163*

San Pedro school, 116

Santa Ana, Cuba, 89, 95

Santa Clara, Cuba: and 1878 education order, 89, 95; and 1893 civil rights orders, 139; education in, 89, 95, 139, 155–56, 157, 158, 172n10; population of color in, 153, 158–59, 172n10; and sugar economy, 158–59

Santa Clara province, Cuba, 158–59

Santa Maria, Havana, Cuba, 117

Santiago, Cuba: and 1878 education order, 97–101, 103–4; location of, 96; population of color in, 96–97, 153; and racial hierarchy, 96; sociedades de color / mutual aid societies in, 125; and sugar economy, 96; teachers in, 106, 113

Santiago de Cuba, Cuba: and 1878 education order, 89; education in, 31, 35, 48, 74, 89, 95, 131, 161; free people of color in, 159; sociedades de color / mutual aid societies in, 118, 119, 131, 133; teacher examining commission in, 77

Santiago de Cuba province, Cuba, 160–62

Santo Domingo, Matanzas province, Cuba, 157

Sarmiento, Domingo Faustino, 8

Sartorius, David, 7, 53, 78, 145

Schools. *See* Escuelitas de amigas / home schools; Municipal schools; Private schools, for students of color; Private schools, White; Sociedades de color / mutual aid societies, schools of

Secretaría de Instrucción Pública. *See* Cuba Department of Public Education

Segregation. *See under* Cuba, education in; Cuba, Spanish colonial government in; Havana, Cuba; Municipal schools; Sociedad

Económica de Amigos del País / Real Sociedad Económica de la Habana / Real Sociedad Patrótica de la Habana; White Cuban Creoles
Serra, Rafael, 10, 108
"'Sewing' Civilization" (Childs), 180n6
Slave and Citizen (Tannenbaum), 172n9
Slavery, in Cuba: during 1868–78 war of independence, 8, 90, 159; abolition of, 1, 2, 3, 14, 90–91, 94, 96, 98, 99, 102, 107, 108, 112, 124, 125, 132, 140, 159; aftermath of, 142, 180n4; and arrival of first enslaved Africans, 3; conspiracies against, 63, 64; and education, 14; expansion of, 1, 27, 172n9; justifications for, 133; and link between literacy and rebellion, 60; and manumission, 3, 8; and racial justice movement, 140; resistance to, 9, 11, 12, 13, 20, 51, 71; and self-purchase, 3; and slave codes, 73; Spanish colonial government and, 66; women and, 13. *See also* Enslaved persons
Slavery, in United States, 1, 13, 60, 69, 172n9
Social Darwinism, 153
Sociedad Abolicionista Española, 139
Sociedad Económica de Amigos del País / Real Sociedad Económica de la Habana / Real Sociedad Patrótica de la Habana: activities of, after passage of 1844 public education law, 74; administration of Cuban education by, 26, 29, 48, 61, 72, 75; and Afro-descended Cuban teachers, 36; and class, 26, 45, 71; and co-ed education, 36; and curricula, 45, 47, 71; and denial of education to Afro-descended Cubans, 26, 33, 34–35, 46, 71; educational surveys/censuses by, 30, 38; education section of, 26, 28, 29, 30–31, 32, 33, 43, 44, 61, 62, 63, 71, 81, 82, 83, 84; establishment of, 26; and expansion of education in Cuba, 27, 33, 34, 36, 41; and free education, 26, 30–31, 33, 34–35, 36, 40–41, 48, 71, 74; and gender, 35, 71; goals of, 71; and maestras amigas, 19–20, 36, 39–40, 42, 43, 46, 47, 169; and national public school system, 33, 43; and patriarchy, 36, 71; principles of, 26; and racial hierarchy, 44, 60; and racial segregation, 33, 44, 45, 47, 71, 77; racism within, 43; and school funding, 31–32, 43; and Spanish colonial government, 29, 32, 48, 72; teachers' rule book by, 32; and teaching licenses, 62–63, 77, 82; White Cuban Creoles and, 6, 26, 30, 31, 35, 39, 43, 49, 57, 64, 169; and White students, 26, 34–35, 60; and White supremacy, 33, 34, 36, 47, 63, 71

Sociedad El Progreso, 114
Sociedades de color / mutual aid societies: activities of, 117, 130; and Black Cuban educational tradition, 170; bylaws of, 117, 118; and civil rights, 18; and class, 18; and Directorio Central de las Sociedades de la Raza Color, 21; and education, 12, 18, 21, 100, 117–18, 120, 121; and Fidel Castro government, 170; increased numbers of, 21, 116, 117; and participation in Cuban social and political life, 122; predecessors of, 111, 140; and racial community and solidarity, 117, 119; as racially separate organizations, 130; White membership in, 117. *See also* Directorio Central de las Sociedades de la Raza de Cloro
Sociedades de color / mutual aid societies, schools of: and access to education by people of color, 3, 21, 88, 89, 111, 119; and adult students, 111, 120, 121, 122; and education for girls, 117, 118, 120, 122; free, 21, 120, 121; funding of, 12, 109, 111, 118, 120, 121, 122, 123, 124, 125; *La Igualdad* newspaper on, 147; leadership of, 111; locations of, 117–18, 120; members' children in, 117; nonmembers' children in, 121; and racial-separatist organization, 125; and racial solidarity, 119; and teachers of color, 2, 89, 111, 118, 119, 125; and tuition assistance, 117; and White students, 12, 21, 111, 119, 120, 121, 122, 126. *See also* Directorio Central de las Sociedades de la Raza de Color; Private schools for students of color
Someruelos, Marqués de, 186n34
Sosa, Ana Joaquina, 119
Sosa, Ramona, 116
South Carolina, 60
Soviet Union, 169
Spain: 1857 education law in, 91; 1876 constitution of, 88, 110, 134, 142, 144, 145; and

abolition of slavery, 90–91; blood purity in, 78; Catholic Church in, 172n9, 173n17; Christians in, 78; and Cuba, 7, 74, 90, 110, 153; Cuban militiamen-teachers of color in, 66; economy of, 173n17; education in, 161, 173n17; and efforts to retain Spanish colonies, 7, 74, 76, 90, 110; and Florida, 60; government in, 74; Jews in, 78; maestras amigas in, 38; Plan de Instrucción Primaria in, 76; political elites in, 173n17; and Puerto Rico, 90; and United States, 158

Spanish colonial government, in Cuba. *See* Cuba, Spanish colonial government in

St. Louis, MO, 155

Stono Rebellion, 60

Tannenbaum, Frank, 172n9

Teachers, Afro-descended Cuban: and 1844 public education law, 72, 75, 76, 77–78, 79, 80–81; and 1878 education order, 89, 105; and armed rebellions, 3, 12, 16, 18, 20; Black Cuban Creoles as, 65; and Black-run schools, 17, 111; and Catholic Church, 79; challenges faced by, 27; and class, 18, 19; and community among persons of color, 28; and concepts of freedom, 13; and education for all Cubans, 17; and education for girls, 17; employment for, 21, 89, 121, 166–67, 168; and equality, 27; and equal school rights, 17, 117; and establishment of schools, 4, 27; and freedom, 28; and free education, 17, 36, 87; free people of color as, 3, 6, 36, 37, 73, 75, 78, 88, 106, 191n58; and gender, 1–2, 37, 68; at Harvard summer school, 114–16; and honorifics, 116, 191n53, 191n58, 192n60; and identity among people of color, 28; ideologies of, 17, 27, 28; and income, 77, 124; and informal schools in homes, 2; lack of historical resources on, 15, 17; lack of pedagogical texts by, 16; and leadership experience, 60; legacy of, 151; and literacy, 28, 73; and magisterio, 106; motives of, 114; mulato/mulata persons as, 3, 6, 13, 16, 18, 73, 75, 82, 86, 89, 106, 113, 121, 122, 151, 168, 191n58; and municipal schools, 89, 106; and national identity/ideology, 27, 28; numbers of, 37, 165–66; and private schools, 111, 112, 113, 117; and public education system, 86, 89, 167; and racial discrimination, 87; and racially integrated classrooms, 17, 36; and racial segregation, 86; and racial solidarity, 73, 86; and rebellion against colonial rule, 12; and resistance to racial oppression, 28, 47; and resistance to slavery, 12; and response to segregation, 11–12; and school desegregation, 12; and school segregation, 20; and social status, 18, 80, 106; and sociedad de color / mutual aid society schools, 21, 89, 119, 125; Sociedad Económica members' disregard for, 36; and Spanish colonial government, 4, 73, 80, 82, 86; and teaching licenses, 2, 3, 4, 5, 12, 15, 18, 20, 54, 73, 76, 77–78, 79–83, 84–85, 86, 87, 89, 106, 110, 111, 113, 114, 116, 118, 123, 166, 167; and ties to slavery, 4; training of, 16, 166; and US occupation of Cuba, 114; valorization of, 22, 125; and well-being of others, 73; and White Cuban Creoles, 18, 106; and White Cubans, 5, 73; and White elites, 9, 16; and White students, 5, 36, 81; women as, 4, 6, 16, 18, 19, 113, 114, 116, 122, 124, 191n58. *See also* Maestras amigas; Militiamen of color, as teachers

Teachers, White: in 1862 census, 86; on education for all Cubans, 121; at Harvard summer school, 106; and honorifics, 105, 191n53, 192n60; male, 37–38, 47; numbers of, 165–66; as replacements for maestras amigas, 47; and students of color, 21, 81, 83, 89, 105–6, 112; and teaching licenses, 47, 78, 84, 89, 105

Tellería, Pedro, 116

Ten Years War. *See* 1868–78 war of independence

Thorpe, Earle E., 14

Torres, Florencia, 113

Trelles, Carlos, 63

Trinidad, Cuba, 95, 106, 131, 133, 134

Trouillot, Michel-Rolph, 16

Turner, Nat, 60

United States: African Americans in, 14, 22, 97, 120, 123, 125, 152, 185n19, 186n2; Africana studies in, 10–11; and agriculture, 166; Black

intellectual history in, 14; caste system in, 132; common school movement in, 147; and Cuban self-government, 151, 152; and Cubans of color, 152, 157; education in, 1, 14, 20, 22, 69, 97, 106, 112, 120, 123, 125, 156, 157, 166, 170, 180n10, 182n42, 184n7, 186n2; and education in Cuba, 151–52, 163, 164, 198n15; gender in, 13; and link between literacy and rebellion, 60; literacy in, 184n7; and literacy of enslaved persons, 172n9; mutual aid societies in, 117; Nat Turner rebellion in, 60; occupation of Cuba by, 17, 22, 105, 114, 116, 150–51, 152–64, 167; and Philippines, 151; and possible annexation of Cuba, 7, 74, 152; present-day racial disparities in, 23; Puerto Rican studies in, 10–11; and Puerto Rico, 151; Reconstruction in, 152; regions of, 97, 117, 125, 152, 170, 182n42; resistance in, 13; scholarship on, 13; slave codes and slavery in, 1, 13, 60, 69, 172n9; and Spain, 158; and Spanish clergy, 168; Stono Rebellion in, 60; teachers in, 184n7; violence against Black schools, teachers, and students in, 185n19; and White supremacy, 22, 152
University of Havana, 94, 138, 141, 143

Varela, Claudia, 4
Vázquez Queipo, Vicente, 32
Velazco, Eugenio, 67
Velazco, Matías, 55, 67, 68
Ventura Olivera, Ana, 116
Ventura Olivera, Flora, 116
Villanueva, A. de, 80, 81, 82, 83, 84
Vinat de la Mata, Raquel, 113
Viosca, Antonio, 98
Virginia, 13

Walker, Vanessa Siddle, 13, 177n41
West Africa and West Africans, 5, 58
Weyler, Valeriano, 150, 151
White Cuban Creoles: and Afro-descended Cubans' place in Cuban society, 104; associations of, 110; and Black Cuban Creoles, 33; and class, 7, 10, 28, 30, 43, 45; and colonialism, 30, 92, 104, 107, 108, 128; and Cuban national identity, 30; and Cuban sugar economy, 29, 30, 44, 45, 71, 102; and Cuban wars for independence, 8, 104; and economic liberalism, 29; and efforts to attract Afro-descended Cuban support, 128; and enslaved persons, 6; exiled, 74, 104; and free people of color, 6; goals of, 26, 71, 74; and increase in Afro-descended Cuban population, 76; and literacy, 154; as local leaders, 104, 106; and modernity, 9; and national identity, 10; nationalist narrative on, 9; and occupations of Afro-descended Cubans, 37, 38; and opposition to Spanish rule, 7; and political autonomy for Cuba, 29, 30; and race, 8–9, 92; and race science, 10; and racial equality, 104, 108; and racial oppression, 22; and racial segregation, 27, 66, 108; and racial solidarity, 104; and racism, 43; as reformers, 9, 26; and slavery, 30, 102, 104; and Sociedad Económica de Amigos del País, 71; and Spanish colonial government, 7, 21, 27, 30, 71, 74, 78, 92, 93, 94, 100, 107, 124; and voting rights, 153; and White supremacy, 7, 30, 44–45, 48, 69, 74. *See also* Cuban Creoles
White Cuban Creoles, and education: and 1844 public education law, 74, 75–76; and 1878 education order, 91, 93, 94–95, 97, 112, 119; and Afro-descended Cubans' access to education, 35, 45, 46, 76, 88, 92, 104–5, 106, 107, 108, 148, 167; and Afro-descended Cubans' place in Cuban society, 91; bypassing of, by Afro-descended Cubans, 100; and control over Cuban education, 16, 17, 26, 29; and curricula, 42, 45, 46; and dismissal of Black Cuban educational tradition, 36; and distain for primary education, 37; and education as prerequisite for self-government, 7, 29, 45, 47; and enslaved persons, 71; and European or White customs, 32; and expansion of education in Cuba, 5, 17, 29; and formalization of Cuban education, 5; and free education, 27, 28, 29, 30–32, 42, 46, 87, 91, 93; and gender, 2, 35, 42, 45, 46; goals of, 8, 33, 34, 35, 44, 74; and maestras amigas, 5, 18, 28–29, 37, 39–40, 42, 43, 44, 46, 49, 57, 68, 71, 169; and marginalization of free people of color, 32; and militiamen-teachers, 18, 57; and national education system, 6, 7;

and opposition to schooling in homes, 29, 40; and political and social order, 45, 104, 107; on quality of Cuban education, 76; and racially integrated education, 49, 91, 94, 110; and racially segregated education, 2–3, 7, 9, 33, 34, 35, 44, 45, 88, 110; and Real Sociedad Económica de la Habana, 26, 28, 30, 31, 35, 39, 45; scholarship on, 26; and schooling for White Creoles, 76; and secondary education, 29; and Spanish colonial government, 7, 27, 29, 30, 31, 32, 75–76, 92, 101–2, 104, 107; as teachers, 33, 57; and teachers of color, 18, 106; and teaching exams, 55; and White supremacy, 9, 93, 105, 108. *See also* Sociedad Económica de Amigos del País / Real Sociedad Económica de la Habana / Real Sociedad Patrótica de la Habana

White Cubans: and 1893 civil rights order, 140–41, 148; and Afro-descended Cubans, 23–24, 133; and city councils, 88; and class, 143, 167; and Cuban nationhood, 148; and education for people of color, 116, 125; and education of enslaved persons, 172n10; as elites, 16; exiled, 16; and honorifics, 105, 191n53, 192n60; and maestras amigas, 19; and militiamen-teachers, 56; and militia service, 52; and occupations, 37; and opposition to abolition, 142; and private schools, 22, 165, 168, 169; and publishing, 16; and racial integration, 21, 142, 143–44, 147, 165; and school registration and attendance, 154, 164–65; and Spanish colonial government, 88, 137; as students, 161; and teaching, 37, 39; and White supremacy, 133–34

Williams, Danielle Terrazas, 4
Williams, Eric, 12
Wilson, James H., 155, 156
Women, 9, 38, 43, 75, 154
Women of color, Cuban: and armed rebellions, 13; and cabildos de nación, 53; and class, 18, 19, 43; as domestic servants, 37; and education, 16; and employment, 154; enslaved, 5; free, 53; in government records, 18; lack of pedagogical texts by, 16; as laundresses, 37; and literacy, 46, 154; and loyal subjectivity, 53; mulata, 19, 43; occupations and activities of, 5, 37, 38, 40; and private and public spheres, 43; and sociedades de color / mutual aid societies, 119; as teachers, 2, 5, 6, 16, 18, 37, 113, 114, 116, 118, 123, 191n58; and teaching licenses, 47, 123; White Cubans and, 5, 38. *See also* Maestras amigas
Women of color, Latin American, 13, 38
Wood, Leonard, 153, 154
Wood, O.M., 155–56

Yacou, Alain, 63

Zambrana Valdes, Ramón, 38
Zerquera, Pedro, 119

Raquel Alicia Otheguy is associate professor of history at Bronx Community College of the City University of New York. Her work focuses on the history of race and empire, the African diaspora in Latin America and the Caribbean, Latinos in the United States, and the history of education. Otheguy was a 2020 National Academy of Education/Spencer Post-Doctoral Fellow. She received her PhD in history from Stony Brook University (SUNY) in 2016. *Black Freedom and Education in Nineteenth-Century Cuba* is her first book.

Caribbean Crossroads: Race, Identity, and Freedom Struggles

Edited by Lillian Guerra, Devyn Spence Benson, April Mayes, and Solsiree del Moral

More than any other region of the Americas, the Caribbean has been continuously defined by the push and pull between global white supremacy and Black liberation, colonial and anticolonial impulses, and the struggle for freedom against externally imposed economies and political systems. This series focuses on these varied and contradictory histories of the region with a particular focus on Cuba, Puerto Rico, Haiti, the Dominican Republic, and their transnational ties. Importantly, books explore the Caribbean as a racialized space and are not afraid to name the ways whiteness and Blackness work in the region.

Black Freedom and Education in Nineteenth-Century Cuba, by Raquel Alicia Otheguy (2025)

www.ingramcontent.com/pod-product-compliance
Lightning Source LLC
Chambersburg PA
CBHW030824230426
43667CB00008B/1363